The LOVE, SEX AND RELATIONSHIP Dream Dictionary

KELLY SULLIVAN WALDEN

AUTHOR OF *I HAD THE STRANGEST DREAM*

Dedication: To the love of my life, Dana G. Walden, for being my partner and fellow explorer in the realm of dreams' greatest possibilities.

Quarto is the authority on a wide range of topics.

Quarto educates, entertains and enriches the lives of our readers—enthusiasts and lovers of hands-on living.

www.QuartoKnows.com

© 2016 Quarto Publishing Group USA Inc.
Text © 2016 Kelly Sullivan Walden

First published in the United States of America in 2016 by Fair Winds Press, an imprint of Quarto Publishing Group USA Inc. 100 Cummings Center Suite 406-L, Beverly, Massachusetts 01915-6101 Telephone: (978) 282-9590 Fax: (978) 283-2742 QuartoKnows.com Visit our blogs at QuartoKnows.com

20 19 18 17 16   1 2 3 4 5

ISBN: 978-1-59233-717-0

Digital edition published in 2016 eISBN: 978-1-63159-162-4

Library of Congress Cataloging-in-Publication Data is available.

Design: Burge Agency
Illustrations: Justin Tran

Printed in China

Contents

Introduction

Whether we admit it or not, we all have love, sex, and relationships on the brain. Whether you're a CEO superwoman, a stay-at-home dad, or a tree-hugging hippie chick, you likely have an unconscious longing for belonging. As much as we'd like to think we are invincible, independent lone wolves who can brave the wilderness of life alone, what we care about most is merging with or relating to our fellow humans.

Our dreams are our secret weapon. If we pay attention to our dreams, we'll discover that these questions (and more) are being answered by them:

- How will I attract my soul mate?
- Will I ever meet the man or woman of my dreams?
- Once I find the love of my life, how do I keep him or her from leaving?
- What should I do with my overpowering sexual attraction for my boss/neighbor/best friend's girlfriend?
- Why am I so afraid my partner will cheat on me, leave me, or stop loving me?
- Why am I afraid to make a commitment?
- How can I reassure my partner that I'll be faithful when I'm attracted to nearly everyone with a pulse?
- How can I fully express my true self and still be loved, admired, and held in the embrace of a relationship?

Here's how it works: Our dominant daytime thoughts and questions are passed on to our dreams, which, in turn, give us clues to effectively navigate the treacherous yet rewarding terrain of love.

The dream scenarios in this book should shed some light on this process. For example, in a TV commercial advertising a new car, a married couple sleeps side by side while Mr. Sandman sprinkles dream dust on them. Through Mr. Sandman's eyes, we gain a glimpse into their dreams. The woman dreams of being swept away by a romance novel–type long-haired hunk on a white horse, riding through a field of flowers.

Meanwhile, the man dreams of speeding around a racetrack cheered on by a stadium packed with bikini-clad supermodels rocking out to Mötley Crüe. Eventually the man breaks through the racetrack barrier into the field where his wife, the hunk, and the white horse are galloping. Upon seeing her husband, the wife dismounts the horse, leaves Fabio and his stallion in the dust, and joins her husband, the hero, in the passenger seat of their new car. This combined dream ends with the sexually charged, happy couple driving into the sunset together.

The dream featured in this commercial hits on several points worth noting.

1. Women and men have different types of sexual dreams and fantasies. In this example, women dream about love, romance, and relationships. Men dream of action, adventure, and seminude supermodels.
2. Even though men and women dream differently, for a variety of valid psychological and biological reasons, we can find a place of connection where our dreams collide and relationship breakthroughs happen.
3. Our sexually charged dreams can turbocharge our relationships . . . if we let them.

This reminds me of "Escape (The Piña Colada Song)" about the couple on the verge of divorce who seek out personal ads to find their true soul mates. They ultimately discover the dream lover they sought was right in front of them the whole time.

In fact, in spite of all the bad news we hear about failing relationships and marriages, it's possible to find true, lasting love even after a decade of marriage. We must harness the power of dreams to heal and reveal hidden relationship resources we never knew we had. This is the underlying intent of this book.

Dreams help us do so many things, from problem solving and making us healthier to giving us insight about how to advance in our careers, as well as providing awareness about growing spiritually. However, for those of us whose love lives are of paramount importance, our dreams might reveal how we can radically improve our intimate, soul-to-soul relationships. This guide will teach you how to interpret the symbols and themes we encounter in our dreams, how to use dreams as a tool for improving our relationships and romantic lives, and how to encourage better, healthier, and sexier dreams.

Chances are good that at least once in your life you've woken up in the morning with a smile on your face from a sexy dream. Sex dreams are common and nothing to be ashamed of. In fact, throughout this book, we'll pull back the covers on what our erotic dreams mean, why they are so common, and what they tell you about your love life and relationships.

Although we might not want to talk about these nocturnal escapades with our friends, colleagues, and mates, there's nothing to be embarrassed about, even if our unedited, lustful subconscious vastly differs from our proper, politically correct daytime persona. But as is the case with most dreams, they are generally not to be translated literally.

In dreams, sex metaphorically connects or integrates the qualities we ascribe to the person (or animal, vegetable, or mineral) in our dream with the person we are "joining." We would be wise to follow the guidance of the Swiss psychologist Carl Jung, who explained that everyone and everything in a dream is an aspect of the dreamer. Sex represents intimate connection with these many pieces of ourselves— not necessarily lust for the person or people featured in our dreams.

Whether the dream includes having sex with a boss, neighbor, favorite celebrity, next of kin, wild animal, or alien, the first thing I ask the brave soul whose cheeks flush crimson in a sex-dream confession is, "What three words would you use to describe the person with whom you had sex in your dream?

I have a client who dreams regularly about a roll between the sheets with the actor Ryan Gosling. I asked what Ryan Gosling represents to her. "Charismatic, risk-taking, and gorgeous!"

My interpretation of her dream was that she was intimately connecting with her own charismatic, risk-taking gorgeousness. I asked her, "Where in your life might you benefit from a surge of masculine energy like that?"

My client became animated as she envisioned embracing her inner Ryan Gosling and responded: "I'm starting my own health and nutrition business and becoming an entrepreneur for the first time in my life. Having my own business requires me to suit up and show up, take risks, and really connect with people. I guess this dream is also telling me to dress up and look my best."

Besides being the result of the primal urge to merge for the purpose of procreating the species, erotic dreams are a natural way to release pent-up desire that may not be appropriate to express in waking reality. Sex dreams are the ultimate safe-sex practice, as well as being a wonderful opportunity for the inner caveman to run wild and express the full-throttled wild man or woman you truly are. I hope my perspective will allow you to revel in the safe-sex wildness of your sleep-time romps, so that you may awaken as the balanced and civilized citizen you are. In *The Love, Sex, and Relationship Dream Dictionary* you will also discover that by paying attention to your dreams, and doing a bit of dream-related introspection, you can:

- Navigate relationships more skillfully and help them thrive
- Revive an ailing relationship
- Heal from past heartaches
- Attract the relationship of your dreams
- Understand aspects of your dreams and relationships that were previously unclear
- Allow your sensual dreams to reignite your passion for yourself and your partner

Who This Book Is For

I'll assume that you picked up this book because, first and foremost, you understand that dreams can be helpful in navigating your life, and the more you understand their wisdom and apply it to your daily life, the better off you will be. We've established that we all share a common fascination with dreams, but what about our love, sex, and relationship status? You may find yourself in one of these scenarios:

- You are single and in pursuit of a meaningful relationship, and want this book to help you decode dreams so as to shorten the gap between where you are and where you'd like to be.
- You are single and happily so, and want this book to help you deeply enjoy being footloose and free and release any and all guilt trips that might block or hinder your full-throttled romps.
- You are in a relationship but aren't sure if it has what it takes to make it through the long haul, and you want this book to clarify whether to solidify your commitment or transition away with as little collateral damage as possible.
- You are in a long-term committed relationship, but it has gotten stale, and you'd like this book to help you discover ways your dreams can revive your love, sex, and relationship.
- You are in a long-term relationship and are in love, and you'd like this book to reveal how dreams can keep your romance growing even stronger.

But you likely also have concerns beyond your sex and love life, like providing for and protecting children, succeeding in business, maintaining good health and fitness, expressing your creative spirit, achieving personal empowerment, and reaching a spiritual state of nirvana. If we look at the motive behind these intentions, which don't at first appear to have anything to do with our love and sex life, we'll find that beneath all of our goals is the core imperative to love and be loved. All of us, regardless of our personal goals or line of work, seek the security we need to feel worthy of enough love, emotional connection, and sex to last a lifetime. Other dream guides decode symbols through the filter of the multiple aspects of life, including work, health, spiritual growth, and family issues. However, *The Love, Sex, and Relationship Dream Dictionary* decodes dream symbols through the steamed-up lenses of relationships, sexuality, and the human imperative to connect with one another. Allow this book to shine a light on your relationship questions and issues. With this book as your tool, you can create a dreamier love life for yourself and those who are lucky enough to share this path with you.

A note for singles: The definitions of the dream symbols in this book are written, for the most part, from the perspective of someone already in a relationship or with a specific mate in mind. I invite you to consider this context as an affirmation that even if your relationship is undefined, your dreams are coming true, and you are closer than you may realize to getting what you want and need.

My Style of Dream Interpretation

Besides being blessed with a younger sister to share dreams with since we were old enough to say, "I had the strangest dream . . ." and beyond my personal fascination with and reliance on the messages of dreams, I've spent more than twenty years as a certified clinical hypnotherapist working with clients to help them interpret their dreams. My training includes being a practitioner of religious science, human-design analyst, Joseph Campbell devotee, goddess-gathering facilitator, spiritual coach (having studied with shamans from around the world), and survivor of a near-death experience. And since I've had the opportunity to publish five books about dreams, I have logged thousands of my personal dreams into journals and have had the privilege of offering my perspective on thousands of dreams shared through personal sessions, emails, social media, radio, and national TV. I am constantly awed by a dream's bizarre ability to help heal and guide our lives.

Here is my basic approach to dream work:

- **Everyone in your dream is you.**
- **Your dreams are an attempt to manage and grow your power.**
- **Your dreams reveal where you resist your wholeness, and creatively lay out clues for reclaiming lost, forgotten, or dismissed aspects of yourself.**
- **Even your nightmares—no matter how frightening—are an attempt to make your life better.**
- **You don't have to immediately know what your dream means to benefit from it.**
- **Remembered dreams require some form of action in your waking life.**

Archetypes

The late, great father of psychotherapy, Carl Jung, believed that dreams had their own language. The symbols in our dreams are not merely signs pointing toward one idea but rather fluid, multidimensional images to which we can ascribe meaning based on our individual experiences. He taught about archetypes—aspects of humanity we all share. For example, we all have an inner child, a higher self, and a shadow side, to name a few. When we identify our inner archetypes, we can better understand different aspects of ourselves and one another. We negotiate with and integrate or repress traits to find balance and harmony.

For example, imagine that in your waking world you're happily coupled and you meet a handsome stranger. That night you dream of running away or being seduced by an alluring dark figure. Meanwhile, a policeman puts you in jail for a crime you know you've committed.

When we understand that every symbol in our dreams is a reflection of ourselves, we begin to understand the meaning of our dream as a whole, and thus the larger pattern playing out in our lives. You might interpret this dream as your inner policeman (rule enforcer) putting you in jail (punishing you) for committing a crime (contemplating breaking the law/agreement between you and your partner). In other words, you, like most people on the planet, may be grappling with how to honor your animal instincts for sexual freedom while desiring the security of a monogamous agreement. This may be an issue you struggle with personally, and yet it is a collective issue for many people in romantic relationships.

Consider dreams from a quantum physics perspective. You are one, intimately connected with all of life. You are the universe in miniature, a microcosm of all life, intertwining with everyone, everything, everywhere, all the time.

As you view your dreams and waking reality through the lens of archetypes (you can even think of them as subpersonalities), you can begin to make choices based on the feedback system and navigational guidance from your dreams. Doing this will help you embrace all aspects of yourself, resolve what might seem to be irreconcilable, and integrate disparate parts of your psyche to become the whole-souled being you were destined to be. You will become irresistible to the many contenders lining up to be your partner, or to that one lucky person who you've already committed yourself to.

For a deeper dive into each archetype, look in chapter 1. The following is a partial list of primary archetypes that appear in our lives and in our dreams:

Authority Figure	Hero/Heroine
Boy	Holy Person (Pastor, Priest, Rabbi)
Bride	Husband
Bridesmaid	Judge
Brother	King
Cheerleader	Mother
Child	Police
Criminal	Prince
Daughter	Princess
Father	Prostitute
Girl	Queen
God	Seducer/Seductress
Goddess	Shaman
Grandfather	Sister
Grandmother	Teacher
Groom	Warrior
Guide	Witch
Guru	
Healer	

Anima/Animus

Any guide to love, sex, and relationship dreams would be sorely incomplete without discussing what Carl Jung called the anima and the animus. According to Jung, there is a masculine soul within women (animus) and a feminine soul within men (anima). Without honoring these aspects of self, we suffer from unnecessary heartache. However, when we are in touch with our anima or animus and awake to their influence, we are able to have love, sex, and soulful, sustainable relationships, and can elevate our self-understanding to a higher level.

The following are a few of the general qualities of the anima/animus to keep in mind:

Anima (Female soul within a man)	Animus (Male soul within a woman)
Emotional	Logical
Feeling	Action oriented
Intuitive	Productive
Compassionate	Manifesting
Sensitive	Protecting
Nurturing	Strengthening
Introspective	Aware of the world
Passive	Aggressive

When securing your relationship with your anima or animus, it helps to think of it as the relationship between expert tango dancers. The woman is feminine yet strong, and the man is powerful yet graceful.

When a woman is in touch with and embraces her animus, she can celebrate the fullness of her femininity, yet she is no pushover. She is able to feel her way to best navigate her relationships and take fierce, decisive action when needed. If a woman is out of touch with her animus, she can't dance, because she can't find her feet. She is the classic damsel in distress—moody, overly emotional, a victim, a martyr, and incapable of standing up for or caring for herself.

When a man is in touch with and celebrates his anima, he can lead, guide, and direct the dance with a simple gesture of his chin, hip, or elbow. He is a good listener and shows sympathy. However, if he is out of step with his female soul, his dance is clumsy, out of rhythm, and more like a bull in a china shop, stepping on toes and bumping into everyone in a macho, unfeeling way.

Here's a dream that demonstrates the dance of the anima and animus:

Laurie is in the backyard of her house, cleaning up after an evening barbecue, when a handsome stranger (animus) appears. He approaches and embraces her with his firm, muscular body and whispers sweet nothings in her ear, offering the most amazing prayer of love and devotion: "You are so beautiful—God's gift to this world—the angels delight at your very presence . . . Your husband is so lucky to have you."

Laurie swoons in his embrace, all her senses fully alive, and she can feel her clothes melting off her body. Just then, she is aware of her husband inside the house. The handsome stranger lets her know that he'll be here, in her dreams, waiting for her. Laurie is brimming over with her own sensuality as she enters her house, and she showers this ecstatic bliss on her husband.

Laurie awakened her inner animus and thus turned on and blissfully reconnected to her own sensuality. She realized that she could let her real life husband off the hook for being the only one to make her feel beautiful, sexual, and loved; she could now draw from her own, perhaps previously foreign, internal source—her animus or male soul aspect.

These sensual dreams don't end when we wake up. By meditating on the energy of these dreams in our waking lives and carrying that energy over to our actual relationships, we will integrate our connection with our inner anima or animus. As we do this, we'll realize the secret recipe for long-term love and a vibrant sex life.

As you view your dreams through the lenses of archetypes and anima/animus, keep the concept of "wholeness" in mind—that's the goal of dream work. With awareness, you'll stop resisting the life that wants to embrace you; you'll stop sabotaging yourself from having the love, sex, and relationships you desire. Instead, allow the blending of opposing forces within you to elevate, strengthen, deepen, uplift, and amplify your personal power. If you can bring together your vast array of subpersonalities and archetypes and embrace them as an essential part of you, you will find ways to ensure that your days of heartache are over. This work helps you to develop the strength and awareness to tend to your own flame, so that the winds of change that come blowing through your life won't blow it out. You'll be able—even in the most difficult moments—to keep the home fires burning as you create the love, sex, and relationship(s) of your dreams.

Finding Balance Helps You Find Love

You may not call it "love at first sight," but you're probably familiar with the experience of seeing or meeting someone with whom you feel an immediate attraction or connection. We can understand this experience by viewing the object of our attraction as an outer projection of our anima/animus that we have not yet embraced. We are drawn to someone who outwardly expresses our soul in ways we have not dared to. This is like Narcissus of Greek mythology, who was proud and disdainful toward his admirers but who ultimately became enamored of his own reflection in a lake and drowned.

Suffering occurs when we refuse to embrace our anima/animus internally but insist on reaching for it externally, and find ourselves drowning in the lake of our own projection.

A client of mine, a self-proclaimed hopeless romantic, tortured herself for years on a romance roller coaster. Her suffering was constant, except for momentary ecstatic blips that would inevitably come crashing down. She was, as it turned out, more committed to her love fantasy than she was to finding real love. She adamantly believed that the men she "fell in love with" (and had mind-blowing sex with) would continue playing out her fantasy beyond one hot week. She refused to take into consideration that the object of her desire was a fallible, flawed, and multidimensional human being, not someone who appeared for the sole purpose of fulfilling her fantasies.

The key to making love stay beyond one exciting week is to embrace the anima/animus within. You can do this by considering that members of the opposite sex who show up in your dreams are symbolic of the current state of balance and imbalance in your life. These people suggest ways for you to be a better partner by incorporating more of your feminine or masculine soul into your awareness and into the ways you date, relate, and mate. And if that doesn't work, here are additional steps to make love stay.

How to Make Love Stay (Beyond One Hot Week)

Anyone can be charming and enjoy a hot and steamy week with an attractive, exciting partner. But to graduate to the next level, and to grow into the kind of person who has the space to accommodate a true, loving relationship that can stand the test of time, you must be willing to go on a hero/heroine's journey. Tom Robbins says it best in his book *Still Life with Woodpecker*:

> Next, she thought, *"When two people meet and fall in love, there's a sudden rush of magic. Magic is just naturally present then. We tend to feed on that gratuitous magic without striving to make any more. One day we wake up and find that the magic is gone. We hustle to get it back, but by then it's usually too late, we've used it up. What we have to do is work like hell at making additional magic right from the start. It's hard work, especially when it seems superfluous or redundant, but if we can remember to do it, we greatly improve our chances of making love stay."* She was unsure if that idea was profound or trite. She was only sure that it mattered.

It's true that we need to work like hell at making magic from the start. Our dreams help us to create that magic by showing us the more shadowy aspects of ourselves (and those of our partner), thereby helping us to emotionally budget space for the less-than-fantastic aspects. After my first relationship, I was sure that finding the secret to making love stay was what mattered, but I've since shifted to thinking of it as allowing love to stay; no one wants to kidnap love, press a gun to its head, and hold it ransom to make it stay. I'd rather have love stay on its own accord. Wouldn't you?

In my opinion, the attempt to make fairy-tale love stay is the cause of most love-related suffering. Newsflash: Fairy-tale love based on fantasy projections isn't built to last! However, real love can stay, as Rumi says in his poem "The Guest House", if we consciously and deliberately make room for all that we and our partner encompass (which is far more than the initial fireworks that take place during one hot night), we could have a lifetime of love.

> *This being human is a guest house. Every morning a new arrival.*
> *A joy, a depression, a meanness, some momentary awareness comes as an unexpected visitor. Welcome and entertain them all!*
> *Even if they are a crowd of sorrows, who violently sweep your house empty of its furniture, still, treat each guest honorably. He may be clearing you out for some new delight.*
> *The dark thought, the shame, the malice, meet them at the door laughing and invite them in.*
> *Be grateful for whatever comes because each has been sent as a guide from beyond.*
>
> —Rumi, "The Guest House"

If we were wise, we would treat our relationships like a guesthouse and welcome and entertain all the unexpected visitors, not just the ubersexy, cologne-wearing, laugh-at-all-your-jokes, all-night love-making version of your lover. This is not to say that we should ever put up with abuse. However, if you can accept that your lover is a completely fallible, mistake-laden human, you might develop the maturity to know when he or she (and you) falls from grace.

Here are six steps to make love stay, based on my decades of field research. I pray this helps you to make love a welcome guest in your dream life and waking love life.

1. Remember: Porcupines Are Little Pricks

Keep in mind that love brings up everything unlike itself. Imagine that we are all porcupines who, when dating, impressing, and seducing each other, intuitively know how to withdraw our spikes, so we can impress rather than threaten our mate. We realize that our spikes, if revealed early on, might send our date running for the hills. However, as courtship graduates to a committed relationship, we begin to relax into each other's loving embrace, and our guard begins to melt. When we relax, our spikes start to poke through our fleecy exterior, and we become little pricks.

The good news is that there is no way to remove our spikes unless they are revealed. The bad news is that our spikes show that we are not always the soft and perfect partner that we first presented. We all know how unpleasant it is to back into our lover's spikes without warning! We feel bamboozled or manipulated, as if Mr. or Mrs. Hyde switched places with Dr. Jekyll, and we wonder about the true identity of our partner.

Once our spikes are out, they can finally be dealt with. With some loving care and attention, these prickly issues and unhealed wounds can be faced, embraced, aced, and replaced by a genuine soul-to-soul connection.

Our dreams during this prickly time reveal the source and location of the spikes, as well as the solutions for how to heal yours and your partner's wounds, so you can avoid pricking each other to death or ending the relationship before it even starts.

2. Take a Look in the Mirror

We attract lovers who resonate on a similar frequency as our own. If we begin to tire of our lovers

and we find a repeating pattern of frustrating flaws, we need to look in the mirror to see the common denominator in these dysfunctional partnerships. If we want a higher-caliber partner, then we need to become a higher-caliber version of ourselves, one who would be a perfect fit for the lover of our dreams.

This is good news. We are victims of our partners no longer! Instead of micromanaging the actions of your partner, especially if you find yourself in a fixer-upper relationship, direct 100 percent of that energy to yourself. As you do, you'll notice that your mate will, as if by magic, begin to shift before your eyes and become someone who meets your needs and matches your heightened consciousness. More often than not, your partner will rise to the occasion without your meddling.

3. Let Your Relationships Be Icing on Your Cake

You are a whole, divine, and sacred being. Regardless of the ridiculous mishaps from your past or the voices in your head, you are a precious, one-of-a-kind creation of love, connected to all the beauty in this universe. The relationships you attract are icing on your cake. They don't make you whole. They simply enhance who you already are.

When you remember this, on a daily or moment-to-moment basis, it helps you avoid investing your time, energy, and money on micromanaging your partner. Instead, you can funnel that energy toward making your cake the most delicious cake it can be.

Speaking of cake, if you dream of pigging out on sweets, it might be a message to stop depriving yourself of love while waiting for your mate to pour on the sugar—you are fully capable of indulging in self-love.

4. Understand the Reason for the Season

Just as the tides move in and out and the moon waxes and wanes, our relationships experience the four seasons, regardless of the time of year.

For example, in the springtime of romance, two people gently flirt with a flicker of attraction for each other. This is the stage of new beginnings. Our romance builds to a passionate crescendo in the summer stage of love, and we feel the heat of desire enflame our bodies. As autumn leaves begin to fall, our libido begins to wane. Our projections start to fade and our resentments pile up, like leaves on the lawn. As the winter of our romance turns everything to ice, including our hearts, we freeze our lover out or feel the chill of being cast out ourselves. We can't remember what we ever saw in this person. Crisis ensues. At this point, the fairy-tale romance may come crashing to an end, or it may be the place where a true relationship begins.

A healthy, mature couple is capable of identifying the season their relationship is in and knows how to ride the tide with patience and a big-picture awareness—to revel in the gifts that come with each season. For example, a healthy, balanced couple knows how to warm themselves during their relationship's winter, so that when springtime rolls around, love bursts forth more potent and energized than ever before.

5. The Acceptance/Freedom Tug-of-War

According to Abraham, as channeled through the trance medium Esther Hicks, we humans are both "harmony-seeking beings" (run by a desire to get along with each other and do what it takes to keep the peace) and "freedom-seeking beings" (run by the desire to do what we want to do when we want to do it and with whom, regardless of whether it will royally piss off our mate).

When we accept that both of these needs (harmony and freedom) are important and worthy of our respect, the complicated drama of romantic love suddenly becomes simple. If we were wise, we would make room in our relationships for both of these needs (e.g., once a month both you and your partner get a wild night out with your friends, a solo road trip, or a dance class sans partner). If we don't have a clue how to reconcile these conflicting needs, our dreams will be our litmus test.

6. Share Your Dreams

After a few years of being in a partnership, even the most juicy, expressive couples can run out of things to talk about. You already know each other's gory ex-boyfriend and ex-girlfriend stories and weird family secrets, and you've seen every new-release movie.

If you get into the practice of sharing your nighttime dreams with each other, you can open doors of understanding into the deeper nature of your loved one and yourself, inviting your partner into your deeper subconscious. It entails a great deal of trust and can open a world of intimacy and insight, not to mention entertainment and an endless menu of new things to talk about.

I'll offer a word of caution when sharing dreams: Be mindful when sharing sexual dreams that involve people other than you or your significant other (especially if they are with someone you truly lust for in your waking life). I once had a boyfriend who thought it was cool to share, in detail, his Salma Hayek sex dreams. It did not bring us closer. Not a bit.

Remembering and Decoding Your Dreams

At this point, you are no doubt sold on the notion that dream work can be a powerful asset to your relationships. However, you may be one of those people who have a difficult time "catching" their dreams. Fear no longer—this section is for you. To better remember your dreams, set a powerful intention before you go to sleep that you will remember them. Back that up with action by placing a journal on your nightstand, and incorporate the following suggestions in your early morning awakening routine to become a more masterful dream catcher.

Don't Move a Muscle!

As you lie on the bridge between asleep and awake after a night spent journeying through your multidimensional dreamscape, don't move at all. Remain in the position you were in while dreaming. Your body's position, the particular crumple of your blanket, and the fold of your pillow are part of the container for your dream. If you move too much, your dreams will evaporate like smoke. To the best of your ability, maintain the position you were sleeping in, or climb back in to bed and do your best at re-creating your body's sleep position to catch your dream(s).

Ask the Right Questions

Often, people don't remember their dreams because the first question on their mind when they wake up is, "What do I have to do today?" This question leads to an onslaught of ten thousand other concerns, which switches your brain waves from theta or delta (deep, dreamy relaxation) to beta (stressed-out work-mode brain state) and sends your adrenal glands to the races. In ten seconds flat, your dream is gone. However, if you resolve to make the very first question you ask yourself, "What was I just dreaming?" you will have an excellent shot at catching your dream(s).

Rewind, Replay, Review

Now that you've been able to catch a dream, before getting out of bed, press the rewind button in your mind and replay your dream at least three times. Don't assume that just because you've been able to recall your dream while lying down in your sleep position that you will recall it once you move your body. Your dreams take place in the part of the brain where short-term memory is located. Within just five minutes of the end of your last dream, half the content is gone. And after only ten minutes, 90 percent is lost. To transfer your dream from short-term to long-term memory, you have to review it several times in your mind's eye before making the journey from horizontal to vertical.

The Snooze Alarm Is Your Friend

In an ideal world, we wouldn't need an alarm to get up—our bodies would complete their sleep cycle and deliver us to our waking state, perfectly refreshed and with detailed dream recall. However, if you are like most people, you need your handy-dandy alarm to make sure you don't sleep through your morning meeting. For most of us who are engrossed in the enchanted and cozy realm of our dreamtime, the blaring siren of the alarm shoots shock waves through our veins and sends our dreams away from our waking memory. But if you have to wake up to an alarm, make good use of the snooze function.

Set your alarm thirty minutes before you actually have to wake up. As soon as you wake and press the snooze button, you are headed right back to dreamland—with an awareness to pay close attention to your dream. Create an alarm sound that will wake you up but not scare the living daylights out of you. I suggest chimes or instrumental music that inspires you. Place your alarm clock where it is easy to reach, to keep movement at a minimum. When you hit the snooze button, you can resume your original sleep position to catch the dream you were just having, or catch a new one.

Put Pen to Paper

Now for the critical last step—to make your dream "physical" by transferring it from the intangible realm of your dreams to the tangible realm of your waking life. The easiest way to do this is to pick up a pen and scribble (as legibly as you can) your dream in your journal, with as much detail as you can remember. Some people prefer to record their dream on a voice app on their phone (check out www.dreamscloud .com). You may be someone who would rather draw a picture of a dream. If this appeals to you, then go for it! Others prefer to roll over in bed and whisper their dream to their lover or spouse. Just make sure you don't interrupt the dream recollection of the person you are sharing your bed with.

How to Decode Your Dreams

Think of your dream world as a dragon: mysterious, otherworldly, fiery, sometimes frightening, and powerful. Gaining mastery of your dream world is not about taming this dragon. If you learn to SADDLE your dragon, and eventually learn to ride fearlessly on its back into the nether world of your subconscious, you will get a glimpse of what your dreams are telling you. In your dream journal or on a sheet of paper, write the word SADDLE across the top:

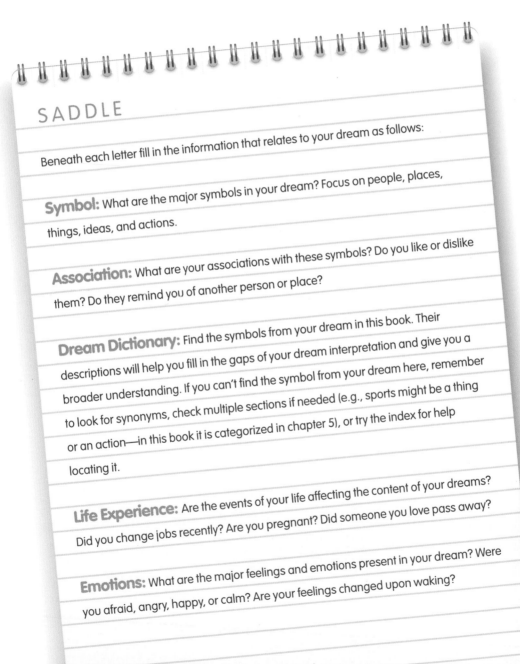

SADDLE

Beneath each letter fill in the information that relates to your dream as follows:

Symbol: What are the major symbols in your dream? Focus on people, places, things, ideas, and actions.

Association: What are your associations with these symbols? Do you like or dislike them? Do they remind you of another person or place?

Dream Dictionary: Find the symbols from your dream in this book. Their descriptions will help you fill in the gaps of your dream interpretation and give you a broader understanding. If you can't find the symbol from your dream here, remember to look for synonyms, check multiple sections if needed (e.g., sports might be a thing or an action—in this book it is categorized in chapter 5), or try the index for help locating it.

Life Experience: Are the events of your life affecting the content of your dreams? Did you change jobs recently? Are you pregnant? Did someone you love pass away?

Emotions: What are the major feelings and emotions present in your dream? Were you afraid, angry, happy, or calm? Are your feelings changed upon waking?

Once you've followed the SADDLE prompt and written your responses, read it all together and take note of any "aha" moments. Ask yourself, "How is this dream helping to improve my relationships, enrich my love life, and deepen my enjoyment of the gift of my sexuality?" Write down your reflections in your journal.

Types of Dreams

Your dreams, no matter how odd, bizarre, scary, repetitive, mystical, or sexually charged, are always coming to you in service of your health, healing, well-being, self-awareness, and growth. However, not all dreams are created equal. In this section I'll describe the most common types of dreams; understanding them will reveal vital clues about the bizarre and brilliant language of your dreams.

- Throughout your day, ask the question, audibly or inaudibly, "Am I dreaming?" As you create the habit of doing this when you're awake, you may begin to do this as you dream.

- If you discover that you are in fact dreaming, check it by flipping a light switch on or off or by looking at a digital clock or any number sequence. A telltale sign that you are dreaming is when you notice numbers getting jumbled.

- Meditate for twenty minutes a day. Ask your partner to join you; this is a powerful practice to enhance intimacy and raise the level of consciousness in your partnership.

- I recommend that you read (together with your partner) *Lucid Dreaming* by Robert Waggoner and *Lucid Dreaming* by Stephen LaBerge.

Lucid

A lucid dream occurs when you become aware that you're dreaming while you're dreaming. These dreams can be invigorating and empowering as they reveal your innate power to change your circumstances and co-create (or at least participate in) the formation of your dreamscape, your love life, and your overall life experience.

Becoming a lucid dreamer brings you closer to being a lucid lover. Awareness is king or queen. The more awake you can be in your dreams, the better your chances of bringing a more lucid and awake version of yourself into your love life.

Some lucky people are naturally talented at lucid dreaming. I unfortunately am not one of them; however, I've had several that were life changing. If you are one of the fortunate ones who can lucid dream with little effort, my hat goes off to you. However, most people must work hard to have a lucid dream. If you want something to jump-start your lucid dreaming and more lucid love life, here are a few tips:

Nightmare

I'm sure at some point in your life you've experienced a scary dream or two. Nightmares can run the gamut from being a mildly disturbing dance with your shadow to preying on your worst fears, waking you in a cold sweat with your heart pounding. I often refer to nightmares as "venting dreams," because I see them on a conveyer belt escorting our anger, sadness, fear, and anxiety out of our body/mind/spirit. By the time we've successfully shown a nightmare to the exit, we are wiser, more compassionate, and more resourceful than we were before. The bottom line is knowing how to work with nightmares so they can become blessings rather than things to fear.

Albert Einstein posed the question, "Is this universe friendly?" The eventual answer came to him after decades of research: a resounding yes! We can apply the "universe is friendly" philosophy to our unpleasant dreams, and thus become grateful for them, because even our nightmares come to us in the service of health, healing, growth, and illumination.

When confronting a scary dream, follow the FEAR Formula: Face it, Embrace it, Ace it, and Replace it.

Think about it. There is virtually nothing that challenges us more than our personal relationships. Once you find yourself stretching the boundaries of your own comfort zone, your nightmares will kick in to help you reveal and heal all your cherished barriers to love. Use the following FEAR formula to better understand your nightmares and to help you grow through this treacherous terrain:

Face It: If you find yourself running, hiding, or avoiding something you are afraid of, realize that what you resist persists. Even though it seems scary or unpleasant, imagine that instead of running, you turn and face the challenging creature. Remember, everyone and everything in your dream is you.

Embrace It: Breathe as you become present. Stand your ground while you get a good look at your foe. Is it a person, beast, monster? What color is it? What does it feel like? What is it doing? As counterintuitive as this may seem, move toward it with open arms, knowing it is an aspect of yourself and your own power and it has a gift for you. Your embrace may be a literal hug, or it may be standing toe to toe as you shift from resisting toward receiving the good intention (the gift) this creature has for you.

Ace It: To ace it means that the hunted becomes the hunter; you conquer it rather than letting it conquer you. Enlarge your personal space. Your consciousness is so big that your nemesis is now inside the belly of the whale that is you and it's no longer a threat. The key to acing it is in your willingness to go beyond your normal, rational thinking and tap into your supernatural power. You may need to open up and accept the cognitive dissonance, to embrace the beauty/ugliness, safety/danger, life/death, creation/destruction, and hold it all within your wide-open consciousness.

Remember that you are a multifaceted individual. Like a mansion with many rooms, you contain many places to explore, and perhaps you've only gotten to know a few of the rooms. A dream that reveals a shadowy character is really an invitation to get to know another room of your love/sex/relationship mansion. It's only in the shadows because you have yet to turn on the lights.

Replace It: If you effectively ace your nemesis, then you have transformed what terrified you into something that can now empower you. Your fear is replaced by fuel to ignite your dreams. Let it make you fearless as you expand and explore the infinite possibilities of your love life.

Here's how Joanne used the FEAR formula to become empowered by her nightmare:

Joanne dreams about a naked Brad Pitt wading gracefully through an enchanted waterway. He comes upon a cave surrounded by murky, dark water. Joanne intuitively knows it's dangerous for Brad to go any farther. She tries to block and protect him from entering. Just then a purple-and-turquoise snake slithers around her belly and bites her on her waist. She wakes up terrified.

Upon awakening, Joanne identified the "snake" as the shadow creature.

- She faced the snake by meditating on it and asking what gift it was trying to give her. She became aware that a snake is a symbol of healing, because it sheds its skin, it is in constant renewal, and it is the symbol of medicine.
- She embraced the gift/message by imagining that she was shedding the skin of her former self, and imagined what it would feel like to be free of past baggage with her new love, her animus (who reminded her of Brad Pitt, by the way).
- She aced her dream by no longer being afraid of this snake and having transformed it from a foe into her ally and trusted advisor.
- She replaced the terror she initially felt with a surge of empowerment, confidence, and excitement about the opportunity to explore a deeper intimate connection with her partner.

Keep the following tips in mind if you want to have fewer nightmares:

- **Refrain from watching the news, horror movies, or action-packed TV before going to sleep.**
- **Watch, listen, or read life-affirming literature, music, or programming before going to sleep.**

If you want a deeper understanding of how you and your mate can turn your nightmares into rocket fuel for your love life, I recommend reading more about it in the FEAR formula section of my book *It's All in Your Dreams*.

Numinous

Have you ever dreamed of flying, floating, communing with an angel, or receiving knowledge from a wise and loving being? Carl Jung defines a numinous dream as an experience that conveys something essential about ourselves that our unconscious wants us to know.

When you have a numinous dream, you may feel spiritually enriched, enlivened, empowered, and renewed. Numinous dreams can also give us a fresh perspective on our love lives, a solution to an issue we've been struggling with, or the confidence to feel worthy of the best that life has to offer.

One way to enhance your ability to have more numinous dreams is to:

- Contemplate the best spiritual dream or uplifting real life experience you've had, and rekindle your connection to the tone of that memory.

- Meditate on your peak spiritual moment just before bedtime (or as often as possible throughout the day), and your dreams will help you take a deeper dive into your spiritual waters.

- Take the action your numinous dream inspires. If the action isn't immediately obvious, meditate on the question, "What can I do to honor this dream?"

- Share this dream with your lover. Numinous dreams connect us with sacred knowledge, and when shared it can deepen the bonds of intimacy.

- Tuck yourself into bed with a spiritually uplifting book or story. I recommend *The Untethered Soul* by Michael A. Singer or *The Alchemist* by Paulo Coelho. If you can share this practice with your lover, it will do wonders to enhance your spiritual connection.

Processing

Processing dreams are not glamorous or steamy, nor do they take you on flights of fantasy. They tend to be simply a rehash of the day's events. If you're overwhelmed because you just met Mr. Right, or if you're stressed out because you've been arguing with Ms. Wrong, your processing dreams help you to find order in the disorder. Processing dreams are more powerful than we give them credit for; they help you solve problems and get your act together so you can continue to improve your love life, even during challenging times.

To get the most out of your processing dreams I suggest the following tips:

- Write in your journal before going to sleep about your issue/desire/challenge du jour, and conclude with this statement (fill in the blanks): "Dreams, thank you in advance for providing me with clarity, insight, and direction regarding my _____ situation with _____."

- Write down your dreams immediately upon awakening, and consider that whatever remembered dream you dredge up from the night before is an answer to your question or a solution to your challenge.

- Apply the guidance you receive from your dream to your waking reality.

- If you need help interpreting your dream, look up the symbols in this dream dictionary.

- If you don't want to have processing dreams (if you've been inundated with them and are hungering for a more fanciful dream experience), read a fantasy book to take your mind off your issues.

Precognitive

Precognitive dreams predict the future. These dreams tend to stand out from the pack because of their intensity and clarity. Of course you won't know for sure if a precognitive dream is in fact a precognitive dream until an event in the future confirms it. However, most people who have well-developed antennae notice a pattern in the way their predictive dreams are presented, for example, in the way they feel or, in some cases, don't feel (e.g., zero emotion during a graphic scene that would normally conjure an emotional reaction).

Precognitive dreams can play a significant role in your ability to successfully navigate your romantic relationships. In fact, many people have found the love of their life simply by paying attention to their dreams and taking action when they discovered elements of their nighttime dreams coming to life.

To enhance your chances of having more precognitive dreams, I suggest that you:

- Practice being bold in the way you honor any psychic nudges you receive throughout the day in your waking state, especially in your love life.

- When you do have a precognitive dream and you see the proof of it show up in your waking reality, resist any temptation to minimize it. Instead, acknowledge and celebrate it. Ask your partner to support you in this endeavor.

- If you don't like the scenario your precognitive dream shows you, remember, it's not set in stone. You can change it if you take preventive measures. Your dream may be showing you what would happen if you continue on a particular destructive path or implement a particular behavior. You can always change the outcome.

- If your dream shows you a desirable future, then keep on doing what you're doing, how you're doing it, and with whom you are doing it.

- Nestle yourself in bed with a great book on psychic development. I recommend Sylvia Browne's *Book of Dreams* or *Blink* by Malcolm Gladwell.

Recurring

Recurring dreams are those persistent nocturnal messages, themes, or scenarios that keep showing up like a vigilante delivery-truck driver hell- (or heaven-) bent on delivering the message you are scheduled to receive. These dreams tend to be critical to your personal development and to the evolution of your love life. You can run but you can't hide from these dreams. In fact, all the sleeping pills in the world won't make them go away until their message is received, decoded, and implemented. As you do this, your inner delivery-truck driver will breathe a sigh of relief as she checks this delivery off her list so that she can get to the business of sending you a new, more interesting type of package next time. To help her do her job, meditate on the following questions:

- What message is my recurring dream trying to send me?

- What is the goal of this dream?

- How is this dream attempting to help me improve my love life?

- What issue is this dream revealing and attempting to heal?

- How would I prefer this dream to unfold? If you feel comfortable, share this recurring dream with your loved one and ask him or her to "dream craft" or role-play the dream with you. For example, if in the dream you are seeking understanding, attention, safety, freedom, sex, or forgiveness, ask your partner to play the role of the person you are seeking those things from. Give your partner the script by writing down exactly what you've wanted to hear, see, or experience. Allow this experience to scratch this recurring itch until it quiets down and recedes to the background.

- For more on dream crafting, I suggest the dream crafting section of my book *It's All in Your Dreams.*

Wet Dreams

A wet dream is when you have an orgasm in your dream and the sexual circumstances feel deeply real. These highly pleasurable dreams are healthy and natural and occur as a result of a lack of inhibition during the dream state. Besides being messy (if you are a male), wet dreams can help you spring forth into your relationship from the right side of the bed.

A wet dream denotes a sense of fulfillment, wholeness, and awareness of your pleasure principle. However, if you deem the content of your dream (and its cast of characters) that led to your dreamtime orgasm an assault to your morality, remember, this dream does not make you a sexual deviant. Your dream characters are symbolic of aspects of yourself seeking integration within you.

These nocturnal emissions that take place during sexual and sensual dreams are literally a release of pent-up feelings, emotions, and energies, as well as an opportunity to allow your inner Eros or Aphrodite to be completely unleashed.

The following tips will support you in having more sensual dreams that may or may not lead to orgasm:

- Explore your sensuality in your waking life by taking note of what arouses you or gives you pleasure. Practice pushing the envelope of what gives you pleasure and give yourself permission to move more deeply into it.
- Prior to bedtime, read literature, watch a sexy movie, or slowly explore your own body's unique pleasure pathways, on your own or with your partner.
- Practice tantric sex. I recommend reading, alone or with your partner, *The Multi-Orgasmic Couple* by Mantak Chia.

How to Use This Book

As a serial monogamist and love pioneer, my other obsession (after dreams) is the realm of love. In my love life, my personal research laboratory, over the past thirty-five years, and my marriage for the past fourteen years, I've learned a thing or two about what not to do . . . and a few things that actually work in terms of attracting a soul mate and maintaining a loving, spicy, long-term relationship.

The intersection of our love lives and our dreams is vital, and one is incomplete without the other. I'd love to say that all you need to do is remember a few dreams and decode them, and you will have profound, meaningful, lasting love and off-the-Richter-scale sex. But, sadly, it's not enough just to dream, decode a few dreams, and fantasize about the relationship you desire. And it's not enough to actively seek love. Love, sex, and relationship success is in the sweet spot where guidance from dreams and dream-inspired action intertwine.

Here's how to get the most from this book:

- Record your dreams on a daily basis upon awakening.
- Decode at least one dream per day by looking up the symbols in this book. You can find them in one of these thematic chapters: People and Animals, Time and Place, Physical Objects, Ideas and Whims, and Actions and Scenarios.
- If you have trouble finding a symbol, reference the index at the back of the book to find the page number or synonym for that symbol.
- Do something each day to honor your remembered dream from the previous night—I call this dream activation—whether it is sharing it with a loved one, wearing something you wore in your dream, or doing something that mirrors or expresses what you did in your dream.
- In your waking life, practice the six steps to make love stay (pages 13–15).

I hope that after you dive in to your dreams and use this book, your own insights will reveal what your dream wisdom is trying with all its might to impart to you.

Sweet dreams . . . and may your wildest and most wonderful dreams all come true!

Chapter 1

People and Animals

(and Their Many Roles and Parts)

The secret to attracting great love and great sex lies not in losing more weight, making more money, or reciting more affirmations. It lies in your willingness to embrace your total self—especially the aspects you find most difficult to accept.

When interpreting your dreams with regard to the parade of humans, animals, and other creatures marching by, you might consider how they reflect the actual people in your life. But, more often than not, according to Carl Jung, the people in your dreams reflect aspects of yourself. In other words, you are the saint, the sinner, the prostitute, the virgin, the howling wolf, the angel in white, and even the transgendered housewife or husband. And your dreams are where you grapple to find a place in your heart to house them all.

When seeking to understand why certain people, animals, and creatures make an appearance in your dream, ask yourself the following questions:

- **What part of me does this being represent?**
- **Am I attracted or repulsed?**
- **Is this being showing me a dysfunctional aspect of myself I would be wise to release, feel, or heal?**

- **Is this an aspect of myself worth celebrating?**
- **How might this creature be teaching or revealing wisdom that would be helpful if applied in my love life?**
- **How is this dream helping me to grapple with my conflicting needs (as personified by two different aspects of self)?**

Keep in mind that our dreams are conspiring on behalf of our wholeness. Our dreams have a "no shadow left behind" policy, and our dream people, animals, other living creatures, professions/roles, and human and animal body parts are helping us to reach a breakthrough that will assist us in loving all aspects of ourselves. They can help us find things worth loving, even our inner-bitch, scaredy-cat, slutty, selfish, hoarding, lying, cheating, controlling, piggish, slothful, awkward, geeky selves. And on the other side of the equation, our dream and dream creatures are helping us accept that we are the sexy, alluring, charismatic, drop-dead gorgeous, talented, enlightened stud we've been chasing in the form of an elusive mate. As we do this, we will, in essence, bring a more accepting, loving version of ourselves to our next date, party, or walk down the aisle.

Accountant

Dreams of an accountant might signify that you're feeling the need to tabulate the pros and cons of your relationship. Consider the perspective that everyone in your dream is you—and no matter how emotional we might be, there is a logical part of us whose job is to run a cost-benefit analysis to reveal how our recent relational or sexual giving/receiving behavior checks out. See also **Money**, page 120.

Acrobat

Dreams of an acrobat signify the need for flexibility or dynamism in your love/sex life. Perhaps you've been doing backflips to entice your lover to fall for you, or maybe you are falling head over heels in love. This dream suggests that your daring, adventurous side is being called to the mat (or the mattress).

Actor/Actress

If you dream of an actor or actress, your dream is giving you a backstage pass to become aware of the roles you play and the lines you say in your love life. Perhaps it's time to shine a light on the characters within you that have been hiding in the wings as a way of bringing more of yourself to your relationship. Or it may be time to take a curtain call, as you remove the mask and let your authenticity take center stage. See also **Celebrity**, page 36.

Adult

Dreams of an adult could be a message to suit up and show up (like a grown-up) in your relationship, even if you are going through a challenging time. Consider what being an adult means to you. For some it represents freedom, for some it represents a burden, for others it means taking total responsibility for your love life. And for many other people, it means XXX-rated adult content.

Agent

Dreaming of an agent can represent a desire or need for an advocate to sell your lover on your best attributes. Perhaps you find it challenging to represent your best self to your partner—or to extoll the virtues of your relationship to your family and friends. This could be a wake-up call to develop your healthy self-esteem and sing your own praises.

Alien

A dream of an alien might be preparing you for a lover from another universe (compared with the typical ones you habitually choose). This dream could be giving you permission to move beyond your longing for belonging and to wave your freak flag with pride so that you can experience out-of-this-world sex. This dream could also be revealing your fear of being alienated if you expose your true feelings. Also, this dream might expose the aspect of yourself that is most alien to you: your power. If you dream of having sex with an alien, you might feel that you and your lover are from different planets and are having a difficult time finding your sexual groove. Alternatively, dreaming of sex with an alien indicates that you may be exploring the pathways to otherworldly ecstasy, connection, and potentially higher love. See also **Abduct**, **Abduction**, page 164, and **UFO**, page 132.

Anal Sex

If you dream of anal sex, you are connecting with a primal experience of domination and submission in your love life. See also **Butt**, page 34, and **Sex**, page 192.

Angel

Dreams of an angel signify that the miracle you've been asking for is at hand. Perhaps you've felt the need for divine intervention to help you through the journey of being in a relationship (or trying to get into one). If so, your dream angel (Cupid) is your answered prayer. An angel can support you in transforming your relationship into higher love.

Animal

Dreams of an animal can signify the need for a primal scream, a howl at the moon, or to tear off your clothes and run naked across your suburban neighborhood. When a creature from the animal kingdom crawls, slithers, sniffs, or pounces into your dream, it comes bearing gifts of untamed power for your relationship. Animal senses are acute and precise. Even if they bare their fangs, often they are offering themselves to you as your spirit animal, should you choose to accept them. Your spirit animal will give you an advantage in your ability to survive and thrive in the jungle of your relationship, as each animal offers a specific strategy for enhancing your love life. The bottom line about dreaming of any animal is a message to stop thinking about the bottom line and reconnect with your natural rhythms, desires, and instincts. Whether you dream of a grizzly bear or a beetle, take the cue from your dream to make room for your animal nature to swing through the jungle, roll in the dirt, and roam free. See also specific animals.

Ant

Dreams of ants could signify that you're getting antsy regarding your love affair. Or perhaps you are letting little things about your lover bug you. In addition to looking at what's gotten under your skin, this dream can also be a message to get your head out of the clouds and pay attention to the details of your relationship—the mundane, ground-level issues that might get overlooked. Because ants engage in teamwork, this dream could be a message to join efforts with your loved ones and your larger network of like-minded friends. After all, it takes a village to raise a relationship. See also **Insect**, page 51.

Architect

Dreams of an architect represent that you are taking responsibility for your life and relationship by creating the blueprint for your dreams and goals. Perhaps you are in the midst of building your relationship from the ground up, or working on a big renovation.

Arm

Arms in dreams are symbolic of a desire, ability, or willingness to embrace the possibilities of your relationship. This dream could indicate a desire to reach out and touch someone, or perhaps that you feel your relationship dreams are within arm's reach. If you are crossing your arms, you may be taking an armored stance against love. Your right arm could signify a desire to be important (your partner's right arm). It may reflect strength, support, and loyalty. Dreams of the left arm represent your ability to flow and allow your mate to lead. You're feeling receptive to the love that is embracing you. See also **Hug**, page 183.

Ass

see **Butt**, page 34.

Astronaut

Dreams of an astronaut symbolize that you are gaining assistance with your ability to break through the gravitational hold on your relationship. This dream is a message to shoot for the stars in your relationship, and realize that even the sky is not the limit.

Athlete

Dreams of an athlete symbolize your winning edge and the stamina to go the distance and overcome hurdles. This dream might inspire you to consider whether it's your competitive nature or your desire to become your personal best that inspires your participation in this love affair.

Audience

Dreams of an audience symbolize a feeling that you are performing in your relationship and are being judged or evaluated or are seeking validation. Consider that the audience is made up of your subpersonalities, including your judge and inner critic. Contemplate the question, "Am I in this relationship because of my heart or my ego?" See also **Theater**, page 90.

Authority Figure

Dreams of an authority figure can relate to your thoughts about, feelings for, and past experiences with specific authority figures in your life. Maybe you've gotten caught in the submit (obey)/rebel cycle in your relationship, and are trying to figure out who has the upper hand. Often a dream of an authority figure, such as a policeman, judge, father, mother, principal, or boss, means we are working out our issues with our parents, teachers, or anyone who has misused his or her power with us. This dream could also mean you are grappling with the part of you that regulates your behavior, informed by your moral compass. If you've been taking risks (e.g., being more flirtatious or promiscuous than you normally are), your inner police might put you in jail. Alternatively, this dream might also indicate maturity, and that you are stepping into a leadership role in your relationship, willing to take responsibility for your life and your choices. See also **Boss**, page 32, **Father**, page 44, **Mother**, page 55, and **Police**, page 58.

Baby

Dreams of a baby signify that you may be renewed or vulnerable in your relationship. A baby is a symbol of a beginner's mind. Although you may feel you've been there, done that, this dream could be a sign to love like you've never been hurt and allow yourself to approach your lover like a virgin. Let vulnerability in and take baby steps again as you approach each moment with wonder. If you are trying to have a baby, this dream may be precognitive or at least affirming that you are on the right track. If you're not trying to have a baby, your dream might be a reminder to use birth control and/or get a pregnancy test.

Dreams of a baby signify vulnerability and renewal.

Bachelor

If you are a man in a relationship dreaming of a bachelor, it might indicate a longing for freedom and independence. If you are a man who is a bachelor, you may be gaining self-awareness as you evaluate whether or not to cast off your single lifestyle for one with more responsibility. If you are a woman, whether single or coupled, dreaming of a bachelor might indicate your connection with your animus, as well as expressing a longing to saddle an available man. See also the anima/animus discussion in the introduction, page 10.

Back

Dreams of a back could signify that you're feeling the need for support, or perhaps you've been spending too much time on your back. A back in a dream could be a message to stand up for yourself. This dream might reflect your level of confidence, inner strength, and ability to stand tall in your relationship. Or you may be wondering if your lover will have your back, want you back, or will back out of your commitment. See also **Body**, page 32.

Ballerina

Dreams of a ballerina are a message to bring more grace, sensitivity, and self-control to your love life. Instead of stomping through like a bull in a china shop, thinking only of your needs, be mindful of the space around you. A ballerina in a dream models how to tread lightly through a challenging situation, inspiring you to stretch and become more flexible than you might otherwise be. See also **Dance**, page 176.

Bartender

Dreams of a bartender could signify that it's time to relax and tell a friendly person your woes to lessen your load. Because bartenders serve wine and spirits, this might be a message that you need to whine (vent) so that you can rediscover the spirit of your relationship once again. See also **Alcohol**, page 97, and **Bar**, page 73.

Bear

Dreams of a bear may help you to get grounded or may be a message to take time out in your cave so as not to lash out in anger. Additionally, you might need a (bear) hug to calm you and to make any relationship challenges bearable. See also **Animal**, page 29.

Beard

Dreams of a beard symbolize masculine power and authority as well as a desire to cover up and hide so that you might appear more powerful, manly, wise, or mysterious than you actually are. A beard might also prompt the questions, "What are you trying to compensate for?" or "What are you trying to hide?" or "Who are you trying to please?" See also **Body Hair**, page 32, **Hair**, page 48, and **Mask**, page 119.

Bee

Dreams of a bee are a message to simply be in the sweetness of your relationship. This dream may also be permission to treat yourself like a queen (whether you are male or female) so that your deliciousness can be shared with the hive. The bee is also a symbol of fertility, hidden wisdom, and a message that the impossible simply means "I am possible." See also **Animal**, page 29.

Best Man

Dreams of a best man are reflective of your supportive, chivalrous, honorable, noble, self-sacrificing, masculine aspect that holds you accountable to do and be your best self in your commitments. Additionally, a best man (just like a maid of honor) is not the center of attention, so this dream might be a message to wait until it's your turn, and know that virtue is its own reward—so support your friends in being the best men and women they can be. Your good karma will ultimately come back around to you and your relationships. See also the anima/animus discussion in the introduction, page 10, **Groom**, page 47, and **Wedding**, page 93.

Bird

Dreams of a bird may be a message to spread your wings and see your love life from a higher, more spiritual perspective. Conversely, maybe you (or your lover) have been flighty, and it's time to rest and nest before you take off in a new direction. If you dream of a hawk or an eagle, you are rising above the mundane issues in your relationship and proving your wisdom can take your love life to higher ground. Dreams of a chicken might be a message that you've been acting like a coward in your relationship, indulging in fear (acting chicken), or keeping love at bay with all your stress (running around like a

chicken without a head). Dreams of a hen might be a message to stop acting like a mother hen, gossiping, and worrying about your relationship. Conversely, you might be feeling henpecked, overly nitpicked by your partner. See also **Animal**, page 29.

Bisexual

If you dream of a bisexual person and don't identify as bisexual yourself, you may be exploring your bicuriosity or expanding your sense of self to include more love, attraction, and possibilities in your life. This dream might be a message to embrace the masculine and feminine aspects of yourself. See also the anima/animus discussion in the introduction, page 10, and **Homosexuality**, page 149.

Body

Dreaming about your or another person's body sheds light on ways to best live in the body, prevent or cure a health or sexual challenge, or reveal whether your love life is full-bodied or malnourished. Body dreams can reflect your self-image and provide guidance about how to take care of your health, well-being, sexuality, and the sustainability of your relationship, as well as your body of affairs. Your body symbolizes what is most personal and natural about you, the center of your self-confidence and sensuality. Note any particular body part highlighted in your dream; it

needs your attention. Because each physical body part we may dream about has its metaphysical counterpart, consider what the body part symbolizes, as well as doing a reality check and seeing a doctor, for example, if a body part is hurt in your dream. See also individual body parts, **Chakra**, page 142, and **Naked**, page 186.

Body Hair

Body hair is symbolic of your primal, wild, ancestral qualities. Your dream of body hair could symbolize that you are longing for warmth or wildness in your relationship. See also **Beard**, page 31.

Boss

Dreams of a boss are symbolic of a desire to be in control, get ahead, get a raise, or come to terms with issues you have with authority figures. Maybe you've been neglecting your relationship in favor of your job, or have been treating your relationship like a job. If you dream of having sex with your boss, see **Sex (with the boss)**, page 192. See also **Authority Figure**, page 30.

Bottom

See page 75 and **Butt**, page 34.

Boy

Dreams of a boy signify that you are connecting with your young, innocent male aspect. Boys are symbolic of feeling impetuous, horny, and foolhardy. You are connecting with the young male aspect of yourself that does not think about future consequences and ramifications of his actions. This dream may be a message to bring more hearty playfulness into your relationship.

Boyfriend

Dreams of a boyfriend could reflect the feelings you have or issues you are grappling with regarding your actual boyfriend or about being a boyfriend. Additionally, the boyfriend archetype represents the romantic, princely young lover, or sexual aspect of yourself. If this dream is pleasant, it reflects your internal state of harmony, self-love, and self-acceptance. If this dream is unpleasant, it could denote feelings of rejection, internal dissonance, and a lack of self-acceptance. See also **Boy**, page 33, **Friend**, page 45, and **Prince**, page 58.

Breast

Dreams of full, ripe breasts represent overflowing nurturing, sexuality, femininity, mothering, prosperity, and abundance. Dreams of small breasts symbolize ripening femininity or perhaps a lack of nurturing in your love life. See also **Body**, page 32.

Bride

Dreams of a bride represent your aspirations, hopes, and projections about romantic love and marriage. If this is a pleasant dream, it suggests that the divine feminine aspect of yourself may be preparing to commit, surrender, and allow your relationship to take the next step toward intimacy. If this dream is unpleasant, consider it an opportunity to grapple with feelings and attitudes about marriage, such as fears of getting close or making a commitment to the wrong person, or for the wrong reasons. See also **Goddess**, page 46, **Groom**, page 47, **Princess**, page 58, and **Wedding**, page 93.

Bridesmaid

Dreams of a bridesmaid signify your supportive, nurturing, helpful, feminine aspect that is holding you and those around you accountable to honor commitments. Or perhaps you are tired of witnessing everyone else's love affair and being in a secondary position, and you're ready to be the bride. This dream might be a reminder that patience is a virtue and that one day you'll have your moment in the spotlight. See also **Bride**, page 33.

Brother

Symbolically speaking, a brother in a dream represents the masculine aspect that has your back (or not); that protects you (or not); and helps you to feel stronger (or not). Dreams of a brother could signify you are processing feelings that relate to your actual brother or to being a brother, and what those qualities represent to you. Additionally, this dream can be symbolic of your desire for brotherly love, being or having a soul brother, and being connected to the sacred brotherhood of men. See also **Man**, page 54.

Bug

Dreams of a bug signify that you may be bugged by your partner, annoyed because you've been sweating the small stuff and it may be making you sick (as in "catching a bug"). This dream may be telling you to pull back and gain a glimpse of the big picture of your relationship and get perspective. See also **Ant**, page 29, and **Insect**, page 51.

Bull

Dreams of a bull could be a message for you to cut the bull (nonsense) and get honest about your true feelings in your love affair. Take the bull by the horns and make your move. Conversely, contemplate whether or not you've been a bull in a china shop in your relationship—inconsiderate as to how your actions are affecting your partner. Perhaps you've been bullish, unwilling to take no for an answer. If this rings true, then practice having some social grace and recognize that your lover has feelings too. See also **Animal**, page 29.

Businessman/woman

Dreams of a businessman or woman might be a message to make a commitment or clarify your relationship agreement. Conversely, your dream may be telling you to take a break from the business of being in love, stop taking everything so seriously, and negotiate some time to have a little fun. See also **Profession**, page 59.

Butterfly

Dreams of a butterfly suggest transformation, rebirth, renewal, and the ultimate culmination, the sweet spot of your love, sex, and romance. Perhaps you are in the early stages of a relationship (emerging from your cocoon), feeling nervous with butterflies in your tummy about being with your lover. Additionally, butterflies symbolize that you and your lover may be preparing to spread your wings and fly to the heights of your full potential together. The two of you are transforming from mere earthlings into the transcendent, liberated beings you are meant to be. See also **Fly**, **Flight**, page 180.

Butt

Dreams of the buttocks can represent issues of feeling behind, the butt of a joke, or that you are doing things ass backwards. Perhaps you're feeling defensive about being made to feel like an ass in this relationship, by revealing feelings before you know if your partner reciprocates. This dream could also signify your fondness of the derrière (or a particular person's backside) and/or a primal desire for sex from behind. See also **Body**, page 32.

Captain

Dreams of a captain or admiral symbolize that you are taking control of your relationship vessel. Because a ship can be considered a phallic symbol, this dream might be a message to stand at the helm of your relationship, claim your authority, and become a more masterful sexual partner. Additionally, this dream might show you how to become more powerful as you navigate through the ebbs and flows, highs and lows of your love/sex life. See also **Profession**, page 59.

Carpenter

Dreams of a carpenter signify that it's time to take your love life into your own hands and craft the relationship of your dreams. You've got the tools, so lay out the blueprint of possibilities with your loved one and start hammering. See also **Jesus**, page 52, **Profession**, page 59, and **Tools**, page 130.

Cat

Dreams of a cat or a member of the cat family (lion, leopard, tiger, cougar, bobcat, and lynx) represent your sensual autonomy and willingness to leap into uncharted territory. Their message to you is to be more self-sourced and sovereign when it comes to your sexual and emotional fulfillment, and withdraw your claws from your lover or those you've depended upon to prop you up. Additionally, cats send the message to be unashamed of carnal pleasure.

Dreams of a **cougar** might suggest its double meaning, as in an older woman seeking a sexual relationship with a significantly younger man. It could be an indication that you are ready to take charge of your love life.

A **lion** (also panther or mountain lion) represents the king or queen of the jungle. You may be feeling a narcissistic sense of royalty, leadership—an alpha, dominant personality. Be brave and make a bold move in your love life. See also **Animal**, page 29, and **Astrology (Leo)**, page 140.

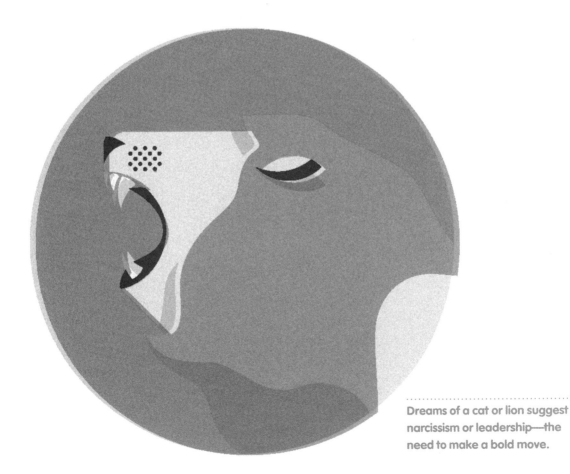

Dreams of a cat or lion suggest narcissism or leadership—the need to make a bold move.

Celebrity

Celebrities often make an appearance in dreams to shine a spotlight on your hidden resources that are essential to your relationship drama. A dream celeb might also make a cameo in your dream to help you develop your own star qualities so that you may step more confidently into the spotlight of your relationship. If you dream of having sex with a celebrity, see also **Sex (with a Celebrity)**, page 192. See also **Star**, page 128.

Cheek

See **Body**, page 32.

Cheerleader

Dreams of a cheerleader might be a message that you are in need of team spirit, or perhaps it's time to become your own champion. Once you believe in yourself, you will find it easier to do backflips for your lover while rooting him or her on in front of a crowd. Conversely, your love life might be so thrilling you wish you could jump up and down and shout it out. If so, don't curb your enthusiasm. Find a healthy outlet for this passion. A cheerleader in a dream is an aspect of your joyous self who is not afraid to show excitement, enthusiasm, and self-love. Be your own number-one fan, and stand up and cheer for how far you've come in your love life!

Chef/Cook

Food is symbolic of thoughts and beliefs, and if you are cooking the food, this signifies you are the one cooking up (creating) your belief system. This dream can be a message to remember, if you don't like what you are serving, you can change the recipe. If someone else is the chef, consider what they represent to you. Consider if you want to swallow their belief system whole, or spit it out. This dream might also prompt you to contemplate what you are hungry for in this relationship and what would feed your soul. See also **Food**, page 113, and **Profession**, page 59.

Chest

Dreams of a chest signify that you are wearing your heart on your sleeve, or you may be puffing out your chest with pride about your amazing relationship. You might even think of your heart as a treasure chest, buried beneath the protectiveness of your chest walls. See also **Body**, page 32, and **Heart**, page 49.

Child

Dreams of a child might reflect feelings you have about your own child in waking reality. Or this dream could represent the aspect of you that is vulnerable, insecure, innocent, joyous, or in need of nurturing and reassurance. It could also be a message to acknowledge the childlike aspect of you and your partner, to stop taking things so seriously and be playful. Perhaps your lover is making you feel like a virgin all over again, all sparkly and new. Dreams of a child indicate that you are feeling safe enough to show your underbelly to your lover. Keep in mind that the child part of you is your most precious and tender aspect, and without it, there is no true intimacy. In any case, this dream may be a message to value your innocence and vulnerability. See also **Baby**, page 30, and **Virgin**, page 67.

Choir

Dreams of a choir symbolize that you and your lover are making beautiful music together and have found harmony. You have found a synergistic way to cooperate and create exponential good vibrations. Additionally, a choir symbolizes strength and power in numbers and the spiritual aspect of your tribe that's singing your relationship's praises. See also **Angel**, page 29, **Music**, page 152, and **Sing**, page 194.

Christ

See **Jesus**, page 52.

Clitoris

Dreams of a clitoris, the only human organ designed purely for pleasure, signify that you may be feeling turned on by life (perhaps by your lover), sensitive, and sexually responsive. Perhaps you feel like a raw nerve, open and ready for love, or at least an amazing sexual encounter. See also **Sex**, page 192, and **Vagina**, page 66.

Clown

If you dream of a clown, it might be a message to lighten up and stop taking things so seriously. Alternatively, you may be putting on a happy face when your heart is broken. You may be clowning around or wearing a mask to cover up your sorrows. This dream may be alerting you to look behind the mask of laughter that is worn by a close friend. Your dream might be encouraging you to be more lighthearted; however, it may be showing you that too much joking indicates insecurity or inauthenticity.

Coach

Dreams of a coach suggest a desire for self-improvement, insight, information, and support to be a better partner and lover. It may be encouraging you to face any challenges and rise to the occasion. A coach symbolizes the encouraging part of yourself that helps you play your A-game and be your personal best, to stretch and grow beyond what you thought was possible. Consider acting on any advice or direction you are given in this dream. See also **Life Coach**, page 53.

Committee

Dreams of a committee signify that you are evaluating the importance of how other people perceive your relationship. Are they approving or disapproving? This dream could reflect your attitudes and beliefs toward your tribe or community, as well as your desire to rebel or seek approval. This dream might also expose the committee in your head (all your subpersonalities) trying to gain consensus and clarity about the best course of action to take in your relationship.

Coroner

Dreams of a coroner signify that it's time to stop beating a dead horse and instead honor what has died. Perhaps it's time to mourn a particular relationship dream, hope, or desire. You and your lover may be saying good-bye to each other, or to a pattern that has run its course. In any case, allow the past to be honored as you lay it to rest; to bring in the new with an equal amount of reverence and respect. See also **Profession**, page 59.

Cougar

See **Cat**, page 35.

Couple

Dreams of a couple represent your feelings, attitudes, and beliefs about relationships, partnerships, romance, love, and marriage. Perhaps you are working through obstacles to intimacy and love, and this dream may be illuminating an objective perspective about your own state of affairs. If you have a positive feeling about the couple in your dreams, they may be revealing a strategy for success in your relationship (or how to attract the relationship of your dreams). If the relationship is unpleasant, it might be revealing a behavior of yours that has been a blind spot, but with awareness can be transformed into support for your current or potential relationship.

Cow

Dreams of a cow signify that you may be craving maternal nurturing in your relationship. It may also indicate that your motherly instincts may be getting in the way of your sex life. This dream could also be a message to milk all the love your relationship feeds you for all it's worth. See also **Animal**, page 29.

Cowboy/Cowgirl

Dreams of a cowboy or cowgirl signify that it's time to dust yourself off and get back on the horse, even if you've been thrown off your game (or out of a relationship). This rugged archetype is a message to come down off your high horse, get grounded, and learn the ropes. See also **Cow**, page 38, **Horse**, page 51, and **Profession**, page 59.

Criminal

If you dream of a criminal, you may be dealing with issues of punishment, forgiveness, guilt, shame, entitlement, or retribution. Perhaps you have been attempting to meet a need in your relationship that doesn't align with your moral code, and this dream could be a call to renegotiate the terms of your relationship. This might be about a shadow aspect that you've demonized as unlovable and put behind bars to punish or do away with. See also **Jail**, page 83, and **Shadow**, page 156.

Critic

Dreams of a critic or someone being critical of you reflect your own judgments, skepticism, self-hatred, or negativity about yourself, your lover, or your relationship. This dream may be helping to illuminate the part of you that is most fearful of making a mistake or looking foolish. Keep in mind that the critic typically shows up during times of great risk or expansion. In shining a light on your inner critic, you can receive the constructive aspect of its message and release any part that might attempt to keep your love light dimmed.

Crowd

A dream of a crowd symbolizes feelings you have about groups of people. If this dream is pleasant, you may be feeling supported, like the crowd has your back. If this dream is unpleasant, then you may be feeling crowded out and need to create space for your individualistic expression of love and sex preferences, apart from the approval of your community. See also **Orgy**, page 188, and **Party**, page 86.

Cult

A dream of a cult signifies a power struggle in your relationship, or perhaps an influence that you inherently know is harmful to you. Consider that you may be feeling seduced by the influential power of your charismatic partner, afraid of the isolation or vulnerability of standing alone. Alternatively, you may want to consider whether or not you are leveraging your charisma abusively.

Dreaming of a crowd of people may suggest that you're feeling supported—or that you're feeling smothered.

Daughter

If you have a daughter in waking reality, then this dream could reflect your thoughts, feelings, and issues you have with and about her. If you are a woman, this dream could reflect your feelings about a younger, more vulnerable you. If you are a man, this dream could also be reflective of your relationship with your younger feminine side (your sensitivity, emotions, and moods) that needs support, care, and direction.

Dead People

Dreams of people who have died can symbolize communication in the form of direct guidance about your love life. This can be a message to support you in resolving grief or pain from loss, so that you can open your heart once again. These dreams are a gift not only to help you stay connected with those you love, but also give you access to life beyond your five senses, and to all that resides on the other side of the veil.

Demon

See **Devil**, page 40.

Dentist

Dreams of a dentist might be a message to clean up the communication between you and your lover. Perhaps your words have been biting and hard to swallow. This dream might be a prompt for you to forgive, make amends, and cultivate a healthier and more effective way of expressing yourself. See also **Profession**, page 59, and **Teeth**, page 64.

Detective

If you dream of a detective this may be a message to do your due diligence about your lover before taking your relationship further. It might be a message to be discerning, read between the lines, and be on the lookout for clues to reveal your next best course of action. Additionally, your dreamtime detective might be telling you to become more curious as you explore the mysterious terrain of your lover. See also **Profession**, page 59.

Devil

Dreams of a demon or devil could represent an aspect of you that brings up shame, fears about being unworthy of love, and your unintegrated shadow. Perhaps you've been feeling self-destructive or trying to deflect the blame ("the devil made me do it") instead of taking responsibility for your naughty behaviors. Keep in mind, what you resist persists, so this dream may be poking you with its pitchfork to take steps toward healing your wounds or shine a light on your self-sabotaging beliefs. This dream could be a predecessor to major transformation. See also **Seducer/Seductress**, page 60, and **Shadow**, page 156.

Dreams of a doctor
suggest your
relationship needs
serious healing.

Doctor

Dreams of a doctor may be a message that your relationship is in need of some emotional or sexual healing. Your relationship's most vulnerable, fragile, and weak aspects, once tended to, can become the most powerful aspects of depth and intimacy. This dream affirms your inner authority to tend to your mental, spiritual, physical, sexual, and relational health—and to inject you and your beloved with the self-care that will bring your relationship back into balance. Additionally, this dream might be a message to go deeper than just putting a bandage on your wound; examine the attitudes and beliefs that are producing the imbalance. Also, this dream could be a message to have some fun playing doctor with your lover. See also **Profession**, page 59.

Dog

Dreams of a dog signify a need for unconditional love, loyalty, fidelity, and to have your lover also be your best friend and protector. If the dog in your dream is angry or vicious, it may represent a disowned part of your nature that is demanding attention. It also may represent your need for protection and boundaries. Dreams of a gentle dog mean that you are connecting to your own innocent vulnerability and sense of true companionship. This dream may be telling you to be your own best friend, and be careful not to get overly domesticated in other relationships; avoid trying to obey your lover's every command. You're no one's lapdog, and your loyalty is a gift that is given to only those who are worthy of your devotion. Bypass your logic and book smarts and follow your animal instincts. Dreams of a coyote are a message to stay on your toes so you don't get tricked. Or perhaps this dream is revealing your trickster strategy for getting your needs met. This dream may also be showing you that your lover may be on the prowl or has tricks up his or her sleeve. See also **Animal**, page 29, and **Wolf**, page 68.

Dominatrix

Dreams of a dominatrix signify a desire to be whipped into shape and told what to do to please your lover or your inner critic. Perhaps you've been slacking off lately in your love affair, and your dream is demanding that you behave, or else. If you dream of being a dominatrix, then you may be stepping into your power, abusing your power, or pushing the limits of how far your desire for control can go. See also **BDSM**, page 168.

Dragon

Dreams of a dragon are symbolic of aggression, anger, violence, or transformational power that could destroy if unharnessed. Perhaps your passion, lust, or excitement feels out of control. If this is true for you, find a healthy expression for the extraordinary, fire-breathing power and passion within you, as it can transform your love life in ways that are supernatural.

Ear

Dreaming of an ear symbolizes your desire to amplify your innate ability to hear what is going on around you and to be listened to. See also **Body**, page 32.

Embryo

Dreams of an embryo signify that you are in the early stages of development and you may be feeling the need for privacy to incubate the potential of your relationship. You may be aware that in order for your relationship to grow its own legs to stand on, it needs care, attention, and gentleness. If this resonates, then keep in mind that this is not the time to pick on each other, but to go out of your way to treat each other with kid gloves. See also **Baby**, page 30, and **Pregnant**, page 189.

Enemy

Dreams of an enemy represent the unintegrated aspects of yourself (shadow, critic, judge) that may be sabotaging your ability to manifest the love you desire. Contemplate the qualities of your dream enemy (cruel, overbearing, critical, selfish) and consider how you demonstrate those qualities in your life, toward yourself or your lover. Once you've explored this, think about alternate, less destructive ways to express yourself and meet your needs.

Ex

Dreams of an ex-lover can assist you in coming to terms with a relationship from your past. They can help you recapture aspects of your power and innocence that you may have left with your former love. Perhaps you are feeling grateful to be on the other side of a tumultuous relationship, or you long for the familiarity of a former love affair. Keep in mind that dreams of an ex don't always mean that you are carrying a torch for that person. If any trauma or heartache from a previous relationship is still left psychologically unresolved, you may dream about your ex. Ask yourself, what does this person represent to me? Strength, innocence, joy, confidence, sexual adventure, or excitement? Exes may be showing up in your dream to help you rediscover a valuable aspect of yourself that has been lost. Your dreams take you back to the scene of the crime, so you can pick up the pieces of yourself—your soul, confidence, and self-respect. Your dreams are also brilliant at helping you see your part in the equation, so you can learn from your mistakes and move confidently into your next relationship, without feeling destined to repeat the past. See also **Sex (with an Ex)**, page 193.

Eye

To dream of an eye could signify an awareness of your identity and self-perception. This dream is also a message to open your eyes and see what's in front of you. In ancient Egypt, the Eye of Horace depicted dreams. Egyptians believed that you were in a highly awakened state during dreamtime. Eyelashes are associated with flirtation, and long eyelashes or batting eyelashes symbolize a desire to seduce. Because eyes are considered the windows to the soul, eyelashes reflect a subtle yet glamorous protective embellishment, or cover-up for the truth of your soul. See also **Body**, page 32.

Face

Dreams of a face signify your ability to face or deal with reality. Dreams of your face symbolize issues of outward appearance, your presentation to the world, your self-image, and your concerns with reputation and the way others perceive you. Alternatively, if you see your face in the mirror, you could be having a lucid level of awareness about who you really are, so that you can face the music and address your relationship for what it is, at face value. See also **Body**, page 32.

Dreams of an ex-lover can help you regain positive traits and feelings from a former relationship.

Fairy

Dreams of a fairy symbolize otherworldly support and guidance happening in your love life. Consider this permission to take things lightly and follow your intuition as you prepare for positive things to come. Conversely, dreams of a fairy might mean that you've been too airy-fairy, or lighthearted, about your relationship expectations, and it's time to come down to Earth.

Family

Dreams about your family members, or of your childhood home, often reflect unfinished or unhealed business you have with them in waking reality. These dreams could also symbolize that you are grappling with issues of loyalty and deeply rooted belief systems from your actual family members or your ancestral line. Psychologically speaking, it is not just you and your partner who are in bed together—you are surrounded by the spirit of both sets of mothers, fathers, sisters, and brothers. Alternatively, you may be feeling the support that comes from knowing you are part of a tribe that's got your back, even as you explore beyond the boundaries of your family tree. If you dream of an inappropriate sexual entanglement with one of your family members, see **Incest**, page 183.

Father

Dreams of a father could reflect your personal feelings or unresolved conflict toward your father, or about being a father. The father archetype within you symbolizes strength, power, guidance, support, and sometimes God. Perhaps you feel the need to handle, or man-age, your relationship. Or you may be feeling rebellious toward a paternal energy you feel from your partner. The father in your dream might symbolize criticism, judgment, and conditional love based on having to prove yourself worthy. A father also symbolizes your ability to provide for or protect yourself from harm and be your own hero. See also **God**, page 46, and **King**, page 52.

Finger

If you dream of pointing a finger, it can be symbolic of blame, shame, scrutiny, or a desire to assign fault. Conversely, your finger may be pointing you and your relationship in a particular direction to explore a new path together. See also **Body**, page 32.

Firefighter

A dream of a firefighter can be a message that there's a relationship fire (crisis) that needs to be put out. Additionally, this dream may signify a longing for a hero or a savior to come to your emotional rescue and prevent your relationship from burning out or going down in flames. This dream may also be prompting your inner hero to come to the surface—the part of you that knows how to go through the fire of relationship initiation and come out the other side unscathed. Also, this dream may be revealing the best way to play with fire and not get burned. See also **Fire**, page 112.

Fish

Because they are aquatic, fish represent the feminine aspect that knows how to go with the flow. This dream might also suggest something fishy going on with your relationship. Or perhaps you've been trying to lure your lover in, or do a bait and switch. Additionally, a fish can be a symbol for Jesus Christ and miracles. Perhaps the miracle you've been praying for is at hand. See also **Ocean**, page 85, and **Swim**, page 196.

Fisherman/woman

Dreams of someone who is fishing could be a message to be patient, quiet, calm, and allow the wisdom from the deep end of your ocean to rise to the surface and reveal itself. A fisherman/woman is related to the water element, which indicates a message to respect the feminine principle of flow. Alternatively, this dream might prompt you to teach your partner to fish for him- or herself instead of being reliant on you for needs to be met. See also **Astrology (Pisces)**, page 140, and **Fish**, page 44.

Foreigner

Dreams of a foreigner can signify that you are feeling out of your element, like a stranger in a strange land. Often what is most foreign to us is our own power—and there is no place where power can be more elusive than in the realm of intimacy. If you dream of making love to a foreigner, it may be a message to try a new position, or approach your familiar lover with fresh excitement, as if it were a foreign affair. See also **Accent**, page 138, **Alien**, page 28, and **Foreign**, page 148.

Foot

Dreams of a foot or feet are a message to come down to Earth and get grounded. The wordplay of this symbol might suggest that perhaps you said something you regret: you've put your foot in your mouth, you're concerned about putting your best foot forward, or perhaps you want to step forward in your relationship with more "soul". See also **Body**, page 32, and **Shoe**, page 127.

Fortuneteller

Dreams of a fortuneteller signify your desire to know how your relationship will turn out. This dream might be a message to receive the reassurance you desire, as well as to connect with your own psychic gifts and abilities, intuition, wisdom, and ability to read patterns. See also **Profession**, page 59.

Friend

If you dream of a particular friend, you may be processing feelings related to your relationship with him or her. Identify the three qualities this person represents to you, and recognize that you are connecting with these friendly aspects of yourself. In general, dreams of a friend signify harmony, fidelity, emotional safety, and an energy within your partnership (and yourself) that is in resonance with your soul. Conversely, if you dream of someone you're in love with wanting to just be friends, you might be processing feelings of being demoted, rejected, or not good enough. This dream might be a message for you to stop throwing yourself under the bus, and become your own best friend.

Frog

Dreams of a frog can reflect that you must search far and wide (kiss many frogs) before you find your prince or princess. Because frogs live in water and on land, they are associated with being able to hop back and forth between emotions and rational thought. This dream may reveal how to transform a challenge into a blessing. Alternatively, it may be a message to stop being superficial and judging a book by its cover, because the frog you are dating or the challenge you are facing in your love life might just be a blessing in disguise. See also **Shadow**, page 156.

Gardener

Dreams of a gardener might be a message to start pulling up weeds (negative thoughts and beliefs) from the garden of your relationship to make room for the new seeds (positive thoughts and beliefs) you'd like to plant. This dream might be a message to get down to Earth and have patience with the cycle of growth, as you prepare to reap what you sow. See also **Profession**, page 59.

Gay

See **Homosexuality**, page 149.

Genitals

Dreams of genitals signify masculine or feminine potency, fertility, vulnerability, pleasure, and masculine or feminine energy and sexuality. This dream might signify sexual desire. See also **Penis**, page 57, **Sex**, page 192, **Testicles**, page 65, and **Vagina**, page 66.

Girl

Dreams of a girl signify that you are connecting to the youthful feminine aspect of yourself. Additionally, a girl represents your virginal, innocent, playful aspect that is vulnerable yet willing to take risks. This dream may be a message to connect with this vital aspect of you, to bring more softness and femininity into your relationship. See also **Virgin**, page 67.

Girlfriend

If you are a woman dreaming of a girlfriend, this could symbolize a desire for feminine support, comfort, and affirmation. Or this dream could be helping you develop a healthy relationship with your own inner feminine energy. You also might be processing your thoughts and feelings about your actual girlfriend. See also **Friend**, page 45.

Goat

Goats can symbolize a calming effect that can help you keep erratic feelings in check, climb upward toward status and recognition, or perhaps push your way through the obstacles to your relationship success. Alternatively, in the tarot, the goat represents Pan, the half-man, half-goat god known for engaging in indulgences, including sex, drugs, food, and alcohol. In fact, this misunderstood archetype is often seen as the devil, as he symbolizes temptation of earthly desires, including power, greed, and selfishness. See also **Animal**, page 29, and **Devil**, page 40.

God

Dreams of God, depending on your spiritual or religious affiliation, can represent supreme judgment or absolute, unconditional love. Dreams of God represent your connection to your divinity and source of love, grace, and miracles. This dream may be empowering you with the capacity to love more unconditionally and forgive more fully, as well as expanding your ability to awaken to your highest form in your relationship and beyond. There's a reason we exclaim, "Oh God!" at the peak of orgasm, where we often find a divine connection. See also **Authority Figure**, page 30, and **Light**, page 151.

Goddess

Dreams of a goddess signify that your love affair is elevating you to the Mount Olympus of your highest possibilities. Perhaps you are calling on a way to find a higher love, or you dream of attracting a goddess or becoming one. This dream may reflect that your relationship is providing the space for you to access your divine feminine nature (whether you are a man or a woman), your psychic, inspired, and most metaphysically powerful aspect. See also **Princess**, page 58, and **Queen**, page 59.

Government

Dreams about the government symbolize the rules for life, conscious and/or unconscious, and your own code of conduct, beliefs, thoughts, and morality that governs your sense of right and wrong, good and bad, acceptable and unacceptable. Perhaps you are becoming aware of the distinction between you (the individual) and the governing body of the collective. This dream might also reflect your issues with authority figures. See also **Authority Figure**, page 30.

Grandfather

If you have a healthy relationship with your grandfather, a dream about him signifies wisdom, authority, and higher guidance. This dream may be an opportunity to grapple with your feelings toward God and male elders, or about aging. If you don't have a positive relationship with your grandfather, you might be grappling with issues that relate to an abuse of power. See also **King**, page 52, and **Shaman**, page 60.

Grandmother

Dreams of a grandmother typically signify your connection with the wise, feminine elder within you, the one who tells the truth and loves you unconditionally. If you don't have a positive, healthy relationship with your grandmother, you might be venting issues of abuse of power or feeling undernourished. In general, dreams of a grandmother are about wisdom and nurturing. See also **Queen**, page 59, and **Witch**, page 68.

Groom

Dreams of a groom symbolize your feelings and attitudes about marriage and commitment. You may be connecting with your higher masculine self, your lover, or an aspect of yourself that is mature enough to make and keep commitments. Consider that you have been grooming yourself for this moment all your life. Or this dream might be a kick in the pants, telling you to man up and stand tall with the divine masculine energy within you that can handle being the counterpart to the divine feminine (goddess/queen) aspect of you. See also **King**, page 52, **Man**, page 54, **Prince**, page 58, and **Wedding**, page 93.

Group

Dreams of a group reflect your thoughts, feelings, and opinions about collective consciousness. You may be attempting to differentiate the way you handle relationships from the way your family or community do. Keep in mind that the power of a group (or group think) can be seductive and empowering if you do things their way, in that there can be pressure to conform that may or may not be good for you. Additionally, this dream indicates that you may be exploring the idea of more than one lover, polyamory or even an orgy. See also **Crowd**, page 38, **Orgy**, page 188, and **Polyamory**, page 154.

Guard

Dreams of a guard signify protection, defensiveness, and the need for rationality in your affairs of the heart. Perhaps you've recently been hurt and your dream is giving you the message to be on guard and tread lightly toward the next level of intimacy. Alternatively, this dream may be revealing the reason you're finding it hard to connect with your lover—a vigilant guard at the gate of your heart. As you learn to trust yourself, you'll find emotional or physical safety and security in a deserving partner, while allowing the possibility of a wonderful relationship to develop.

Guide

Whether you dream of a life coach, angel, guru, or leader, you are connecting with the higher aspect of wisdom, confidence, clarity, certainty, and the answers to your questions. A guide signifies that you are on the right track with your relationship and that you are endowed with the wisdom to navigate your relationship's most treacherous terrain. With the confidence you gain from this connection, you will be more able to open your heart, knowing you have the answers you seek before the questions are even formulated.

Guru

Dreams of a guru (if you have one in waking reality) might be revealing your relationship with this person, and that you are receiving guidance from them. Or perhaps you've abdicated your navigational power from a source outside to a loved one. Always remember that within you is the source of your own higher awareness, wisdom, guidance, and higher knowing, should you take the time to tap into it.

Hair

Dreaming of hair is symbolic of attractiveness, health, memory, and power. If you dream of hair loss, then you might be combing through the ways to hang on to your sexual empowerment in the midst of a devastating loss, or you are no longer tangled up in the primitive game of "who's on top?" and instead may be feeling a boldness in your baldness. If you dream of long luxurious locks (longer than you have in waking reality), this dream might be giving you the message that your current relationship is fortifying you and helping you to be healthier and stronger. The question this dream prompts is, "Are you feeling empowered, lusting for power, or trying to get a grip on the sexual power you do have?" Long hair is also associated with power, attractiveness, fertility, warmth, and protection.

Dreaming of long, healthy hair suggests a strong and healthy relationship.

Hand

Dreams of a hand signify that you feel you have a handle on your relationship, or perhaps you wish your lover would give you a hand and help you out. Dreams of a left hand signify that you are relating to the feminine aspect. Dreams of a right hand reflect demonstrative action, a take-charge attitude, and a connection to the masculine aspect. See also **Body**, page 32.

Harem

For a man, dreaming of a harem, besides being a sexually charged dream or fantasy, symbolizes that you are intimately connecting with your feminine side. Perhaps this dream balances out your overly masculinized side (doing, building, creating, and proving). Conversely, this dream could signify that you've been resting on your laurels, and it might prompt you to examine your beliefs around fairness, entitlement, receiving, and being taken care of in your love life. For a woman, this dream might be a message to investigate whether or not your mate has another lover. Additionally, your self-esteem might need a boost, to move you out of the framework of being just one of the pack to being someone's one and only. See **Orgy**, page 188, **Polyamory**, page 154, and **Prostitute**, page 59.

Head

Dreams of a head represent your mental process, logic, rational thought, critical awareness, or a desire to get ahead. This dream might be showing you that you need to either be more mindful in this relationship or get your head out of the clouds and come down to Earth. Alternatively, this dream could be wordplay for your desire for a blow job. See also **Blow Job**, page 164, **Body**, page 32, and **Chakra**, page 142.

Healer

Dreams of a healer signify the need for balance and guidance related to your love life. This dream could be revealing your inner shaman/goddess that knows just the right soul medicine to prescribe for the challenges you are moving through. This dream may be prompting you to consider that when you learn a lesson from the School of Hard Knocks (like when you heal a wound), the blessing in disguise is that you have a lesson and a blessing to give to others. With that in mind, your dream might be illuminating the path to becoming a healer based on the wisdom you've been earning and learning. See also **Doctor**, page 41.

Heart

Dreams of a heart signify the status of your love life. Consider the form of the heart in your dream (e.g., a child's drawing, an actual heart, a heart being repaired). This dream could be revealing the wisdom, resilience, courage, and power of your heart as it relates to the heart of the matter in your love commitment. This dream also affirms your ability to have a hearty relationship. See also **Love**, page 185.

Heel

A dream of a heel might signify feelings of vulnerability, as in your lover knowing your weak spot (your Achilles' heel). This dream might indicate that you've been acting unkind (like a heel) and you or your relationship are in need of some healing. A dream of toes symbolizes that you are getting a grip and seeking balance in your love life. Consider whether or not you have been paying attention to the little things, or perhaps you have been counting on your partner to keep you grounded. See also **Body**, page 32, and **Foot**, page 45.

Dreams of a hero/ heroine reflect your healing abilities and willingness to make sacrifices.

Hero/Heroine

Dreams of a hero or heroine reflect your connection to this powerful archetype within yourself. The true love you desire requires sacrifice of the small self, to emerge into the hero or heroine you truly are. The hero within you is symbolic of your higher, most exalted self, your healing ability, and your willingness to do what it takes to keep loving in spite of the challenges you face. Alternatively, this dream could reflect an attachment to the role of rescuer or of needing to be rescued in your relationships. See also **Rescue**, page 190.

Holiday

See specific holidays. See also **Vacation**, page 92.

Holy Person (Pastor, Priest, Rabbi, etc.)

Dreams of a priest, priestess, pastor, rabbi, or other holy person signify spiritual authority, devotion, dedication, and sacrifice. This dream reflects that you may be discovering how to relate to your lover (and even to lovemaking) from a spiritual perspective. You may be working through any guilt you have about your sexual needs or desires.

Homeless Person

If you dream you are homeless, you may be expressing your fear of being alone, uncoupled, and cast adrift. You may be feeling disconnected from your mate or from the hope of ever being at home in a relationship. You may be working out the stress or victimhood of having lost a significant relationship and connection to what home means to you. Alternatively, you may be feeling completely untethered from all restrictions, confines, and obligations, so that now you can define home the way you most desire.

Homosexual

See **Homosexuality**, page 149.

Horse

Dreams of a horse signify that you may be fooling (horsing) around too much and not taking your relationship seriously. Or this dream is helping to give you the horsepower to rein in your lover and saddle up to put on the bridle. Your dream could also reflect your desire for a stallion. See also **Animal**, page 29.

Husband

Dreams of a husband can reflect your feelings about your husband (if you have/had one), and all that he represents to you. A husband symbolizes the masculine aspect that is hunter/provider/ protector for the family. If you are an unmarried woman, this dream may be an expression of your "dream" of what your future husband will one day be. If you are a man, this dream may help you to gain clarity about the kind of husband you want to be, or the kind you are rebelling against based on your past associations.

Insect

Dreams of insects often reflect that you've been letting the little things bug you, get under your skin, and cause friction in your relationship. Keep in mind that when you sweat the small stuff, you might be missing out on the greater good of what your love affair has to offer. Alternatively, this dream might be a message to pay attention to the minutia of your relationship agreement.

Dreams of a beetle signify that your relationship might be served if you stepped outside your preconceived ideas of how it should be and flew in a new and different direction. Dreams of a dragonfly signify that great change and transformation are occurring in your relationship. Allow yourself to approach this change in your love life with a light and joyous heart, trusting that something wonderful is around every corner. See also **Animal**, page 29, and **Bee**, page 31.

Intruder

Dreams of an intruder can suggest the presence of an unwanted person or energy in your love life. Perhaps you feel boundaries have been violated or you have not stood up for yourself to make needs clear. An intruder represents your unintegrated shadow—an aspect of your pain, shame, or blame that you'd prefer not to embrace. However, you'll discover that if or when you do embrace it, it will leave or change of its own accord. Alternatively, if you dream you are the intruder, your dream may be giving you the message to only go where you are invited, wanted, and desired, and not to waste time on people who don't see you as a blessing. See the FEAR formula discussion from the introduction, page 20. See also **Shadow**, page 156, and **Stalker**, page 63.

Dreams of an intruder suggest a shadowy, unwanted presence in your love life.

Janitor

Dreams of a janitor are a message to clean up your act, make amends, ask for forgiveness, and be willing to take out the trash and release the past. This dream also suggests your desire or compulsion to clean up after your lover's mess, cover for his or her mistakes, or obsess over spilt milk. See also **Clean**, page 174, **Maid**, page 54, and **Profession**, page 59.

Jesus

Dreams of Jesus represent unconditional love, higher consciousness, miracles, and enlightened relationships. You may be connecting with the aspect of yourself that is transcendent. If you dream of Christ, this dream might be showing you where you are acting like a martyr, putting your needs on the back burner. Perhaps someone has wronged you in the past. If so, this dream may be a message to turn the other cheek and forgive, so that you can be resurrected from your greatest heartache into a renewed, eternal version of yourself. Alternatively, maybe you identify with Mary Magdalene (the sacred prostitute archetype), and you're looking for your animus in Jesus, for spiritual partnership or for redemption. Take note of any direct guidance or advice you receive from this dream. See **Crucifixion** page 175, and **God**, page 46.

Judge

Dreams of a judge may symbolize your inner critic or a desire for fairness, justice, or redemption. Perhaps you've been feeling guilty, or a need to prove your innocence to your lover. A judge may be holding court in your dream to help you rule and be discerning about a relationship decision you must face.

King

Dreams of a king signify empowerment—you may be feeling sovereign in your love affair, like the rules of the rest of the world don't apply to you. The king is symbolic of masculine nobility, the father archetype, God, higher knowledge, vision, and ambition. Be aware of how you're using your influence. Additionally, this dream might indicate that you are rising above the masses in terms of status and inner wealth because you are connecting to your higher purpose. This dream may also reflect that you have taken the throne of your birthright and are willing to take responsibility for your power.

Knee

Dreams of a knee beg the question, "Are you feeling needy?" Because knees bend, they symbolize flexibility and a willingness to bend to meet your lover. Alternatively, this dream could be a message that your rigidity might be cutting you off at the knees. Maybe your lover is making you weak in the knees. If you dream of being on your knees, then you have fully surrendered your heart to love and perhaps have found the person you'd like to propose eternity to because they fulfill your needs. See also **Body**, page 32.

Lawyer

Dreams of a lawyer might be a message to reevaluate the laws, regulations, agreements, and parameters of your relationship so you can negotiate whether or not this arrangement works in your best interest. Consider whether the lawyer in your dream is operating on your behalf by seeing your innocence, or against you by prosecuting you as guilty. This dream might also reflect your need for justice and fairness. See also **Profession**, page 59.

Legs

Dreams of legs can be a message that it's time to stand up for yourself, your standards, your foundational principles, and the morals that uphold your integrity. Legs in a dream can also be a message to get a move on in your love life, or walk away from a situation that may be harmful to you. If someone is pulling your leg, they may be lying to you. Instead of standing still, waiting for someone to notice you (or move your relationship forward), give yourself the leg up you need and take steps toward your desires. See also **Body**, page 32.

Lesbian

If you dream of a lesbian and identify as one in waking reality, you may be processing your feelings and thoughts about what that means to you. Let this dream help you vacate any judgment or shame that would prevent you from feeling a sense of pride about your sexual identity and preferences. If you are a heterosexual woman, dreaming of a lesbian may suggest the need for additional feminine support and a message to embrace your inner self-loving lesbian. If you are a man dreaming of a lesbian, besides the sexual fantasy this might be, you are connecting with your inner feminine qualities (such as intuition and sensitivity), perhaps to help bring your masculinity into balance. See also **Homosexuality**, page 149.

Life Coach

Dreams of a life coach represent your desire to seek higher guidance and to connect with your own inner champion. This dream may be an answer to a question you've had regarding your relationship, by connecting you with an empowered viewpoint. Consider the guidance, as it might be the wisest advice that money can't buy. See also **Guide**, page 47.

Lips

Dreams of lips can reflect a desire for communing (kissing, talking, or connecting in an intimate way). This dream might be a message to be aware of gossip ("loose lips sink ships") or to be mindful when you and your lover "give each other lip," or speak disrespectfully. Keep in mind that all paths within your body lead to the throat, and lips are the gatekeepers of your self-expression. Also, because the vagina has lips, you might contemplate what your vagina would say if she could speak. See also **Kiss**, page 185, and **Vagina**, page 66.

Lover

Dreams about a lover represent feelings of desire, passion, sex, and romance. Perhaps this dream is revealing your wild side in the realm of romance. Alternatively, if you are having an affair, you may be processing guilt about your pleasure at the expense of someone else's feelings. See also **Love**, page 185.

Magician

Dreams of a magician are a message to allow the magic and mystery of your relationship to surprise and delight you. It might indicate that your relationship has mystical potential. So don't be surprised when blessings show up seemingly out of thin air. See also **Profession**, page 59.

Dreaming of a lesbian may suggest the need for feminine support.

Maid

Dreams of a maid are a message to clean up your side of the street. Explore where you might need to make amends or have judgmental thoughts cluttering up your heart space. This could also be wordplay for "made" as in "you've got it made in the shade." See also **Clean**, page 174, and **Janitor**, page 52.

Mail Carrier/ Messenger

Dreams of a mail carrier, messenger, or delivery person are alerting you to be prepared to receive an important message. Perhaps you are receiving life-altering news, or maybe someone in your life is about to deliver a baby. Also, avoid taking your feelings (good or bad) out on the messenger. You may have an important message you'd like support in ensuring its delivery. See also **Profession**, page 59.

Man/Men

Dreams of a man often reflect that you are connecting with your masculine (animus) energy, strength, demonstrative energy, initiation, decisiveness, and the force to make things happen in the world. Perhaps you're heading the call to man up in your relationship or manifest your relationship dreams to come true. If you dream of a man you are in a relationship with, consider the qualities he represents and what he means to you. Dreams of a young man, as opposed to a boy or a full-grown man, symbolize masculine energy, outwardly manifesting strength and assertiveness; that is, maturing. This dream might reflect the way you feel in your love life, or that your relationship hasn't completely found its stride yet but is on its way.

A club or group of men signifies the power of team spirit and strength in numbers. A unified group of men in a benevolent (even sexual) manner signifies that you are in harmony with the brotherhood of man, feeling empowered, and that the universe has your back. If the men in your dream are against you, then you may be dealing with issues of paternal approval or fear of being overpowered.

If you dream of men in a sexual context, you might be working out a traumatic experience, as in having been raped or abused, where you were victimized by a mob mentality. If this resonates, this dream may be helping you to get your power back, or to discover how to use your power in a way that is benevolent instead of destructive. If you are a man dreaming of having sex with multiple men, see **Homosexuality**, page 149. See also anima/animus discussion in the introduction, page 10, **Boy**, page 33, **Brother**, page 33, **Father**, page 44, **Group**, page 47, **Husband**, page 51, **King**, page 52, **Rape**, page 190, **Sex**, page 192, and **Violent, Violence**, page 192.

Mechanic

If your car is your vehicle through life, then dreams of a mechanic symbolize energy that can help you get through your love life more powerfully and repair problems with your momentum along life's path. This dream may be a sign for you to check your fluids and consider whether you are drinking and eating properly. Consider the thoughts with which you are fueling yourself. It may be time for a relationship overhaul. See also **Car**, page 104, and **Profession**, page 59.

Mermaid

Dreams of mermaids symbolize that you've found a comfort zone in the deep end of your love affair. A mermaid is symbolic of the feminine aspect of you that has oceanic wisdom, power, and beauty. Conversely, this dream may indicate that you have overly indulged in your emotions and it's time for you to come up for air, find your legs, and become more grounded and logical.

Millionaire

Dreams of a millionaire signify that you may have hit pay dirt in romance. Money in a dream (especially lots of it) symbolizes power. If the millionaire you dream of is benevolent, it may be a sign that you're learning to use your personal mojo in a sustainable and beneficial way. If the millionaire in your dream is greedy, look at where you are holding back your love. This dream may be showing you that you're stockpiling your affection in an attempt to save it for someone worthy. This dream may be telling you that the way to keep your love "bank account" in the black is to open the wallet of your heart and love the ones you're with. See also **Lottery**, page 185, and **Money**, page 120.

Monster

See **Shadow**, page 156, and **Devil**, page 40.

Mother

Are you feeling the need for some mothering? Dreams of a mother symbolize nurturing, caretaking, unconditional love, support, and understanding. Consider that this dream may be helping you process your feelings and thoughts about your own mother. Additionally, dreams of a mother could be about your own biological clock ticking, and your views of motherhood. Or this dream could signify that it is time for you to cultivate your own inner mothering skills to make you an even better partner.

Neck

Dreaming of the neck can represent flexibility, vulnerability, or stubbornness and rigidity, depending on the feeling tone in the dream. This dream may reveal that you or your relationship is under scrutiny and you feel you've been sticking your neck out. Or perhaps you, like animals in the wild, know intuitively that the best way to wave the white flag of surrender is to reveal your neck. See also **Body**, page 32.

Neighbor

Dreams of a neighbor reflect your relationships with other people and your issues with boundaries. Perhaps you're beside yourself, feeling the need to put up a fence and create some space between you and your lover or an ex-lover. If you dream about an actual neighbor (or of having a fling with the girl or boy next door) you could be processing your feelings, thoughts, or fantasies about him or her. In general, a neighbor symbolizes a friendly aspect of yourself that knows how to live side-by-side in harmony with the other aspects of you.

Nose

Dreams of a nose represent your instincts and intuition necessary to sniff out a situation. Perhaps you are feeling nosy about your lover's business. You may be sticking your nose where it doesn't belong, because something doesn't smell right. The answers you seek may be right in front of you. See also **Body**, page 32.

Nymphomaniac

Dreams of a nymphomaniac represent your animal and sexual nature seeking expression. Perhaps you've been suppressing your wild side for too long. Allow yourself to express it and make up for lost time. Dreams of having intercourse with a nymphomaniac represent your desire to be at one with freedom, liberation, and pleasure; to let your animal instincts run wild. See also **Addiction**, page 138, and **Sex**, page 192.

Owl

Dreams of an owl symbolize wisdom, patience, and intuition. This nocturnal bird also reflects the aspect of you that sees things in the dark that go unnoticed in your day-to-day consciousness. In Shamanism, the owl represents a creature that travels between worlds—between life and death, the underworld and the upper world. This dream may be helping you connect to your logic, wisdom, and higher view to guide you with matters of the heart. See also **Animal**, page 29.

Oyster

Oysters symbolize the wisdom that is earned through struggle. Just as a pearl is formed by sand, a painful irritant, your dream may be telling you not to give up on your relationship five minutes before the miracle—and to appreciate the gifts and blessings you've gained through all the trials and tribulations of your relationship. An oyster can also be seen as a metaphor for the vagina. Either way, this dream points toward personal power found via vulnerability. See also **Pearl**, page 123.

Parents (Mother or Father)

Dreams of your parents might be a message to parent or take care of yourself. This dream might also signify that you may have adopted some of your mother's or father's behaviors. Have you been playing out a parent–child dynamic in your relationship? Remember, you're meant to bring the best of your inherited qualities into your relationship. This dream might be a message that your success formula in relationships is to evolve what your parents have taught and modeled for you and take it to the next level (or many levels higher). See the archetypes discussion in the introduction, page 9. See also **Family**, page 44, **Father**, page 44, and **Mother**, page 55.

Passenger

If you dream of being a passenger in a car, it signifies that you are letting someone else do the driving (take control) of your relationship's direction. You may be deliberately playing a passive role, or this may be an unconscious pattern. If you like where you're being driven, then sit back and enjoy the ride. If not, consider that it's time to pull over and take control in a new direction.

Pastor

See **Holy Person**, page 50.

Peacock

Dreams of a peacock signify that you are feeling proud of the wisdom you've received along your relationship journey. A peacock, with its lavish display of tail feathers, symbolizes pride, vanity, and a desire to be noticed, praised, adored, and respected. The peacock can also represent immortality and alchemy, because it's believed that it receives its feathers' glorious color because of the poison from the thorns it eats. See also **Bird**, page 32.

Pedophile

Dreams of a pedophile reflect an uneven playing field in your relationship, a parent–child dynamic, or that you may be processing a real life wound from having been on the receiving end of an abuse of power. This dream could point to why you may find it difficult to let your guard down. Additionally, it could be a venting dream where you're releasing fears of being taken advantage of (or of abusing your power when you are in a superior position). This dream may be taking place so that you can resolve and heal the trauma of having your innocence taken from you. See also **Rape**, page 190.

Penis

The penis is a symbol of masculine power, strength, fertility, passion, and creative energy, and perhaps that you've been feeling cocky lately. If the penis in your dream is erect, then you are feeling virile, potent, sexual, and capable of producing and manifesting the relationship of your dreams. If the penis in your dream is flaccid, it may be a sign that your feelings about your current relationship are limp, and your partner may not be rising to the occasion. Or you might be feeling temporarily emasculated or powerless to manifest the love life of your dreams. See also **Blow Job**, page 169, and **Sex**, page 192.

People (in general)

Dreams of people reveal your thoughts and feelings about groups of people. Do you feel harmonious and supported, or do you feel like an outcast and rebellious? If this is a particular group of people that you already know, then you may be processing your thoughts and feelings about your relationship to them and perhaps working out how to integrate your love life into your social scene. See also **Group**, page 47.

Pet

Pets in dreams often reflect our domesticated wild side—the part of us that is untamed but has learned to conform in order to be accepted and loved. Additionally, our pets can be like our children, or the tender, vulnerable part of ourselves, which needs to be taken care of. Perhaps you're at the stage in your relationship where you've become comfortable with your sweetheart and you feel adored and adoring toward them. Dreams of a pet represent an adored, lovable, and innocent aspect of yourself. This could also be wordplay for foreplay, as in heavy petting.

Pig

Dreams of a pig signify you've been getting down and dirty in your sexual affairs, perhaps even lying and cheating. They might suggest that you've been greedy, selfish, slothful, or have an insatiable appetite for sex, love, or attention. Keep in mind that we can never get enough of what we don't really need. See also **Animal**, page 29.

Pilot

Dreams of a pilot are a message that you are taking the throttle of your relationship's higher trajectory. You may be realizing that if you want to reach a higher plane in your love affair, you must reach for the stars. This dream may be a message that your relationship is taking off and reaching skyward. See also **Airplane**, page 72.

Pirate

Dreams of a pirate are about rebellion, breaking the rules, anarchy, or seeking a treasure buried out of sight of your lover's or your own egotistical desires. Because a pirate is a thief on the ocean (a symbol for emotion), someone may be taking advantage of your sensitivity, or you might be feeling manipulated or manipulating someone else's emotions. See also **Thief**, page 65.

Plumber

Dreams of a plumber or of plumbing signify that you are attempting to unclog old belief systems, pain, and trauma that could relate to your emotions. You may be feeling that your sexual organs are not functioning properly and hindering your ability to go with the flow in your sexual experiences. Perhaps your pipes have been clogged while you've been holding back your feelings. Or maybe you've become so turned on that you can't turn it off. Either way, this dream is a message to release what's in the way and develop skill and mastery when it comes to turning on and off the faucet of your full-blast passion. See also **Faucet**, page 111.

Police

Dreams of the police signify you've been harboring guilt over a past transgression. Perhaps you broke your relationship agreement and you're afraid of being caught, or maybe you suspect your lover of foul play. A dream about police may be helping you to process issues that relate to keeping the peace within yourself or your sense of morality, justice, and fairness. Keep in mind that your inner police squad's job is to be vigilant about the rules, fairness, and keeping the peace in your relationship. See also **Handcuff**, page 115, **Jail**, page 83, and **Profession**, page 59.

Polyamory

See page 154.

Polygamy

See page 154.

President

Dreams of a president denote that you are connecting with your ultimate authority, sovereignty, and empowerment. You are taking total responsibility for your experiences and perhaps realizing that much is expected of someone who has been given so much. If you want to change the status of your relationship, you have the power to do so.

Priest/Priestess

See **Holy Person**, page 50.

Prince

Dreaming of a prince signifies that you are connecting with your ideal masculine aspect—the noble hero that will save you, whisk you away, and elevate you to a higher love. If you are a man dreaming of a prince, you may be working toward becoming this ideal in your relationship, activating your inner hero. If you are a woman, you may be pining for this chivalrous mate and comparing your real life lover to your fantasy . . . and your real life mate may be coming up short. Consider that this dream could reflect your animus, your masculine soul. For more on animus see page 10. See also **King**, page 52.

Princess

If you dream of a princess and you are a male, you may be connecting with your inner anima (your feminine soul) and your ideal feminine energy (your dream girl), and identifying a strategy for how to be in a relationship with such a being. If you are a woman dreaming of a princess, you are identifying with your royalty, beauty, preciousness, and how to bring your best self to your relationship. For more on anima see page 10. See also **Queen**, page 59.

Prostitute

A prostitute in a dream is a reality check to decide if the kind of relationship you want is worth the price you might have to pay. This dream might suggest you are selling yourself out or using your sexual power to get what you want or need. This dream might be a nudge to consider your values, morals, and ethics before putting on the red light.

Profession

Dreams that feature someone in a particular professional role can reveal a certain pattern, dynamic, or archetype you've been living out in your relationship. These dreams can also shine a light onto what may be needed (e.g., the particular point of view or type of support) to help you and your relationship thrive. You may be realizing that great relationships don't just fall from the sky—they require work. See specific professions or roles that may reveal themselves in your dreams to help you gain a glimpse into the type of work your relationship requires to make the grade, or even get a raise. See also individual professions.

Queen

Dreams of a queen signify that you are realizing that to attract the relationship of your dreams, you need to bow to your inner feminine nobility. If you dream of a queen and you are a woman, you are connecting with your royal highness—the part of you that is powerful, beautiful, and knows you are worthy of having it all, including the relationship of your dreams. If you are a man dreaming of the queen, as in the game of chess, the queen is the symbol of your ultimate success, achievement, and status. This relationship may be meeting your needs and filling you with royal self-esteem. Conversely, you may be feeling that your relationship or marriage is arranged—as in coupling for reasons other than love and genuine attraction. Perhaps you feel that to have the wealth, status, or circumstance your ego desires, you must sacrifice your deeper, nobler feelings of love and soulfulness.

Rabbi

See **Holy Person**, page 50.

Ram

Dreams of a ram reflect that your sexual desire or anger may be getting the best of you. A ram is related to the astrological sign Aries and is synonymous with springtime fertility, sexual excitement (horniness), and putting yourself and your sexual needs first. Additionally, this dream may be showing you the strength of your desire to meet your needs in your relationship regardless of the ramifications. See also **Animal**, page 29, **Astrology (Ram)**, page 140, and **Ram (verb)**, page 190.

Reptile

Dreams of a reptile can be symbolic of an unfeeling aspect of self, like calm and rational logic. If you've been overly emotional lately, this dream might be helping you swing your pendulum back toward a more logical or cold-blooded attitude. See also **Snake**, page 62.

Sailor

Dreams of a sailor might be a message to respect the ebb and flow of your relationship, to honor the motion of your emotion in the sea of intimacy. A sailor is also known for promiscuity (having a girl in every port). The wordplay of "sea man" relates to semen, so this dream may be about a desire to come into your oceanic sexual expression. See also **Captain**, page 34, and **Profession**, page 59.

Salesperson

Dreams of a salesperson might be a message that to have the relationship of your dreams, you've got to be sold on the fact that it's possible. Or maybe you need to convince (sell) your lover of your passion. Conversely, dreams of a salesperson could mean that there is an underlying meaning or message to your lover's advances. This dream might also alert you to your lover's or your own opportunistic tendencies, to make sure you are getting a good deal in this relationship, or to evaluate if the price you pay for what you want might be too high, or just right. See also **Promote, Promotion**, page 189, and **Sell**, page 191.

Savage

A savage in a dream is a symbol of your most wild, lusting, and primitive aspects of self, busting through the walls of social propriety to inspire the questions, "Where have I been overly buttoned up in my life?" and "Where do I need to create more room and space for my inner wild man or woman to breathe, express, and let loose?" Consider whether this dream is a message to button up and clean up your act, or to drop all convention and let your wild child free. See also **Animal**, page 29.

Scientist

Dreams of a scientist might be a message to treat your relationship like a laboratory and take risks experimenting, particularly with any new qualities, new sexual experiences, or love explorations. Release your prejudices regarding trying to perfect your relationship. This dream might be a message to free yourself so you are able to think outside the box, create your own breakthroughs, and discover a relationship that the world has never seen. See also **Profession**, page 59.

Seducer/Seductress

Dreams of a seducer or seductress (Don Juan, Casanova, or a femme fatale) symbolize sexual desires, manipulation, and short-term ego tricks to gain momentary power. This dream may be an opportunity for you to vent out your struggle with what you want versus what you know is good for you.

Shaman

Dreams of a shaman (healer, sorcerer, or medicine man or woman) signify that you are connecting with your own higher self that is wise and interdimensional. The implication could be that you have what it takes to heal any imbalance you find. This dream might indicate that you are challenged with a difficult time in your relationship, which is prompting you to call on supernatural assistance. This difficulty might just be your initiation to bring forth your latent abilities as one who can live, dream, and heal between worlds. You are waking up to your true potential. See also **Healer**, page 49, and **Wise Man or Woman**, page 68.

Shark

If you dream of a shark you may be feeling out of your depth. Perhaps you or your lover have been insensitive, cruel, or critical. Maybe you or your lover have been on a mission to get what you want without regard to how it leaves the other feeling. Or this dream is helping you to negotiate the terms of your relationship in a cut-and-dried, non-emotional way. See also **Animal**, page 29.

Shoulders

Dreams of shoulders represent strength, confidence, responsibility, and your ability to shoulder the blame or consequences of your behavior. This dream might reflect that you need a shoulder to cry on or that you are carrying the weight of the world. See also **Body**, page 32.

Sister

Dreams of your sister could be about processing your actual feelings about a sister. Dreams of a sister could also symbolize a younger or older feminine aspect of you. If you are a man, you might be experiencing the feeling of brotherly love (platonic and supportive; nonsexual) toward your sister, or processing any guilt or shame you might have regarding sexual thoughts about your sister. See also **Family**, page 44.

Skeleton

Dreams of a skeleton symbolize the primary structure of the belief systems, promises, and basis of your partnership. This dream could symbolize that your relationship isn't feeding your soul or nurturing your body's needs. Also, skeletons can represent secrets you've been keeping from your lover that may be rattling at the closet door.

Slave

Dreams of a slave represent that you are venting out energies related to being either the victim or the victimizer, operating on the misconception that you or anyone else has the right to own someone else. Perhaps you feel like your lover owns you, or you may be exploring your possessive tendencies. This dream could reflect that you are grappling with a desire for freedom from negative influence, including your own thoughts, habits, and addictions.

Snake

Dreams of a snake can be a message that you are tempted to slither away, or you might wonder if you are being seduced or deceived by your lover. Because snakes are hard to tame and seem to slither into whatever hole they can find, it may indicate that you've got wanderlust or are questioning whether or not your partner has been faithful. What most people don't know is that snakes are an ancient symbol of healing, not just a phallic symbol. Because snakes shed skin, your dream could reveal that you are healing in the place where you've been wounded. These dreams can also represent your ability to release old incarnations, attachments, and identities in your love life so that you can reinvent yourself. Many religious teachings depict the snake to be evil, as in the Garden of Eden, revealing temptation, a lover being deceitful, or even the devil. However, ancient Hermetics teach that the snake represents wisdom earned from facing and embracing your shadow. See also **Animal**, page 29, **Devil**, page 40, **Penis**, page 57, and **Shadow**, page 156.

Many people don't realize snakes are an ancient symbol of healing.

Son

If you have a son in waking reality, then this dream could be assisting you to process your feelings and thoughts about him. If you don't have a son in waking reality, then this dream could be a message for you to tap into the younger male aspect of yourself that is impetuous, carefree, or vulnerable, with bravado and a "you're not the boss of me" attitude that masks insecurity. This dream could be inspiring you to create space for the younger masculine aspect of yourself to run wild, and in doing so, let it lighten up your life and fill you with a sunny disposition. See also **Child**, page 36.

Spider

Dreams of a spider are the ultimate message that you are weaving your dreams into reality. Because spiders weave a web that draws their sustenance to them, this dream may be a message to stop running around, slow down, make your space appealing, and await the energy and attention that comes to you. If you dream of a black widow (a poisonous spider or also a woman who kills her lovers), it may be a warning to be on your guard. See also **Seducer/Seductress**, page 60, and **Web**, page 134.

Spouse

If you have a spouse and dream about him or her, you may be processing or working out aspects of your relationship. Contemplate what your spouse represents to you—perhaps commitment, support, devotion, obligation, grounding, or home. Whatever he or she symbolizes, you are integrating and embracing these qualities within yourself. If you're not married and you dream of a spouse, you are paving the way, preparing yourself to have the relationship of your dreams one day. See also **Husband**, page 51, and **Wife**, page 68.

Stalker

If you dream of a stalker, this could indicate that you may be trying to outrun or hunt down an aspect of yourself that you've not yet embraced. Shamans believe that we are always being stalked by our disowned power, as it is trying to be reunited back into the embrace of our whole being. If you dream of being stalked, you may be releasing feelings of victimhood. If you dream of stalking someone, then you've placed someone on a pedestal (your anima or animus) and are trying to incorporate them into your soul; you will come to realize they are already there. For more on anima/animus see page 10. For the FEAR formula see page 20. See also **Intruder**, page 57, and **Shadow**, page 156.

Stomach

Dreams that feature a stomach symbolize your primal, primitive survival awareness. This dream may be prompting you to contemplate what your gut instinct has to say about your relationship. For many of us, there can be a gap between our logical and rational thought and our deeper knowing. However, if we were wise, we'd let our gut be our navigational guide. Have you been trying to stomach an aspect of your partnership that is hard to digest? If so, spit it out and communicate your feelings to your lover. See also **Body**, page 32, and **Pregnant**, page 189.

Stranger

Dreams of a stranger reflect your relationship journey that may be transporting you to foreign territory, leaving you out of your element, like a stranger in a strange land. A stranger can also represent a shadow aspect of you or your relationship that you haven't yet been introduced to. Keep in mind, what is most estranged from us is our own power. See also **Foreign**, page 148, **Foreigner**, page 45, and **Shadow**, page 156.

Stripper

Dreams of a stripper could reflect your desire to be completely revealed in your relationship, to strip away all that stands in the way of your being emotionally, sexually, and sensually naked in your relationship. This dream could also be shining a light on the ways you are willing to dance to the beat of your lover's drum to get the payoff you desire. See also **Dance**, page 176, and **Prostitute**, page 59.

Student

If you dream of a student, you might be receptive to new things, ready to be challenged, and willing to be taught a lesson. You may have a particular teacher–student relationship with your lover, as you move through a rebel–submit cycle. Or this may be an aspect of your sexual fantasy, whereby you, a powerful teacher in your own right, defer your power and allow someone else to take the lead. Additionally, consider that the beginner's mind is an enlightened state. See also **School**, page 88, and **Teacher**, page 64.

Swinger

Dreams of a swinger can reflect a fear of intimacy or an adventurous, daredevil approach to love, swinging outside the lines. This dream might also symbolize your willingness to explore your inner Tarzan (or Jane) and expand the emotional, spiritual, and physical territory of your relationship. See also **Polyamory**, page 154.

Tadpole

Dreams of a tadpole are symbolic of sperm, reflecting an urge to impregnate or inspiring a pregnancy test in waking reality. This dream might also reflect the embryonic aspect of you that has a yen for the water (the female, emotional element) and might be a tad squirmy but is finding its fins in the realm of intimacy.

Tail

Dreams of a tail could signify that you're allowing yourself to be the follower (not the leader) in this relationship. If this is true, then this dream might encourage you in waking life to develop eyes in the back of your head; that is, become discerning and don't just take your lover at face value. Or maybe this dream is revealing that you or your lover are just interested in having sex (getting a little tail). Perhaps you feel that your lover is leading you around by the tail, or telling you lies (tall tales). You may be feeling like an ass for being a step behind your lover's agenda. See also **Butt**, page 34.

Teacher

To dream of being a teacher signifies that you are processing your thoughts and feelings about authority, mastery, and legacy. Often the teacher archetype is depicted with a student; this dream may be showing you where you and your partner have a give and take, where you both can learn, grow, and benefit from your partnership. Are you trying to teach your partner a lesson? Consider whether the scales are balanced or not, or if it feels that what you have to teach or learn is being received or falling on deaf ears. This dream may be connecting you with your inner wise man or woman who has the answers (from the teacher's manual) to every question on which you're being tested. See also **School**, page 88, and **Student**, page 63.

Teenager

Dreams of a teenager signify that you are in the midst of growing pains in your relationship as you try to find your voice, or are feeling out-of-control horniness without thought to the long-term consequences. Dreams of a teenager represent an awkward transition from one stage of your relationship to the next. This dream could reflect a new desire budding within you. It could also be a message to watch out for immature tendencies that are not necessarily reflective of the wise adult you are presently. You might want to get your hormone levels checked if you're feeling imbalanced.

Teeth

Dreams of your teeth reflect communication issues. Perhaps you've been biting back (withholding) the words or backbiting (saying nasty things). Either way, this dream might be a message for you to say what you mean, without having to say it mean. Your teeth are the gatekeepers for your self-expression, so make sure your communication empowers, uplifts, and enlightens. If you dream of teeth falling out, you may be feeling insecure and hungering for support or protection. Or you may also be processing an argument. Take this dream as a message to chew on your thoughts before you make relationship agreements, so you can express yourself impeccably with mindfulness. If you dream of strong teeth, then you may be feeling confident about speaking your needs and desires.

Testicles

Dreams of testicles might prompt you to evaluate whether or not you have the balls for this relationship, because it may demand that you grow a pair. This dream may be raising awareness about your mojo, gall, and willingness to assert your desires to get what you want and to lay claim to the relationship of your dreams. Alternatively, you might consider the irony of how, even though they are symbolic of power, strength, and masculine energy, testicles are vulnerable and easily hurt. This dream might be showing you how to remain humble even as you are coming into your relationship mastery and power. See also **Ball**, page 99, and **Penis**, page 57.

Therapist

Dreams of a therapist signify that you and your partner are discovering thorns that come with your relationship's rose, and you are receiving dreamtime help from your inner therapist to discover solutions for your relationship issues. A therapist in a dream is related to your higher, wiser self that encourages total responsibility for the part you play in your relationship. You would be wise to heed your own guidance. The wordplay, as harsh as it sounds, is "the rapist," which may be a message to take back your energy and power from any authority figure to whom you have given your life force. See **Authority Figure**, page 30, **Life Coach**, page 53, and **Shaman**, page 60.

Thief

Dreams of a thief signify that you lack consciousness in your relationship. Perhaps you either fear losing what you have or want to take what isn't yours. Perhaps you feel entitled to more than what you have in your love life. A fear-based consciousness tends to attract more to be fearful about and can rob you blind. Conversely, this dream might be a message to be grateful, appreciative, and take care of what you do have. Thus, your lover or potential lover will be drawn more deeply toward you. See also **Shadow**, page 156.

Thigh(s)

Dreams of a thigh signify that you are standing strong in your sexual power and your sexual preferences and that you have the endurance to stand up for yourself, if need be. Additionally, a thigh signifies that you have the ability to walk toward whatever or whomever you want. If the thighs in your dream are spread, this denotes receptivity to a sexual exploration. If the thighs are closed, this signifies an instinct to close yourself off. See also **Body**, page 32.

Throat

A throat in a dream prompts the question, what are you trying to say? This dream might signify a desire for communication, expression, creation, and manifestation. You may be realizing that your words have power and the potential to make or break your love affair. This dream might be a message for you to speak up for yourself or to realize that sometimes silence is golden. This dream might also be related to "deep throat"— the desire either to keep a secret or to provide pleasure. If this resonates, see **Blow Job**, page 169. The throat also represents your vulnerability or your issues with betrayal, as in someone going for the throat or being cutthroat. See also **Body**, page 32.

Thumb

Dreams of a thumb could be about the way you rate your lover (thumbs-up or thumbs-down). Also, consider whether or not this dream is sending you a message that you're under your lover's thumb. If so, this dream could be a wake-up call to change your current circumstance and get a handle on your power. Consider trying to pick something up without using your thumb. It is important when it comes to gaining control or getting a grip on your life. See also **Hand**, page 49.

Tongue

Dreams of your tongue are related to self-expression, speech, taste, preferences, likes and dislikes. Anything related to your mouth represents communication and a desire to aptly let your lover know how you really feel. If you dream of French kissing or using your tongue in a sexual way, this means you are expressing the language of your soul. The tongue is like a miniature sword, and the words we use can heal or injure. This dream might be a message to choose your words wisely. See also **Body**, page 32, **Cunnilingus**, page 176, and **Kiss**, page 185.

Transgender, Transsexual, or Transvestite

Dreams of a transgender, transsexual, or transvestite individual symbolize your awareness that you are every woman and man, and that all aspects of humanity and sexuality are within you. Perhaps you've been curious about how the other half feels. Or maybe you've been feeling overly in touch with your masculine side (if you're a woman) or overly in touch with your feminine side (if you're a man). Your dream might be helping you to find balance, acceptance, and celebration of the unique and wonderful being you are. See also the anima/animus discussion the introduction, page 10.

Turtle

Dreams of a turtle signify that you've been overly sheltered, feeling protective of your sensitive underbelly. Perhaps you're recovering from having been hurt and overexposed. This dream may also be a message that it's okay to take your time coming out of your shell and slowly reveal yourself as you get to know your lover, one step at a time. See also **Animal**, page 29.

Twins

Dreams of twins can be symbolic of the two sides of your or your loved one's personality. This can also reflect or indicate duplicitous behavior. Alternatively, this relationship may be bringing you double the pleasure compared to what you're used to. See also **Astrology (Gemini)**, page 140.

Umbilical Cord

Dreams of an umbilical cord represent your depth of connection to your mate. This dream might be revealing the maternal-like (mothering) bond you share with your lover. Alternatively, this dream may be revealing that you've become overly dependent, and this is a wake-up call to reattach your umbilical cord (plug in or connect) to your higher power, to have a more balanced and less needy relationship with your lover. See also **Cord**, page 108.

Uterus

Dreams of a uterus can reflect a desire to go deep with your lover. This dream may reflect that you are connecting with the sacred feminine (the goddess within) or perhaps your desire to be internal with your relationship (stay indoors, beneath the sheets, in your own little womb). Consider the wordplay of uterus, "you tear us," which invites the question, "Where might you be sabotaging your relationship—tearing (being overly critical or rejecting) at the very fabric that is being created?" See also **Pregnant,** page 189.

Vagina

A vagina is the quintessential symbol of all that is feminine. It represents receptivity to love and openness to be penetrated by your lover's intent and desire. A vagina can also be seen as a symbol of fertility, desire, sensuality, vulnerability, and sacred feminine power. Perhaps you are feeling open to love and to being loved, and this dream is helping you feel connected to the essence of your femininity. See also **Body**, page 32.

Vampire

Dreams of a vampire are symbolic of parasitic, addictive behavior that tries to live off the energy of another. Perhaps you feel your lover is sucking you dry, demanding too much of your time and attention. Or you may be feeling overly needy in your relationship. This seductive dream could be a message to become responsible for your own well-being and to tend to the relationship you have with your eternal source so that you don't have to fall into unsustainable power struggles with your mate.

Victim

Perhaps you've allowed your relationship to sap your strength, because you've given all your power over to your lover. Dreams of a victim might shine a light on unresolved issues resulting from a relationship power struggle that needs to be revealed and healed. See also **Rescue**, page 190.

Virgin

Dreams of a virgin represent vulnerability, a beginner's mind, curiosity, innocence, and that your love affair is causing you to feel brand-new. This dream might be revealing that your best relationship strategy is to act like you've never been hurt and contemplate who you would be if you knew you were whole, complete, and safe. Even though you may have been around the block a few times, perhaps there's a part of your heart that has been healed, that you're allowing to be touched, as if for the very first time. See also **Child**, page 36.

Voyeur

If you are watching a sexual act in a dream, this may reveal your aloof, detached relationship strategy: being more comfortable dreaming about the relationship of your dreams than realizing it. Conversely, dreams of a voyeur can help you can gain objectivity about your strategies. Additionally, this dream may be telling you that if you remain aloof in your relationships—avoiding the pain of being on the playing field—you may be allowing your love life to pass you by.

Warrior

When this fearless, ruthless, powerful aspect reveals itself, it is usually because you're feeling threatened, mistreated, or in danger and in need of protection. Your inner warrior can give you a boost of confidence, knowing that you have it in you to survive the crisis you are moving through. The battle you're in may be an actual fight (intense disagreement with your mate) or a war within yourself, feeling torn between conflicting needs and determining which one will win out. Your dreamtime warrior reflects that all your resources need to be rallied to attention, because what you say and do during a period like this can make or break your relationship. This dream might also be helping you to pick your battles, and to know when to lay down your arms, when to stand firm and take charge, and how to create a win-win situation in all your relationships. See also **Battle**, page 168.

Whale

Dreams of a whale signify that you are connecting with your oceanic power. Perhaps your love affair is stimulating deep feelings from your ocean floor to rise to the surface. Alternatively, you may feel you are in SOS mode, overwhelmed by your whale of a relationship, or need to cry (wail) a river. Whales, because they are aquatic, are associated with the deep feminine, the psyche, the soul, and your sexuality. Keep in mind that your power is always stalking you and there is no place where power (your true mojo) plays hide and seek more than in the ocean of our intimate relationships. See also **Animal**, page 32.

Wife

Dreams of a wife reflect your feelings, thoughts, and associations with marriage and what it means to be or have a wife. If you are married and dreaming about your wife, then you might be working through issues that relate to her. However, a wife symbolizes the feminine archetype most identified with the caretaking of her husband—above her career, herself, and even her children—and being the woman he needs her to be. This might be an ideal dream to you, or you might rebel against the institution and feel the need to revolutionize your relationship and what it means to be committed (spiritually, physical, or legally). See also **Husband**, page 51, **Marriage**, page 83, and **Spouse**, page 63.

Wise Man or Woman

Dreams of a wise man or woman are a blessing in that they offer you guidance through a challenging moment in your relationship. This man or woman may be related to your higher self; it might be a spiritual guide, or a departed loved one's enlightened message to you. See also **Grandfather**, page 47, **Grandmother**, page 47, **Guide**, page 47, and **Shaman**, page 60.

Dreams of a wolf suggest you may be on the prowl for a loyal life mate.

Witch

Dreams of a witch may signify your connection with the crone archetype—a symbol of great wisdom and empowerment. If the witch in your dream is malevolent, she may represent a dark feminity that is hell-bent on revenge. She may represent the shadow aspect of you that feels scorned, disrespected, or treated unfairly and will not sit meekly by and allow it. Often a dream visitation of this kind is a message that it's time to adopt a more raw and authentic version of yourself. If the witch in your dream seems more like an earth-goddess type or Wiccan, your dream may reveal that when you harness the potency of your true nature, your words have the power to create worlds and you are a force to be reckoned with.

Wolf

Dreams of a wolf signify that you may be grappling with a relationship strategy that is sly, cunning, and predatory. Additionally, this dream may be showing you that you don't have to be a lone wolf for the rest of your life, and perhaps you're on the prowl for someone you can mate with for life. You have proven that you are resilient and resourceful, but it may be time to risk joining your wild side with that of your true love. Perhaps this

dream is preparing you to meet or recognize the person you will pledge your heart and loyalty to. See also **Animal**, page 29, and **Dog**, page 41.

Woman/Women

Dreams of a woman are symbolic of intuition, receptivity, nurturing, sensuality, and caretaking. A woman (as opposed to a young girl) might be reflecting your own maturity regarding feminine traits—for example, to receive rather than take or to control emotions without their controlling you. Dreams of a young woman, as opposed to a girl or a full-grown woman, are symbolic of your feminine aspect (sensitivity, intuition, emotionality, nurturing) and your maturing relationship. This dream might signify that you are finding your ability to harness your emotions and channel them in a positive, life-serving way in your relationship. It might be telling you that there is room to grow your love affair but to take heart in knowing that you are making progress as you bloom. Perhaps you are feeling idealistic, overflowing with emotions as you swoon in the direction of your romantic dreams being realized. Dreams of women or a group of women can reflect that you are coming into a relationship with the vastness of your emotions, intuition, sensuality, and nurturing.

Conversely, from the shadow side perspective, this dream could signify that you've been overindulging in your emotions, passivity, jealousy, or victimhood. If you dream of a group of women in a sexual context (e.g. a harem), you might be expressing a need to feel special, adored, and lavished with goddess attention (supernatural femininity that evokes healing and gives rise to the higher self). See the anima/animus discussion in the introduction, page 10. See also **Crowd**, page 38, and **Yin Yang**, page 161.

Womb

Dreams of a womb are symbolic of depth, intimacy, and the need to cocoon yourself away from the world, or to nurture the early growth of a new or potential relationship. Perhaps you are looking for a safe place to hide or are hoping to feel safe enough in this relationship to take your lover into your inner sanctum. See also **Pregnant**, page 189.

You

When you make an appearance in your dreams, whether in the first or third person (you can see yourself, you feel that you are there, or you know you are perceiving the dream through your unique lens), it signifies that you are gaining an objective view into what makes you tick. This dream may shed light on your love life strategy, how you get your relationship needs met, your deeper feelings, and a holistic view about how your actions and behavior affect your partner.

Zombie

Dreams of a zombie are a message that you've become listless and are sleepwalking in your relationship. Perhaps all work and no play has made Jack or Jill a dull boy or girl; you've been working hard in other aspects of your life—career, fitness, hobbies, or friendships—and have no juice left for your relationship. This dream could be alerting you that you've allowed your partner to take over your mind and you've joined the walking dead. If this resonates for you, it's time for you to snap out of it and regain your power. This dream may be a call for help, yelling at you to make a concerted effort to bring your liveliness to your relationship.

Chapter 2

Time and Place

(and Seasons, Locales, and Events)

Just as the saying goes, in the real estate world there are three things to remember when valuing a property: location, location, location. In the dream world, the same is true when evaluating your love life.

The time, season, locale, or event in which your dream takes place can reflect the state of your relationship. Whether your dream environment is messy or clean, urban or old-fashioned, natural or man-made, opulent or basic, foreign or familiar, the house you grew up in or outer space circa 2150, it reveals a great deal about the context of your love life. When seeking to understand the time or place, of your dream, consider that it is revealing insight about the phase you and your beloved are moving through (or have gotten stuck in), so that you can discover a new route to your desired destination and the best timing to get you there.

Think about how in your waking reality, when a friend asks you, "How are you and [insert your significant other's name] doing?" you may find yourself answering, "We're in a good (or not so good) place."

Our relationships will either take us where we want to go or not, and our dream locale is our inner GPS alerting us as to whether or not our love life can stand the test of time.

When contemplating your dream time or locale, ask yourself these questions:

- **How do I feel about this place?**
- **Does this time of day, season, or location give me a positive or negative feeling about my love life?**
- **Am I trying to get out of this place, or am I trying to get into it?**
- **What part of me is this dream locale revealing?**
- **What are my feelings or memories associated with this time in my life or with this place?**

In general, our dream locale will reflect our personal state of mind/spirit so that if we like where we are, we can take that as a message to unpack our bags and stay awhile. However, if we don't like where or when our dream takes place, it might be a sign to look for the nearest exit door out of our personal rut or out of our relationship.

Afternoon

Dreams that take place during the afternoon signify lucidity. The lights are on, and the sunlight of your awareness is shining at full force. You and your love might consider some afternoon delight and take time for fun during this sunny time in your romance.

Aging

See page 165.

Airplane

Dreams of an airplane signify that your relationship dreams are taking flight. This dream might also signify your desire to elevate your relationship to a higher plane, perhaps the next stage of commitment. It could also be a nudge to drop your ego and earthly baggage, to see things from higher up. If the airplane in your dream is experiencing turbulence, you might be in the midst of dramatic change in your relationship. If it is on the ground, then you are being guided to have patience as you make sure you're equipped and prepared for your next relationship journey to take off. If you are soaring through the air, you are well on your way to manifesting your heart's desires. See also **Fly, Flight**, page 180.

Airport

Dreams of an airport symbolize a waiting room between flights, an opportunity to ensure that your mind/body/spirit is tuned up before you take off, or to regroup after having just landed (hopefully not from a crash landing). Perhaps it's time for you to refuel by preparing for your next relational/sexual flight of fancy. Contemplate if you are actually ready for your relationship dreams to lift off. Often it's easier to fantasize about the relationship of your dreams, but it might be an entirely different story when it comes to having the audacity to actualize them. See also **Airplane**, page 72, and **Fly, Flight**, page 180.

Alley

Dreams of an alley may reflect a shadow aspect of yourself or an avoidance behavior. Ask yourself if your front entrance matches the behind-the-scenes aspects of your love life. These dreams may be a cue to take those aspects you'd rather leave hidden behind a dumpster, clean them up, and embrace them in the light of day.

America

See **Country**, page 78.

Amusement Park

Dreams of an amusement park could signify that you feel your relationship has been an emotional roller coaster. Or perhaps you've been given a pass to revel in the joy of your relationship, and this dream might be a message to enjoy the peaks and valleys, highs and lows, bumps and grinds of your relationship. See also **Park**, page 85.

Ancient

See **Old**, page 85.

Anniversary

Dreams of an anniversary signify that you are connecting with the rewards of your staying power and the strength of your commitment, endurance, and fortitude.

Attic

Dreams of an attic symbolize that your relationship is taking you to higher ground. An attic is often related to the mind, where your belief systems, inherited thoughts, and customs (that you'd forgotten about) are stored. The wordplay of attic could also be "addict," so consider whether this dream could be shining a light on addictive tendencies or memories you've packed away. See also **House**, page 83.

Autumn

If you dream of autumn, it might signify that your libido is beginning to wane. Perhaps your relationship or sex life has reached a plateau stage, and you may be negotiating your way through the individuation stage in the relationship. Additionally, you may be wondering whether to let your feelings pile up, like leaves on the lawn, or to address your concerns, so that you might fall back in love again. See also **Season**, page 88.

Back Door

Dreams of a back door symbolize your awareness of the finite reality of your relationship, and perhaps an escapist tendency to explore what lies beyond the door. Perhaps you fear intimacy or you've been looking for a passive-aggressive way out of an argument, commitment, or opportunity to talk about your deeper feelings. Maybe you need an escape, even a brief one, from your relationship or commitment. A back door can also be sexual innuendo for anal sex.

Backseat

If you dream of being in the backseat, it might indicate that you've given your partner the steering wheel, so that you can be more passive about the direction of your relationship. Or maybe you've allowed your sensuality to take a back seat to your more rational, grown-up sensibilities. Additionally, this dream might reflect that you've been a micromanaging backseat driver in your relationship. If you dream of making out in a backseat, you could be reconnecting with your wild, adolescent, sexual self whose rational mind has taken a backseat to your sexual impulses. See also **Car**, page 104.

Balcony

Dreams of a balcony symbolize the need for some fresh air, an outside perspective, and a desire to see the events of your relationship from a higher view. A balcony also intimates romance (as in Romeo and Juliet).

Bank

Dreams of a bank symbolize that you may be grappling with whether or not to bank on or trust your lover. You may be getting ready to invest your time, energy, and mental and emotional capital in the love of your life, and this dream could be helping you evaluate the solvency of the arrangement. This dream could also be helping you process money issues that may have to do with your self-confidence, security, and sense of worth. See also **Money**, page 120, and **Number**, page 153.

Bar

Dreams of a bar or nightclub might prompt the question, "Are you raising or lowering the bar of your romantic standards?" Consider whether or not it serves your best interests to bar or "barricade" yourself from unsavory customers or contenders. Keep in mind that you reserve the right to refuse business from anyone who doesn't seem worthy of you. Since in waking reality a bar is a place where alcohol is served, and where people go to hook up, it could signify your desire to break loose, go wild, and drop the ordinary formalities of your persona. See also **Alcohol**, page 97, and **Barricade**, page 99.

Barn

Dreams of a barn symbolize a storehouse for your wild self and a place to care for, feed, and shelter animal instincts, power, and resources. Perhaps you are preparing for the opportunity to "unleash the beast" with your lover (let your animal aspect out of the barn) when you feel it is safe and appropriate. See also **Corral**, page 78.

Basement

Dreams of a basement signify the energies that underlie your motivation for love and sex. The basement is where your deepest primal beliefs, fears, and unconscious ancestral energies are stored. It's also where the bodies are buried, so to speak: unresolved memories of unrequited love, past heartbreaks, and shameful secrets. This may be a message that it's time for some show-and-tell with your lover—a time to reveal your secret qualities or dark past by bringing them into the light. Unpack those boxes and share the deeper (and perhaps darker) aspects of yourself in the soft glow of the daylight. See also **House**, page 83, and **Shadow**, page 156.

The beach is a place where all the elements collide, and thus it is a symbol of transformation.

Bathroom

Dreams of a bathroom symbolize the need for a good flush, an attempt to release, unclench, and shed your worries, anxieties, and fears down the drain. A bathroom also suggests that you might need some privacy—time away from your lover—while you let loose (cry, scream, have a temper tantrum), so you can emerge feather light and refreshed.

Beach

The beach is a place where all the elements collide, and thus it is a symbol of transformation. Here you bring all elements of yourself into your relationship (earth, wind, fire/sun, water). The beach can also relate to your empowerment, synchronicity with the movement of the tides, and the cycles of your relationship's flow. The beach in your dream might suggest that your relationship has oceanic potential. See also **Ocean**, page 85.

Bed

See page 100.

Bedroom

To dream of a bedroom could indicate that you're ready for a sexual awakening. In dreams, your bedroom symbolizes your inner sanctuary and the aspects of yourself, your life, your past, and your sexual self you'd prefer to keep private. Ask yourself, "What part of myself do I want to keep hidden behind closed doors?" or, "What aspects of myself and my sexuality am I ready to reveal in the light of day?" You may opt to keep your sensuality private; however, just like skeletons in the closet that make noise, we are as sick as our secrets. This dream may be an invitation to remember that your sexuality is healthy and beautiful, so you can feel free to be more energetically and physically naked, honest, and vulnerable with your lover (or at least with yourself). Conversely, because your bedroom is the one place where you are revealed as you truly are, this dream may be showing you that you have a need or desire to drop the curtains, close the door, and take a respite. So that when you are ready, you can allow your lover to see the true, raw, intimate you. See also **House**, page 83, and **Room**, page 86.

Birth

See page 168.

Birthday

Dreams of a birthday signify a new beginning of a growth cycle or opportunity in your relationship. You may be feeling seen, appreciated, and celebrated in your relationship. If, however, this is not a joyous occasion, you might be grappling with issues of getting older related to your lovability and sexual attractiveness. If this dream is unhappy, you may be feeling disappointment that your relationship is not seeing or reflecting your best. See also **Party**, page 86.

Boat

Because water is symbolic of feelings, sensuality, and the mystery of love, dreams of being on a boat reflect that you are floating just above the depths of your emotions. This dream might also reflect the status of your relationship; for example, it may be smooth sailing or on rocky waters, or your relationship has set sail and you are navigating your way through the ocean of your emotions. See also **Ocean**, page 85, and **Ship**, page 88.

Bottom

Dreams of being on the bottom, sexually speaking, can symbolize a passive state of surrender, submission, and allowing. Perhaps you want to empower your partner to be on top. If this dream feels good to you, then you are altruistic, allowing others' needs and desires to take precedence. However, if this doesn't feel like an empowering dream, it may be a message to be more assertive and speak your mind about what you need, so as to rise to a higher level and not be overlooked in this relationship. This dream could be about your bottom line, symbolic of a desire for clarity and clear-cut agreements, or possibly even issues having to do with money. See also **Butt**, page 34.

Bridge

A bridge in a dream signifies your connection to the past and the future of your relationship possibilities. Additionally, this dream could reveal your ability to mediate and see both sides of conflicting aspects of yourself and your loved one. If a bridge is in need of repair, your dream may be telling you to slow down in your new relationship or business venture. If a bridge is burned, this may mean a relationship has been severed or is in the midst of major transformation. If you are crossing a bridge, you are moving forward in your relationship.

Brothel

Dreams of a brothel signify your connection with the prostitute archetype, prompting you to ask yourself if you are selling yourself out in this relationship.

Every relationship requires compromise; however, what price are you willing to pay to have the love, sex, and relationship you desire? This dream could be a wake-up call to be aware of where you might be seduced into undervaluing yourself for short-term gain. Alternatively, this dream could suggest a desire to act out on forbidden desires. See also **Prostitute**, page 59, and **Red Light**, page 124.

Building (noun)

If you dream of an actual building, this could be helping you see the kind of relationship you have built. Is the building in good shape or in disrepair? The status of the building will reveal the status of your relationship. Additionally, if an aspect of the building is emphasized, it can draw attention to where your relationship is focused. If you are on the lower level (basement), this denotes an emphasis on the primal/sexual/instinctual aspect. If you are on an upper floor, penthouse, or roof, it means that you and your lover are connected to your higher purpose and spiritual reason for being together. If you are somewhere in the middle, your relationship is seeking a balance between higher consciousness and your sexual/primal selves. See also **Build**, page 171.

Cabin

To dream of a cabin might suggest you are hiding away from love. Alternatively, the cabin could symbolize that you and your sweetheart need time alone in your natural habitat. Dreams of a cabin can be a message that you have found your center, sanctuary, and inner haven. Because you've found a cozy place nestled within yourself, you can be self-reliant and independent in your relationship.

Camp

See page 172.

Car

See page 104.

Car Park

See **Parking Lot**, page 86.

Carnival

A dream of a carnival is a message to don a mask and drop your inhibitions, shame, and perfectionism in favor of wild abandon or a romp on the wild side. This dream might prompt you to take a risk, put your hands up, and enjoy the ride of your life. A carnival can represent permission to be free and live out what normally would be socially frowned upon. See also **Celebration**, page 172, **Mask**, page 119, **Party**, page 86.

Castle

Dreams of a castle signify magic and that you view your relationship as if it were a fairy tale. Because a castle is, in essence, a fortress, this dream may be asking you to become aware of hiding or protecting your wealth, resources, talents, prominence, and magic from your lover. See also **Fairy Tale**, page 147.

Cemetery

Dreams of a cemetery suggest an ending to either a pattern or a relationship. This dream could signify that it's time to lay a belief system to rest. You may be grieving and moving through the bittersweet sorrow of missing your connection to an ex or a departed loved one, or you may be releasing a cherished attachment. Pay respect to your former self and prepare for a new and better incarnation. See also **Death**, page 177, and **Dead People**, page 40.

Christmas

Dreams of Christmas suggest that you are reveling in the gift of your love affair. You may be feeling present to the miracle of transformation that happens when you unwrap your heart and are willing to be a giver in your relationship. Christmas is a symbol of the Christ-like aspect (higher love) of you and your relationship. See also **Jesus,** page 52, and **Gift**, page 114.

Church/Temple/ Mosque

Dreams of a church, temple, mosque, or other holy place symbolize your relationship with spirituality. This dream might also be revealing your most cherished beliefs regarding your love and sex life. If this dream is unpleasant, you may be working through fundamental judgments about sexuality or your relationship preferences. This dream may be helping you to release self-doubt, drop the garments of limited beliefs, and discover your ability to create a sacred relationship and divine trinity between you, your lover, and a higher power.

Dreams of a circus suggest you are stretching your boundaries for your lover.

Circus

Dreams of the circus suggest that you are going to extremes in your relationship. Perhaps you're discovering a personal edge in your self-expression. Perhaps you feel like you're doing death-defying flips, swallowing swords, walking on glass—all in the name of stretching your boundaries for your lover. Additionally, you may feel that your love affair has become a three-ring circus. If so, consider running away, taking some private time away from the scrutiny of your friends and family so you can explore the unique and maybe larger-than-life qualities of your relationship out of the limelight. Additionally, this dream could signify that your love life may be bringing out some extraordinary qualities of your genius that you might have previously deemed freakish.

City

If you dream of a city, it symbolizes your constructive, manifesting, masculine side that is building your relationship, hopefully on solid ground. Perhaps you are feeling out of touch with your sexual/animal nature because you've been caught up in the traffic, noise, and hustle and bustle of your daily life.

Cliff

Dreams of a cliff signify that your relationship may be taking you to your edge and beyond. Perhaps you are on the verge of taking the leap into intimacy, and this dream is showing that you are at a life-altering point in which you either leap and build your wings as you go, or run in the other direction.

Closet

Dreams of a closet are shining a light on secrets you think could be cause for rejection if discovered. A closet also symbolizes a safe hideaway for your innermost feelings or secrets. If you dream of being in the closet, it might mean you are grappling with becoming public with your sexual preferences, or with your shadowy parts seeking recognition. If your dream scene involves actually coming out of the closet, it may be telling you to be public about your feelings and that your ego is strong enough to handle it, regardless of how others may judge you or your relationship.

College

Dreams of college suggest that you seek a higher degree of love or sex or a higher-level relationship. You may feel you are in a love-life learning phase, being tested and stretched beyond your comfort zone. This dream may reveal that every challenge you face is a learning opportunity. The dream may also relate to significant relationships (unfinished business) from back in your college days. See also **School**, page 88, **Student**, page 63, and **Teacher**, page 64.

Concert

Dreams about a concert symbolize harmony, resonance, and the complementary energies flowing with synergy between you and your lover. It could be that you two are making beautiful music together and it's time to make it public. See also **Music**, page 152.

Convention

See page 175.

Corral

This dream might be a message to rein in your (horse) power and learn to manage your personal responsibilities so that your passion doesn't run off without you. This dream could also suggest that you are feeling fenced in by your relationship and are grappling with conflicting needs of freedom and security. See also **Horse**, page 51.

Country

If you dream of your country of origin, it may be challenging you to discover your sense of belonging and self-identity within the territory of your relationship. This dream may be supporting you as you grapple with your desire for the comfort of being at home and simultaneously expanding your borders and seeking new horizons that may be off the beaten path. Contemplate the primary adjectives you'd use to describe what your country and its customs mean to you (e.g., home, free, comforting, constricting, judgmental, supportive, conservative, liberal, etc.), and consider that they describe the backdrop of what may be informing your relationship. See also **House**, page 83. If you dream of a foreign country, see also **Foreign**, page 148.

Court

If you dream of a court, you may be feeling like you're on trial, under scrutiny, guilty about a past transgression, or you need to stand up and prove your innocence. You may be attempting to judge whether or not this relationship is the one for you, or if forgiveness is an option. Alternatively, you might be in the courtship stage of your romance—proving, evaluating, or judging whether or not your partner is the right person for you. Additionally, this dream may be telling you it's time to lay down the law in your relationship. See also **Judge**, page 52.

Crossroads

A dream of being at a crossroads symbolizes that you need to make a choice in your relationship and evaluate the pros and cons of the decision. This dream may be a message to tap into your higher self to bring lucidity to a life–altering decision you are about to make.

Cruise

See page 176.

Date

Dreams of a date can be a preparation or rehearsal for how you would like your next courtship to go (or continue as the case may be), and a sign that you're ready to put yourself out there. This dream might also be inspiring you to romance yourself. Alternatively, you might be feeling time-bound and have a preconceived idea that your romance should meet certain milestones by a preordained day on a calendar.

Death

See page 177.

Desert

Dreams of the desert symbolize that you may be having a relationship dry spell. You may be feeling like you're in no-man's land, en route to where you'd like to be but not there yet. Although your love life may look bleak right now, you're moving toward more fertile ground. Conserve your energy, because you'll soon get a chance to quench your thirst.

Dinner

Dreams of a dinner or any shared meal suggest a shared belief system. Dinner also signifies a social time for bonding and feeding yourself some social sustenance. Perhaps you hunger for a delicious date or a zesty courtship.

Dungeon

Dreams of a dungeon symbolize that you are exploring your feelings around punishment, shame, and blame. This dream might also spark a desire to explore the shadow side of your sexual interests. See also **BDSM**, page 168, **Jail**, page 83, and **Shadow**, page 156.

Earth

Dreams of the Earth might signify that your lover means the world to you. Earth is a symbol of your body and the world of your relationship. If your dream features Earth in a state of harmony, then this is a reflection of your relationship. If the Earth in your dream is in distress, your relationship might also be in trouble. Pick your battles and look for a win-win situation. See also **Ground**, page 114.

Eclipse

See page 178.

Elevator

Dreams of moving up in an elevator signify that you desire to elevate your relationship status or move up in the world together. This dream may be showing you that you know where the buttons are, so you can advance in your love life with a sense of confidence and control. If the elevator in your dreams is moving down, you may be feeling a loss of control, moodiness, or depression. Moving down could also signify your desire to seek depth in your partnership. If your dream elevator is moving sideways, you might fear that you are making lateral moves and not necessarily progressing in your relationship. Additionally, sex in an elevator is a popular fantasy, which denotes that you are thrill-seeking and willing to take risks. See also **Escalator**, page 79.

Escalator

Dreams of an escalator symbolize moving at a quick clip toward your relationship desires. If the escalator is moving up, then you are feeling optimistic about your love life. If the escalator is moving down, you may be coming down from a high, going in the wrong direction, or exploring the depths of your nature. See also **Elevator**, page 79.

Fall (season)

See **Autumn**, page 73.

Forest

Dreams of a forest indicate that you've been so fixated on the big picture that you haven't been allowing yourself to see the details. A forest reflects being in touch with your primal nature, the true nature of your relationship, unexplored regions of your love life, animal instincts, healing, and enchantment. This dream could indicate a need to step away from your preconceived ideas, get back to the wilderness of your organic way of being, throw off your clothes, and let your love life unfold the way Mother Nature intended it. See also **Tree**, page 132.

Garden

A garden is symbolic of your blooming relationship finding its way into organic maturity and growth. This dream may be a message to ensure that your love life gets the nurturing, time, attention, and care it deserves. Perhaps it's the season to prune back thorny aspects of your behavior (e.g., anger issues or resentments). If you feel that your relationship is overgrown with weeds, then this dream is a nudge to trim back on time together and allow space to grow in the sunlight of your own spirit. Keep in mind that the best relationships know how to compost the destructive energies and turn them into fertilizer for their internal gardens to grow and flourish. See also **Flower**, page 112, and **Fruit**, page 113.

Graduation

Dreams of a graduation signify that you have completed a cycle of growth and are ready to walk across the threshold to a higher realm of love. You no longer have to suffer or struggle with the issues that have been familiar to you up until now. You have paid your dues and passed your tests with flying colors, and you can now move on as you enroll your energies in higher degrees of mastery in love and romance.

Grocery Store

Dreams of a grocery store signify that you are at a decision point and are being mindful of the thoughts, beliefs, and mental constructs into which you invest your energies. You might consider what thoughts you've been buying into lately regarding love and sex, and whether or not they feed your soul or nurture the body of your love life. Consider what you buy. See also **Shop**, page 194, and **Store**, page 90.

Gutter

See page 115.

Gym

Dreams of a gym signify the need to work out an issue with which you and your partner have been grappling. This dream might be giving you the reassurance that with each challenge you work your way through, you are developing stronger relationship muscles (discipline, determination, and heart), so you can handle the heavy lifting that comes with the journey of true love.

Halloween

Dreams of Halloween signify the thinning of the veil between worlds. Halloween means "all hallows eve," a time to honor the dearly departed, and when you dream about it, you may be reviewing what you've learned from past relationships. You might be finding the treat in all the places where you've felt tricked or betrayed in a relationship. This dream is an opportunity to give the past its due, honor it, and give it a proper burial. Additionally, it could bring awareness to the different masks or disguises you wear and to the social roles you play in your relationship. See also **Costume**, page 108, **Mask**, page 119, and **Shadow**, page 156.

A garden is symbolic of your blooming relationship finding its way to organic maturity and growth.

Hallway

If you dream of being in a hallway, you may be transitioning from one place to another, one state of consciousness to another, or one relationship (or sexual partner) to another. A hallway is symbolic of having options, and you get to choose or commit which way you will go. Because a hallway is a transitional space between where you've been and where you are going, this dream signifies that you are exploring beyond the confines of what is normal and habitual, but you haven't yet found what you're looking for. Perhaps you are feeling the need for a hall pass from your relationship.

Hanukkah

Dreams of Hanukkah signify that the lights are on in your love life. Because Hanukkah is about the gift of light during a dark time, this dream is a symbolic message of hope if you've been discouraged or disenchanted in your relationship. The blessings new love brings can heal past heartaches and deliver you to a new dawn.

Hell

Dreams of hell signify that you may have hit a rough patch in your relationship. Keep in mind that the darkest hour is before the dawn. A dream of hell is a clue to stop blaming your partner and take responsibility for your part of the relationship that has gone wrong.

Highway

Dreams of a highway can be a message to drive—engage your will—as you take your relationship to higher ground. It is encouragement to go above and beyond and do what it takes to gain a higher view of your current situation. See also **Road**, page 86.

Hill

See **Mountain**, page 83.

Holiday

Dreams of a holiday signify a reprieve from the struggles in your love life. You may be feeling a holy (whole, fulfilled, content, satisfied) bond with your lover. This dream may also be a message to become present, take a reprieve from past squabbles or future yearnings, and enjoy the gift of being together in this moment in time. See also **Vacation**, page 92.

Home

See **House**, page 83.

Honeymoon

A honeymoon is symbolic of a delicious getaway to establish your relationship, whether you are headed to the altar or not. This dream might reflect the desire to get away from the beehive of life and hibernate with your lover without outer influences buzzing in your ear.

Hospital

Dreams that take place in a hospital signify a need for healing in your relationship. Keep in mind that you can't heal what you can't feel. So if this dream is shining a light on your big relationship wound (or the wound that triggers your mate), you are halfway to the healing you desire. Additionally, there may be a desire on your part to play doctor with your lover.

Hotel

Dreams of a hotel symbolize impermanence and a temporary place to lay your head, as in a one-night stand. You may be feeling that you are not with Mr. or Mrs. Right but with Mr. or Mrs. Right Now, and that it's okay to love the one you're with. Alternatively, this dream may be letting you know that the phase you are going through in your relationship is transitory—a passing blip on the radar screen of your eternal love story.

House

Dreams of a house symbolize your view of yourself, your body, and the body of your relationship. The levels of the house represent different parts of your relationship (e.g., the attic is higher consciousness; the main floor is mundane/ego perspective; the basement is unconscious/primal point of view). On a physical level, the shape, size, and decor of a house, as well as the activity within it, are a reflection of how you think and how you see yourself within the four walls of your love life. If you are uncomfortable in the home, this dream may be recommending self-improvement or couple's therapy. If you are comfortable in the home, you are at home within your relationship and growing strong roots. Additionally, you and your beloved might be in the beginning stages of your romance and you may be playing house and contemplating moving in together. Or, if you've been together awhile, you might be moving into a deeper level of comfort together.

Jail

Dreams of jail might signify that you've been feeling smothered in your relationship. Perhaps you've been feeling trapped by your commitment. Or you may have ventured too far outside your relationship/sexual comfort zone and you're paying the price behind bars of guilt and shame. This dream might be a message for you to think before you indulge in a behavior that could bring an undesirable consequence. Remember, forgiveness is the key that can set you free. See also **BDSM**, page 108, **Handcuffs**, page 115, and **Police**, page 58.

Lake

Dreams of a lake are associated with the water principle: intuition, sensitivity, emotionality, and flow. Perhaps you are feeling refreshed by your relationship or desire, taking a dip in the calm, cool waters of your relationship. Conversely, this dream might signify your relationship is at a standstill. Either way, it indicates that you are aware of the ripple effect your relationship has on your circle of life.

Lift

See **Elevator**, page 79.

Marriage

See **Marry**, page 186.

Maze

Dreams of a maze symbolize your desire to find your way through the land mines of emotional drama. Perhaps you're realizing that your relationship is more than a game but a true hero's journey, fraught with tests and difficulties. Ultimately, if you continue to rise to the occasion, you will find your way to that elusive center and the success and happiness you have been dreaming about.

Mountain

Dreams of a mountain or hill reflect the way you handle obstacles, challenges, or difficulties in your relationship. If you dream of walking, climbing, or driving uphill, then you are facing and surmounting the challenges presented by your lover. If you try to go around the mountain, you may be avoiding an uncomfortable confrontation. If you are at the bottom of the mountain looking up in frustration, you may feel that your relationship is an uphill battle. If you are on top of the mountain, you are likely feeling victorious, empowered, and clear that the ups and downs of your love life were worth it. A dream of a mountain could be a message that you want to mount or be mounted by someone. You may be working toward your sexual peak. Because hills and mountains can resemble breasts, this might signify a need for nurturing before your next big adventure.

Oasis

Dreams of an oasis can signify that you have found or soon will find the relationship of your dreams. After time spent in a relationship or sexual drought, you're headed toward a heart- and soul-filling experience. Remember this fertile feeling, for it can support you to enhance your relationship and soak in all that you've been thirsting for.

Ocean

Dreams of the ocean are symbolic of being in touch with your feminine side and preparing yourself to take the plunge into the deep waters of intimacy. Water is a symbol of the feminine energy within you, and the ocean symbolizes the vastness of your passion and spirituality, the motion of your emotion, the rhythm of nature, and the ebb and flow of your feelings, creativity, and cycles. This dream could be a message for you to let go of any firm, rigid ideas about how your relationship should unfold and instead to go with the flow. Take time to delve into your feelings, cry your eyes out, and open to the mysteries of your femininity. Remember, you are comprised of at least 70 percent water, so flowing is your natural way. If you dream of the ocean and have a pleasant experience, you have a harmonious and trusting connection with your inner mystery, emotions, and ability to be current with life. Water is essential to life, and water and the ocean symbolize someone or something essential to your well-being. Dreams of ocean creatures (e.g., fish, dolphins, whales, and mermaids) signify your connection with your own multidimensional wisdom, intelligence, and healing.

Old

Dreams of something old or antique can signify something that gains value as it ages—like fine wine or a relationship—or something that has lost its charm. This dream might be prompting you to address your feelings about aging, to keep your relationship fresh and new (even if you've been together forever), or to respect the fact that time under your belt doesn't necessarily make you wise—it's what you do with your time that counts. Perhaps you're coming to value your lover or friends who have earned your respect, credibility, and authority and have stood the test of time.

Overpass

See page 122.

Paris

Paris is symbolic of the ideal romantic rendezvous. Your dream might be inspiring you to put a bit more amorous effort into wining and dining your lover. You may be creating an affair to remember. If so, allow your lover to sweep you off your feet.

Park (noun)

Dreaming of a park could signify a desire to connect with nature, or with your authentic nature. This dream could be a message to spend more time outdoors (outside the four walls of your relationship), or to think outside the box of your relationship to breathe some fresh air into it. A park is also a place where children play, so it might be guidance for you and your lover to take some time out of your ordinary, serious life to play.
See also **Park (verb)**, page 188.

Maze dreams (page 83) challenge you to find the elusive center—success and happiness in your relationship.

Parking Lot

Because dreams of a car symbolize your ambition or drive, a parked car can mean that you feel stalled in your love life, need a break from the fast lane of your relationship, or are in need of a tune-up—a physical check-up to make sure all your body's systems are running smoothly. If you dream you're looking for where you parked your car and can't find it, this may be a message to keep track of your commitments, promises, and the energy that drives your pursuit of a relationship. This dream may be cautioning you to be aware of the allure of the bright and shiny aspects of a new person that might cause you to forget where you parked your current relationship. In other words, don't abandon the care you've been giving to your current lover without being truly mindful of the consequences. See also **Car**, page 104.

Party

Dreams of a party signify that it's time to have some fun in your relationship. Perhaps you've been making your relationship all about hard work, or maybe you think it's always supposed to be fun and games. Dreaming about a party symbolizes multiple aspects of your subpersonalities harmoniously interacting. Whether the party is joyous or uncomfortable, it reflects your level of self-integration. If this is a joyous occasion, this dream is celebrating the strides you've made in your relationship. See also **Celebration**, page 172.

Prison

See **Jail**, page 83.

Restaurant

Because food symbolizes beliefs, thoughts, and nurturing, if you dream of dining in a restaurant, you are opening yourself to the thoughts of others. This dream may be showing you that you allow yourself to be fed and nurtured by relationship beliefs other than your own. Consider what type of food is being served on the menu and who is serving it. Keep in mind that you are always making choices. See also **Menu**, page 120.

Road

Dreams of a road symbolize the journey of your relationship. You may be gaining perspective that you are in this for the long haul. Consider the state of the road (bumpy or smooth, sharp curves or straight as an arrow). If it feels like you're on the right track, then stay the course. If it feels that you're on a road to nowhere, then this dream may be telling you to pull over and consult your internal GPS. See also **Highway**, page 82.

Room

Dreams of rooms in a house reflect whether or not you are making room for all aspects of yourself and your lover in the house of your relationship. Or you might be getting so hot and heavy that you need to get a room—some privacy to express yourselves sexually. Additionally, each room in a house signifies an aspect of your physical body, your meta-physical body, and the space you create to nurture your relationship. For example:

Bathroom: cleansing/release

Kitchen: nurturing/feeding

Bedroom: sexuality/privacy/relaxation/intimacy

Living room: social/ego expression

Attic: higher consciousness

Basement: unconscious feelings/desires

Front porch: outer presentation/facade

Backyard: primal expression

A dream about school (page 88) signifies the learning phase of your relationship.

Salon

Dreams of a beauty shop or a hair salon suggest a desire to look good in your relationship, to put your best foot forward, to be admired, and to appear more alluring and attractive on the outside than you might naturally feel on the inside. This dream might be a message for you to prepare for the relationship game. Conversely, this dream might reveal how you rely on superficial attributes to lure your lover in. Keep in mind that if you want a love that will stand the test of time, you've got to let your lover see you with your hair down. See also **Hair**, page 48.

School

In dreams, school signifies a learning phase in your relationship, as you grow and grapple with issues relating to independence and dependence. School dreams may hearken back to the first time you felt pressured to fit in or make the grade in a relationship, or when you had your first kiss or first sexual experience. This dream may also be testing you. These dreams may help you find redemption so you can remove your heavy backpack of insecurities and graduate to a more empowered relationship. Most people who have recurring school dreams are highly driven, success-oriented individuals who are constantly testing themselves. See also **Test**, page 130.

Season

Dreams that feature a particular season provide an insight into the current temperature of your love life. Seasons in dreams can give you practical guidance as to how to weather any storm that may be blowing through. See also **Autumn**, page 73, **Spring**, page 88, **Summer**, page 90, and **Winter**, page 43.

Ship

Dreams of a ship reflect the status and seaworthiness of your relationship. If the ship in your dream is in good shape, then it has what it takes to carry you through the long haul. If the ship in your dreams is in disrepair, then there may be issues that need to be tended to in order to support your passage on the high seas of intimacy. Because a ship in waking reality is large and can travel across deep water, it may be a message that your relationship is carrying the goods to go the distance. If you dream of a yacht, your relationship is rich, in terms of love and all that you need for a joyous voyage together. See also **Boat**, page 75.

Shop

See page 194 and **Store**, page 90.

Spring

If you dream of spring, you are in a phase of new beginnings in romance, whether you've been with your partner forever or you just met. This dream may be a message to see your partner with new eyes, and to become like a virgin again by making love, kissing, dating, and beholding your partner as if for the first time. See also **Season**, page 88.

Staircase

Dreams of a staircase can signify ambition and a desire to go places. Perhaps this dream could also signify your step-by-step play toward achieving the love, sex, and relationship you desire. If you dream of ascending a staircase, then you are moving up in the world with your partner and discovering higher, loftier, perhaps more spiritual aspects of your love life's possibilities. If you dream of descending a staircase, then you and your lover may be spiraling into a negative pattern, or you may be exploring the basement of your house together (a place of depth and grounding). See also **Elevator**, page 74, and **Ladder**, page 117.

Dreams of a staircase signify your step-by-step play toward achieving the love, sex, and relationship you desire.

Store

Dreams of a store reflect the beliefs, desires, and thoughts you are buying into about your relationship. This dream might be revealing all the choices that are available to you, and prompting you to consider them before investing your time and energy. If the shop belongs to you, consider what you are selling. What traits or ideas are you trying to get your partner to buy into? See also **Shop**, page 194.

Stream

Dreams of a stream (and water in general) reflect your feminine aspects: intuition, sensuality, compassion, empathy, and nonresistance. Your dream stream might also symbolize that your love affair is bringing you into the current of the present moment—where the continuity of true love runs in perpetuity. This dream could also reflect an easy-breezy stage in your relationship, a time for taking it easy, resting, and allowing your love to flow, "merrily, merrily, merrily—life is but a dream." See also **Water**, page 93.

Summer

Dreams of summer signify a passionate stage in your relationship. This dream may be a message that you can take the heat, so allow yourself permission for as much pleasure as you can handle. See also **Season**, page 88.

Sun

See page 129.

Supermarket

See **Grocery Store**, page 80.

Theater

Dreams of a theater suggest that you have a desire to allow your inner drama queen/king to act out. This dreamtime theater may be helping you to gain awareness of the roles you play, masks you wear, and scripts you write in your relationships. Additionally, you may desire exposure, expression, and recognition for your feelings and creativity. You may also be gaining objectivity about the contrast between your backstage persona and what you present to the world. See also **Costume**, page 108, and **Play**, page 188.

Time (in general)

Dreams of time could be a message that it's time for a reality check regarding your relationship. Perhaps you've been taking your time, and this dream is spurring you to get a move on. Or this dream could be alerting you to the reality that you've been allowing external factors to impact the internal, organic unfolding of your relationship's natural flow. If you are a woman and are taking any form of birth control, you may be concerned about your period being late. You may be coming to your senses and expressing your fear of this. See also **Clock**, page 106, **Date**, page 79, and **Watch**, page 93.

Time of Day

Dreams that clearly reveal the time of day, just as a season or a day of the week, may reveal an underlying feeling, tone, theme, message, such as:

Morning: Suggests a fresh, clean start; a sunny, joyous feeling; optimism; naïveté; or an open mind.

Noon: Signifies that the spotlight of clarity and illumination is upon you, revealing the truth of the situation. This dream could also reflect your hot feelings of passion or anger, or your productive, work-oriented attitudes.

Midday: Suggests a slightly more somber tone than other times of day, a more sober outlook and feeling about your relationship.

Night: Signifies romance, a more relaxed, seductive time of day when your love life gets the focus of your attention.

Midnight: Signifies the darkest hour before the dawn, a dark night of the soul, and a bewitching hour when you feel related to the world between worlds.

Tomorrow

A dream about tomorrow might indicate that your relationship goals are only a day away. The message of this dream is to be patient as you prepare yourself mentally, emotionally, and spiritually for what you want to create in your relationship.

Tower

Dreams of a tower could reflect that you've put your lover on a pedestal, or he or she has put you on one, and you may find yourself or your lover falling back to earth. A tower, in addition to being a phallic symbol, can represent great success. The message of this dream might be to build your relationship on strong foundations so that it won't falter when the winds of change blow. Additionally, dreams of a tower can be about power and intimidation, as in towering over someone. In fairy tales the princess gets locked in the tower, which could reflect that your relationship has been isolating, creating an unhealthy disconnection with the rest of the world. This dream might prompt you to contemplate whether or not your relationship can stand up to the changes you're going through. What changes to the tower should you make so it won't fall down? In tarot, a tower signifies a foundation that can be rocked if it is not stable.

Dreams of a tower can be about power and intimidation, as in towering over someone.

Tunnel

Dreams of a tunnel could reflect that you and your partner have discovered a hidden passageway to explore previously undiscovered dimensions of your body, mind, and soul. Perhaps you or your partner have tunnel vision, in which case this dream may be nudging you toward a broader perspective. Conversely, a tunnel could symbolize a depression, or even a dark night of the soul. If so, don't forget to look for the light at the end of the tunnel. Dreams of a tunnel could also symbolize a vagina or uterus, reflecting that you may be opening yourself for your lover to find the hidden feminine treasures of your heart, mind, body, and spirit.

University

See **College**, page 78.

Vacation

Dreams of a vacation symbolize a desire for change or an escape from hard work, whether that is your job or your relationship. Vacation dreams can also prompt you to open your mind, expand your horizons, and contemplate new ways of mating and relating. This dream might signify that it would be wise to take a break from your loved one and from the stress of life and relationship drama.

Vault

Dreams of a vault signify your secret feelings and resources that perhaps have been hidden from view. This dream might prompt the question, "What is it you don't want people to know about you?" or, "What is it you don't want to let yourself consciously know about your partner?" Often treasures or great sums of money are hidden in a vault, so this dream signifies that you have inner riches that you have yet to discover or reveal to your loved one. See also **Safe**, page 126, **Treasure**, page 131, and **Warehouse**, page 92.

Volcano

See page 134.

Warehouse

Dreams of a warehouse signify untapped resources within you. Perhaps you're waiting to lavish affection on your loved one someday. This dream may be revealing that there's more to you than meets the eye, or more to your lover than you realize. Perhaps you are coming to realize just how powerful and fully stocked you are. If the warehouse is empty, this could signify that you are open and available for a fresh delivery of love, sex, and untold delights.

Dreams of a vacation symbolize a desire for change or an escape from hard work, whether that is your job or your relationship.

Watch (noun)

Dreams of a watch may signify that your biological clock is ticking. Perhaps you are aware that your timing regarding the progression of your relationship may be different than your lover's. Conversely, if you are a procrastinator, your lover might be the one watching out to see if you are going to make your move. If this is the case, then know that time is on your side. See also **Clock**, page 106. For **Watch (verb)**, see **Voyeur**, page 67.

Water

Dreams of water are often related to the mystery of all that is feminine (sensitivity, feelings, sensuality, sexuality, emotions, creativity, intuition, deep unconscious, and even dreams). Biologically speaking, because we consist mostly of water, it is symbolic of our being in touch with our deepest essence. To have the relationship of your dreams, you must learn to go with the flow. Water can take myriad forms in dreams, from a cool drink to a full-blown tsunami and everything in between, just like the span of your relationship. See also **Ocean**, page 85.

Wedding

Dreams of a wedding represent the joining of the divine masculine and sacred feminine within you. If the wedding in your dream is a joyous affair, then you are connecting with the ways to harmonize your relationship with your partner, as well as your relationship between the opposite energies within you. If the wedding in your dream is stressful or chaotic, you may be releasing your fears, worries, stresses, and discordant thoughts about your actual wedding or the aspects of your own psyche you are trying to bring together. Because weddings are such an ideal in the minds and hearts of many women, there is a lot of pressure for perfection put on them. Your dreams may help you bring sanity to such an event, both physically and metaphysically. See also **Commitment**, page 174, **Husband**, page 51, **Wife**, page 68, and **Marriage**, page 186.

Winter

Dreams of winter signify a chilly period of your romance, perhaps even a crisis. Your heart may have turned to ice, or your partner may be acting like an ice king or queen. You may be going through the autonomy stage in your relationship, where you find your sense of independence apart from the relationship. At this point, your fairy-tale romance may seem to be crashing down,

or, if you can figure out how to stay warm, this may be the place where true love actually begins. See also **Season**, page 88.

Yacht

See **Ship**, page 88.

Young/Youth

Dreams of youth, the fountain of youth, or of young people symbolize that you are in touch with the wellspring of vitality within you. This dream may be sending you a message for you and your lover to have more fun in your relationship, take things more lightly, and make more time to play. You may be discovering that your relationship is not a problem to be solved, but a magical treasure hunt to explore.

Zoo

Dreams of a zoo represent your attempt to cage in your animal instincts, primal urges, and sexual drives. Alternatively, you might be attempting to display only the aspects of your sexuality that you want your lover to see. This dream might be giving you the message to find your natural habitat so you can unleash your urges and let your inner Tarzan and Jane roam free. See also **Animal**, page 32.

Chapter 3

Physical Objects

(the Visible and Tangible)

It may surprise you to discover that a great love affair, sexual relationship, or long-term partnership takes work. Sure, the initial spark of attraction is easy and sometimes comes when you least expect it. However, to make love stay, you've got to tattoo this mantra to your forehead: "It works if you work it!" In other words, a great love affair is not likely to fall into your lap from the sky without some participation by you.

When interpreting the stuff of your dreams, ask yourself: "How does it work? And what is its function?" For example, if you dream of a phone, its function is to help you connect or communicate with someone. Now that you've identified the object's function, think about its functionality: Is this thing working?

I'm sure you've heard the terms functional and dysfunctional to describe a family system or a relationship that is either harmonious or has become a sideshow act. The object in your dream will reflect the state of care/carelessness, balance/imbalance, and connection/disconnection within your relationship. If the thing in your dream is broken or malfunctioning, it may reflect that your relationship is missing a few screws. If the thing in your dream is doing its job, then congratulate yourself for ensuring your relationship remains a well-oiled machine. To understand the objects in your dreams, contemplate these questions:

- **How do I feel about this thing?**
- **What does this remind me of?**
- **If it is broken, how might it be repaired? Or is it broken beyond repair?**
- **Is this a message to look at my love life more objectively?**
- **Am I feeling like an inanimate object, robotically going through the motions?**
- **Am I treating my partner like a thing or a tool?**
- **Have I been tending to the soul of my relationship?**

Whether you dream of a shoe, hammer, or doorknob, every thing serves a purpose, represents a particular aspect of yourself, or reflects your relationship functionality. Once you unpack the deeper meaning of what these dream objects are trying to tell you, you can fix what's broken, grease the wheels of what is working, and transport your love life beyond the owner's manual into a realm that makes the intangible—love, awe, ecstasy—tangible.

Accelerator

Dreams of an accelerator signify your need for speed: a desire to stimulate your relationship to hurry and catch up with your aspirations. Or this dream may be the speed bump you need to slow down. Take a breath and become present with each moment. Your dream may be about your foot being stuck on the gas, unable to stop from careening out of control. Perhaps this dream is a message that your lover is driving you crazy with his or her ambition to take your relationship farther and faster than your comfort zone can handle. If so, consider this to be a message to pull over and create a new relationship road map. See also **Car**, page 104, and **Drive**, page 177.

Ace

Dreams of an ace denote good luck and success in your love affair. This dream may be revealing that you've been hiding your winning attributes (trump card) up your sleeve. Perhaps you feel that your relationship has been testing you, and this dream is prodding you to make the grade and ace the test. See also **Ace (verb)**, page 165, and **Gamble**, page 181.

Acne

Dreams of acne can represent shame, self-criticism, unexpressed rage, and adolescent feelings or expectations about your lover. Consider that puberty is an accelerated time of sexual awareness, so perhaps you're feeling like a teenager again, in the awkwardness of a new relationship, noticing the out-of-control feelings you've been holding back.

Acorn

Dreams of an acorn signify that you are in the early stages of great possibilities in your love affair. Within the acorn is the blueprint for the mighty oak tree, which is symbolic of great potential and indicates that your highest relationship destiny is taking root within you. The acorn in your dream could represent that your relationship is capable of being larger than life. Alternatively, this dream might be a message of literal or metaphorical pregnancy, or that your relationship may be driving you nuts. See also **Seed**, page 126.

Advertisement

Dreams of an advertisement could signify that you want to be seen and recognized in your relationship. There may be a message you want to send to your loved one in BIG BOLD LETTERS. Dreams of advertisements can

symbolize that it's time to be bold and upfront with your needs. It could also be a message to pay attention to signs the universe is sending you regarding your love life.

Air

See **Wind**, page 161.

Air Conditioner

Dreams of an air conditioner can represent a subconscious desire to chill out your internal thermostat. For example, if you and your lover have been running too hot and heavy, allowing passion and impetuousness to overheat you, then your dream may be alerting you to take a cold shower to achieve balance. Or if you've been playing it too cool, this dream may be a message to turn up the heat of your attention and affection in your relationship.

Airplane

Dreams of an airplane signify that your relationship dreams are taking flight. This dream might also signify your desire to elevate your relationship to a higher plane, perhaps the next stage of commitment. It could also be a nudge to drop your ego and earthly baggage, to see things from higher up. If the airplane in your dream is experiencing turbulence, you might be in the midst of dramatic change in your relationship. If it is on the ground, then you are being guided to have patience as you make sure you're equipped and prepared for your next relationship journey to take off. If you are soaring through the air, you are well on your way to manifesting your heart's desires. See also **Fly, Flight**, page 180.

Alarm

Dreams of an alarm are a message to wake up, pay attention, and be present, because something important is happening or changing in your relationship, and it would be a shame if you missed it.

Alcohol

Dreams of alcoholic beverages represent a desire to pour more spirit into your love life. Conversely, dreams of alcohol can symbolize a desire for abandon, an escape, or a diversion from your present state of affairs. Perhaps this dream is revealing that you've been numbing your relational/sexual pleasure or pain and that it is time to look through sober eyes at what's working and what's not in your relationship. If you dream of cleaning with alcohol, you may have an emotional wound that needs healing.

Almond

Dreams of an almond signify that your relationship may be making you nutty. Or perhaps your outer shell that is designed to protect you is actually keeping intimacy at bay. Because of its husk, an almond represents substance hidden behind a rough exterior; your ego might be obscuring your open and loving heart and soul for fear of being swallowed whole.

Altar

Dreams of an altar symbolize a willingness to alter and transform your relationship and bring it to a higher level, which could imply marriage or perhaps simply a desire to bring your love life to higher, more spiritual ground. See also **Ceremony**, page 142.

Ambulance

Dreams of an ambulance signify a dangerous imbalance in your relationship. Perhaps you are having an emergency, make-it-or-break-it moment in your love life, or you've let yourself get carried away in a fit of passion, or you've held back your feelings and you are reaching the breaking point. See also **Accident**, page 164.

Amulet

Dreams of an amulet signify that you may feel the need for supernatural support to help you with your love life. This dream might also be helping you evoke power, strength, and wisdom from a higher source to lend you a hand during a challenging time in your relationship. See also **Jewelry**, page 116.

Anchor

Dreams of an anchor might signify that you've been feeling adrift on the stormy sea of your relationship and you desire security, to feel grounded, or to be tied down. Alternatively, this dream might reveal how to become free from any binding chains, so you can explore intimacy in the vast ocean of your emotions. See also **Chain**, page 105.

Anesthesia

Dreams of anesthesia suggest that you're feeling numb in your relationship or that an issue may have emerged in your love life that seems too much to bear. This dream is telling you to pay attention to your body's wisdom. Keep in mind you can't heal what you can't feel. See also **Drug**, page 111.

Apple

Apples represent a healthy, nubile relationship. Dreams of an apple also symbolize the vagina, fertility, health, and the divine feminine. Alternatively, this dream could signify that you've been feeling tempted by forbidden fruit. See also **Fruit**, page 113.

Arrow

Dreams of an arrow signify that you are trying to hit the bull's-eye of your lover's affection. Considering the context of the dream, arrows represent direction, focus, and the ability to be clear about what you want in your love affair. An arrow might also relate subconsciously to the Greek god of love, Eros (otherwise known as Cupid, a cherub with arrows), representing a desire for a heart-piercing love affair that can catapult you and your sweetheart into higher love.

Art

Dreams of art or an artist can be about your need or desire to express your passionate, creative heart with your loved one. Alternatively, many creative people receive their best inspirations in dreamtime. If you are viewing or creating nude art or art that is of a sexual nature, you might be trying to cultivate a taste for the finer things in the realm of your sexuality.

Ash

Dreams of ashes denote that the fire has been extinguished from your relationship. Perhaps you are laying it to rest and it's time to let it go, like dust in the wind. Just like fertilizer in a garden, ashes help new life to grow. Take heart in knowing that the wisdom of what you've learned will support a new insight to spring forth.

Ass

See **Butt**, page 34.

ATM

Because money is what you deposit and withdraw from an ATM (automatic teller machine) and money is a symbol of power, a dream of an ATM suggests a desire or need for instant gratification. The ATM is the financial equivalent of a sexual quickie, a short, sweet, and efficient affirmation of love, connection, and reassurance that you are both being provided for and empowered in this relationship. See also **Money**, page 120, and **Number**, page 153.

Autograph

If you dream of receiving an autograph from someone, the qualities you ascribe to that person are being valued or endorsed. If you are the one signing an autograph, you may be coming into your signature style of success and influence while making an impression on your lover and those that admire you. Also, you might ask yourself, "What agreement(s) am I cosigning?" In other words, what are you saying "yes" to in your relationship? Consider that the person who is signing an autograph may be righting a wrong or endorsing your relationship, choices, or behavior. Additionally, the act of writing your name in a dream is symbolic of assigning your support, friendship, or affinity. See also **Celebrity**, page 36, and **Signature**, page 128.

Award

Dreams of an award symbolize that you've made great strides in your love life and are (or soon will be) recognized for them. This dream might affirm your worthiness, self-love, and empowerment, perhaps for having forgiven your lover for something you previously thought unforgivable. You've learned to respond rather than react to things that your lover does that used to trigger you, you've opened your heart after you swore you'd never be vulnerable again, or you've learned the skills to be a truly sensitive lover. This dream is a message to take a deep breath and receive your well-earned praise. See also **Trophy**, page 132.

Back Door

See page 73.

Backseat

See page 73.

Bag

Depending upon the type of bag (paper, shopping, or Gucci), this dream symbolizes the baggage you carry in your love life and the way/style/strategy with which you carry it. Your baggage could be concealed beliefs, attitudes, wounds, and expectations. Consider the contents of the bag. Does it weigh you down, does it lighten your load, or is it a secret? See also **Box**, page 102, **Luggage**, page 118, and **Purse/Wallet**, page 124.

Baggage

See **Luggage**, page 118.

Ball

Dreams of a ball symbolize your playful spirit that comes from feeling whole and complete, within yourself and in your relationship. A ball could also symbolize the need for a well-rounded approach to your love affair that might include more silliness and less seriousness. Alternatively, a ball can suggest a need to have your (or your lover's) testicles looked at or cared for to ensure you they are healthy. If you dream of a ball, as in a dance, this suggests that you are in the midst of an epic love story, celebrating a turning point or rite of passage.

Banana

See **Fruit**, page 113.

Bandage

Dreams of a bandage symbolize the need for healing the wounds that come from the rough terrain of a relationship. Perhaps you feel that your heart has been cut or bruised. Know that the healing process has already begun and help is on the way. Alternatively, a bandage can symbolize an attempt to find a quick fix to a larger problem.

Banquet

Dreams of a banquet symbolize that you are aware of the ways your relationship feeds your soul and you are ready to feast on the bounty of your relationship. Perhaps this is the delicious love and sex you've been hungering for. You may be realizing that in this relationship you can have your cake and eat it too. Give yourself permission to indulge in all that your lover feeds your soul.

Bar

See page 73.

Barricade

Dreams of a barricade suggest that you are encountering a fear of or block to love. Perhaps this barricade is an opportunity to stretch beyond your comfort zone and take a risk. If you dream that you are barricading yourself away, this might reflect your internal resistance to someone with whom you are contemplating crossing the threshold. There may be a good reason for this resistance and it may be a message to be critical and discerning about the person with whom you are considering taking a deeper dive. It can't hurt to do your due diligence before or if you proceed. Alternatively, this dream might be a message to create firm boundaries with your sexual partner in order to manage your own self-care.

Baseball

See page 167, and **Ball**, page 99.

Basket

If the basket in your dreams is full, it suggests that you are feeling carried, contained, and supported in this relationship. If the basket in your dreams is empty and your needs aren't being met, then this dream may be prompting you to speak up or make adjustments in your relationship. Or perhaps you aren't bringing enough to the table, expecting your lover to do all the providing. If your dream involves weaving a basket, you may be mentally integrating your love wisdom, thus allowing it to powerfully carry you through your life. This dream might also prompt you to contemplate whether or not you've put all your eggs in one basket, thus relying too much on your lover.

Basketball

See page 167, and **Ball**, page 99.

Battery

Dreams of a battery represent the energy level, passion, and stamina you have for your relationship. If your battery is fully charged, then you are a vibrational match and are turned on by your relationship. If you dream of batteries running low, then this symbolizes your need for down time to recharge and perhaps plug into a new way of relating (maybe a new sexual position) that stimulates and revitalizes the situation. You might consider plugging yourself in and charging your own batteries, so that you can be your own vibrational match.

Beard

See page 31.

Bed

There is no other location that better represents letting it all hang out than a bed. For this reason bed is the ultimate symbol of relaxation, rejuvenation, sexuality, intimacy, privacy, and vulnerability—a message that you can allow your walls and inhibitions to come down and rest in the comfort (and the pleasure) of the love you make, give, and receive. Additionally, this may be a message to stop taking your relationship lying down. See also **Bedroom**, page 74, **Blanket**, page 101, and **Cover**, page 175.

Beer

Dreams of beer, wine, or alcohol represent a desire to be drunk in love, in the spiritual aspect of your relationship. Beer can represent infatuation or being slightly bubbly or out of control, in a semi-conscious stupor. See also **Alcohol**, page 97.

Belt

Dreams of a belt are symbolic of authority and that which secures the pants in the family. A belt can also be symbolic of discipline and punishment, a desire to assert authority and control, or the wish to be controlled. See also **BDSM**, page 168.

Bicycle

Dreams of a bicycle might symbolize that you are in sync with the cycles of your relationship, finding your balance, and advancing along the path of intimacy. This dream could also be wordplay for bisexual.

Billboard

See **Advertisement**, page 96.

Binoculars

Dreams of binoculars symbolize a desire to explore what's out there in the future of your relationship. This dream could also reflect your interest in what's happening next door, rather than what's happening in your own backyard. See also **Voyeur**, page 67.

Birth Control

A dream of birth control, besides being a message to be mindful in your use of contraceptives if you're taking them, may suggest taking a time-out from your love affair and doing some reflecting. Consider your right to choose what kind of commitment, relationship, or romance you want to bring forth into life. Alternatively, this dream could also reflect where you've been holding back feelings or sabotaging your creative juices from flowing with your lover. This dream might be a reminder for you that your body is a temple and you have the right to choose the experiences you want to birth. In any case, this dream is pointing you toward taking responsibility for your creative power. See also **Condom**, page 108.

Blanket

Dreams of a blanket beg the question, is there something that you're covering up? Or perhaps you are feeling the need to withdraw from the world, pull a blanket over your head, grab your lover, and take cover. This dream may be a message that you and your beloved need some alone time, sheltered from the world, to grow a sense of safety, security, trust, warmth, comfort, and love. See also **Cover**, page 175, and **Safe**, page 126.

Blender

See **Blend, Blender**, page 169.

Blindfold

Dreams of a blindfold might indicate that there is something about your lover or relationship you don't want to see, or perhaps it is you who is hiding something from your lover. Depending upon the spirit in which the blindfold is put on, it can be symbolic of a friendly game of hide-and-seek, where you're pretending your power is just slightly out of reach. Or it can be symbolic of the fact that you are blindly in love and you need to wake up. If the blindfold in your dream is put on in a sexual context, it could mean that you have a desire to be led blindly into a new experience and be in the passenger seat while someone else takes control. See also **Blind, Blind Date**, page 169.

Boat

See page 75.

Bomb

Dreams of a bomb signify anger, radical change, a devastating loss, or the need to vent unpleasant feelings. A bomb can also symbolize transformation, whereby old structures, patterns, and belief systems that used to support your ideals are blown to bits so a radically new way of mating and relating can emerge. This dream may be sending the message to take responsibility for your incredible power and to keep in mind that destruction precedes creation. See also **Anger**, page 140.

Bone

Dreams of a bone symbolize the fundamental strength and structure of your relationship. It can also be seen as an affirmation that you or your lover are doing something right, as you would reinforce good behavior by giving a dog a bone. If you dream of a broken bone, it suggests that you may have some healing to do to mend a broken promise, heart, or some disruption to the integrity of your relationship. Bone can also be wordplay for boner (erection). See also **Body**, page 32, **Penis**, page 57, and **Skeleton**, page 61.

Book

Dreams of a book indicate a desire for understanding and knowledge. It should encourage you to read between the lines of what your lover is trying to communicate to you. Alternatively, you may be realizing that you have the power to rewrite your history by changing your belief systems. Dreams of a book could be suggesting that you are the creator or writer of your relationship. See also **Sacred Text**, page 126.

Bottom

See page 75 and **Butt**, page 34.

Bowl

If you dream about an empty bowl, ask yourself what's missing in this relationship. If the bowl in your dream is full, then consider this an affirmation of a fulfilling relationship.

Box

Dreams of a closed box are a message to contemplate what secret feelings, resources, talents, or memories you may be keeping under wraps. A box signifies that you may be hiding or protecting an aspect of your vulnerability, beauty, or deeper feelings of love. If you dream of an open box, then you may be realizing that there is more to you and your lover than meets the eye, and you may be ready to have a more authentic, transparent, out-of-the-box relationship. Dreams of an open box, as in Pandora's Box, may also be a message to be mindful when you unleash the beast of your anger, sadness, or jealousy. If the box is ornate, it signifies that you prefer to hide your jewels, your innermost feelings, behind a fancy and distracting facade. If it's a safety deposit box, then you may have forgotten that you've left an aspect of your beauty, wisdom, talent, or innocence in the box and out of reach from your partner, or you may be saving it for when the timing is right. If you dream of a treasure chest, you may be realizing the depth and exponential value of your inner wisdom. Also, box can be slang for vagina. See also **Safe**, page 126, and **Vagina**, page 66.

Bra

Dreams of a bra signify a cover for your maternal feelings. Conversely, this dream could reflect a need or desire to highlight, support, and uphold your feminine and maternal instincts, or your desire for maternal affection. Additionally, if the bra is lacy and padded, it could reflect an inherent insecurity and a desire to embellish your desirability and femininity. A utilitarian or sports bra denotes that you are in a comfort zone in your relationship. Perhaps the sport of relationship is like a game to you, which you are trying to win. See also **Breast**, page 33, **Clothing**, page 106, and **Underwear**, page 132.

Braid

Dreams of a braid signify that you and your loved one are weaving and intertwining aspects of your thoughts, beliefs, and relationship philosophies. A braid can also signify a desire to blend families, schedules, or even bank accounts. Additionally, the way hair is braided can denote youth, a youthful mindset, or royalty. See also **Blend, Blender**, page 169.

A dream of branches signifies a desire to connect beyond where you are currently rooted.

Brakes

Dreams of putting on the brakes suggest a need to slow down, pause, or stop the flow of your relationship so that you don't break (up). Perhaps you've been going too far too fast, so before you crash, pull over to the side of the road and allow your engine to idle to gain clarity about your next move.

Branches

Dreams of branches signify a desire to reach out, branch out, and connect beyond where you currently are rooted. Branches also signify that you are growing in an organic way. You may be expanding beyond your family tree or the belief systems of your community garden and going out on a limb. Branches could also suggest a grappling between yearning for more relationship experiences and the notion of blooming where you are planted. See also **Tree**, page 132.

Bridge

See page 75.

Brush

Anything related to the head, like hair, is symbolic of thoughts. If you dream of brushing your hair, you may be attempting to unravel thoughts and beliefs about romantic love or your notions about sex. Dreams of a hairbrush could also be wordplay—you are processing a brush with death or brush with temptation. Additionally, if you are brushing your hair, it reflects willingness to clean up your act, play up your assets, realign your thoughts, and be present and presentable. See also **Hair**, page 48, and **Salon**, page 88.

Bullet

Dreams of a bullet suggest that you may be processing an argument from your waking life, where verbal attacks were fired. Perhaps it signifies your desire to find the magic bullet to quickly end an argument, or even end your entire relationship. A bullet can also signify anger, aggression, and judgmental words that could undermine or destroy the fabric of your relationship. This dream may be a reminder to be more mindful of the words you speak and the impact they have. Additionally, because a gun is a phallic symbol, a bullet could represent sperm, impregnation, or that someone is shooting blanks (has a low sperm count). See also **Gun**, page 114, and **Shotgun**, page 127.

Cabinet

Dreams of a cabinet symbolize what you may be storing, waiting to share if and when the time is right. This dream implies you may have hidden resources, wealth, or passion saved away for a rainy day. See also **Closet**, page 77, and **Shadow**, page 156.

Cage

Dreams of a cage symbolize that you may be suppressing your true feelings for fear of what might happen if they were expressed. A cage denotes animal instincts feeling trapped, smothered, powerless, or victimized. Perhaps you have a desire to break out of, leave, fight, or flee the love affair you've been in. See also **Jail**, page 83.

Cake

Dreams of a cake symbolize that it's time for your just desserts, or your desire to have your cake and eat it too (why not?). Perhaps you and your partner have successfully made it across an important threshold and you deserve a celebration, acknowledgment, and reward for your hard work. See also **Dessert**, page 109.

Calendar

Dreams of a calendar could be a reminder that time is passing, asking you to pay attention to what you schedule and what you don't. This dream could be a nudge to make a special plan or date with your lover. Consider if a particular day or month is highlighted and what that could mean to you. See also **Clock**, page 106, and **Time**, page 90.

Camera

Dreams of a camera symbolize a need to imprint a precious moment in time with your loved one, a desire to capture a special feeling and grow it (not to take it for granted). Conversely, this dream could suggest that you are holding tightly to your past memories that may be getting in the way of your being totally present with your lover in the here and now. See also **Photograph**, page 123, and **Selfie**, page 191.

Candle

A candle symbolizes a flicker of an attraction, a romantic mood, or the glow of love burning in your heart. Also, because a candle emits light, it indicates awareness, lucidity, and consciousness in your relationship, which might inspire you to wax poetic. A candle is also an old-fashioned way of brightening a dark room, so you might consider what part of your ancient past is now being brought to light and healed by the love in your relationship. If the candle is being used in a sexual way (as in dripping candlewax on a body), this dream may be lighting the path to turn your pain into pleasure. See also **Light**, page 151.

Candy

A dream of candy may be symbolic of the need to lay it on thick with your sweetheart and give him or her (or yourself) a reward as acknowledgment of all he or she (or you) is doing right in your relationship. This dream may signify you are craving sweet nothings from your partner. Perhaps you've become overly focused on the meat and potatoes of your relationship, and this dream is a message to sweeten your relationship. See also **Dessert**, page 109, and **Sugar**, page 129.

Car

Dreams of a car can symbolize ambition (drive) and the desire to make tracks. The question to ask is, who is driving this relationship? If it isn't you, consider whether or not you are going along for the ride, allowing your dreams and desires to take a backseat. If you are driving, then give yourself a pat on the back for taking initiative in your love life—but make sure to consider whether or not your partner is enjoying the ride. If you dream of steaming up the windows in the backseat of a car while making out, ask yourself whether you are enjoying the caress or if you are careening toward a dangerous romance. Consider this as a message to pay more attention to your internal GPS, so you can enjoy the ride of your relationship or sexual adventure as you cruise down the road of intimacy.

Card (Greeting)

Dreams of a greeting card are a message to spell out what you want to say. If you're dreaming of receiving a greeting card, then this dream might be revealing an affirmation and acknowledgment of how far your relationship has come, as well as your state of receptivity and positive expectations regarding love and messages of love. If you are the one sending the card, then consider what magic spells you are creating with your words. See also **Credit Card**, page 109, and **Tarot**, page 158.

Card (Playing)

Dreams of playing cards symbolize risk-taking behaviors; you may be treating your romance as if it were a game. This dream should encourage you to ask if you and your lover have cards up your sleeves. Are

you dealing with a full deck in your relationship? Do you feel like this relationship is a gamble or a sure bet? This dream may be reminding you that life is 10 percent about the cards you're dealt and 90 percent how you play them, so go ahead and lay your cards are on the table and let your true feelings show. See also **Gamble**, page 181.

Carrot

See **Vegetable**, page 133.

Cash Point

See **ATM**, page 98.

Cell Phone

See **Phone**, page 123.

Chain

Dreams of chains might reflect that you are struggling with your current relationship situation and it's leaving you fit to be tied. Perhaps you've been feeling torn between the restriction of commitment and your desire to belong, feel special, and have an unbreakable bond with someone who loves you. Alternatively, if you dream of pleasure associated with being shackled, then you may be exploring your desire to relinquish control.

Champagne

Dreams of champagne suggest celebration, success, and orgasmic delight between you and your lover. You may be feeling uncorked, bubbly, and willing to fully release the love, joy, and passion in your heart and to get drunk on love. Additionally, the popping of the cork can be associated with a sexual or emotional release. See also **Alcohol**, page 47, **Celebration**, page 172, and **Party**, page 86.

Cherry

Dreams of a cherry can symbolize the vagina, hymen, sexual innocence, or sensuality so sweet and ripe it's falling off the vine. This dream might also reflect that you've been tempted by forbidden fruit, or that you're feeling like a virgin all over again and you desire to be plucked. A cherry often symbolizes that you're enjoying your just desserts, and the cherry on top is that you get to share it with your lover. See also **Food**, page 113, **Fruit**, page 113, **Vagina**, page 66, and **Virgin**, page 67.

Chocolate

Chocolate is the ultimate symbol of a desire for love and affection. You may be craving sweetness in your relationship. This desire could come as a result of having survived a bitter breakup and the need for kindness to melt away your pain. Also, dreams of chocolate symbolize a reward for having embraced an aspect of your shadow, as in finding something delicious in the darkness. See also **Candy**, page 104, and **Dessert**, page 109.

Cigarette

Dreams of a cigarette, depending on the feeling tone, signify addictive, self-destructive habits in your love or sex life. Alternatively, Sigmund Freud would say that a cigarette is a phallic symbol and that sucking on it (smoking it) is a symbol of fellatio. Cigarettes are also related to your need for a break from your relationship or to having just completed a sex act. Dreams of a cigarette might be a message that you need to take a break, so that you can relax into your relationship. See also **Blow Job**, page 169, and **Smoke**, page 128.

Cliff

See page 77.

Clock

Dreams of a clock signify that time is of the essence, and that it may be time for a reality check. This dream may reflect a desire to evaluate next steps for deepening your level of commitment. See also **Time**, page 90.

Closet

See page 77.

Clothing

Because clothing covers up your nakedness and authenticity, clothes in a dream represent the aspects of your persona or ego you are reflecting in your relationship. Consider what your dress says about you. For example, a wedding dress suggests the dreamer is marriage-bound, idealistic, or in touch with her sacred feminine self; a pair of ripped jeans with a leather jacket suggests the dreamer is rebellious, single, or unapproachable. See also **Dress**, page 111.

Coat

Dreams of a coat signify the need for protection from the cold. Perhaps you are in a chilly period in your relationship and need extra care, comfort, and to be reassured that you are loved and loveable. Additionally, this dream may be revealing that you've been hiding or protecting your true feelings from your lover, perhaps because you need to feel warm and safe. See also **Trench Coat**, page 132.

Coffee

Dreams of coffee signify a desire for stimulation in your relationship. Perhaps your love life is beginning to perk up. This dream could also be a wake-up call, alerting you to bring the best to your love affair. Maybe your relationship is in the early stages, where he or she gives you the jitters or a buzz that lasts all day.

Collar

Dreams of a collar signify restraint and that you are negotiating with animal instincts that want to run wild. It could also reflect that your relationship-oriented aspect wants to belong to someone. This dream may be helping you find clarity about commitment, monogamy, power/submission issues, or your willingness to pay the price for being chained or unleashed in your love affair. Also see **BDSM**, page 168.

Clothing is a representation of your persona or ego in a dream.

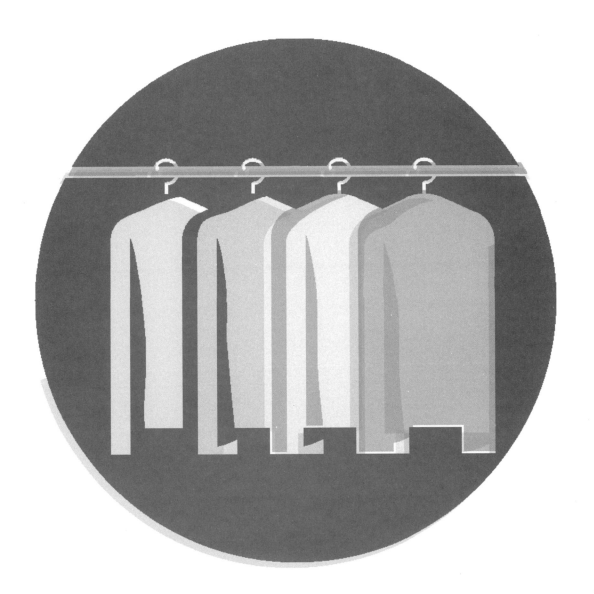

Compass

Dreams of a compass signify a desire for direction; it may be telling you literally which way to turn, or the best way to navigate the hero's journey of love, sex, and relationship. This dream may be helping you stay on course. See **Directions**, page 144, and **Map**, page 119.

Computer

Dreams of a computer reflect your mental process, memory, and your ability to download new software, get a mental reboot, and delete old files that keep your bandwidth from opening to maximum capacity. This dream may be a message to upgrade your love-life relationship program to version 2.0. The computer also symbolizes the universal mind of creation and your unique access to that mind, as well as your desire to connect with and express yourself to others. Additionally, the dream might be suggesting you are spending too much time in front of the computer. Perhaps it is time to unplug and spend actual face time with your loved one. See also **Internet**, page 150, and **Online Dating**, page 186.

Condom

Dreams of a condom, besides being a literal message to have safe sex, symbolize a desire for protection, perhaps due to a fear of intimacy or of impregnating someone else with your energy. Additionally, dreams of a condom are a message to proceed with caution in your love affair, take responsibility for your sexual power, and remain lucid. See also **Birth Control**, page 101.

Cord

Dreams of a cord are about your level of attachment and bonding with your lover, and also your dependence upon him or her. Consider whether or not your connection is energizing or draining you, plugged in or unplugged. Additionally, you might feel "tied up" in your love affair. Perhaps you feel an unbreakable bond to your partner, as in a bondage-related expression. If you like the way this feels, then remain plugged in. If not, exercise your will and pull the plug.

Cosmetics

See **Makeup**, page 119.

Costume

Dreams of a costume suggest you may be stuck in a role or that you want to break free from a mask you've been wearing in your love life. A costume, like a mask, can bring an aspect of you and your power to the surface that might otherwise remain obscured. Perhaps you feel the need to become someone else to please your partner, or wish your partner could be different in order to please you. This dream might also suggest that you are covering up a secret. Consider the type of costume and what it represents to you to better understand this dream. Keep in mind that you should bring your true self to this relationship. See also **Clothing**, page 106, and **Dress**, page 111.

Couch

Dreams of a couch represent a desire for a soft place to land. Perhaps you are looking for a kind and gentle way to couch or present your wants, desires, and needs to your lover. A couch also signifies a desire for relaxation, comfort, and a cushion to soften the rough edges of a difficult situation in your love affair. Alternatively, a couch can suggest that you may be too apathetic—resting on your laurels, acting like a couch potato, or couch surfing—and that perhaps if you still really want the kind of love, sex, and relationship you have desired, you need to get moving and put it into action.

Crack

Dreams of a crack signify a broken heart, thwarted promise, or fracture in the foundation of your love affair. See also **Break**, page 170. If you dream of the drug crack or cocaine, see **Drug**, page 111.

Credit Card

Since money is a symbol of power, influence, and energy, a credit card is about taking credit for that which isn't truly yours, living on borrowed wealth, or being indebted to your lover; one day there will be a payback. Conversely, dreams of a credit card might also suggest that you want appreciation or acknowledgment (credit) where credit is due. See also **Money**, page 120.

Cross

Dreams of a cross suggest that you are at a crossroads in your relationship and are hoping or praying for divine guidance in making the best decision. Perhaps you've had a cross to bear (secret, burden, weight of the world on your shoulder), and this dream may be a message to stop being a martyr in the name of love. Alternatively, because a cross symbolizes the intersection between the divine and human as well as heaven and earth, this dream may be a message that you share a holy connection with your lover, and to remember to treat each other as sacred.

Crown

If you dream of a crown, it signifies that you are accessing higher consciousness and thoughts aligned with royal self-esteem. You may be stepping into an aspect of your confidence, authority, and prominence. The shadow message of this symbol is that you may be feeling holier than thou, entitled, or arrogant, or you may be misusing your power. See also **King**, page 52, or **Queen**, page 59.

Crucifix

See **Crucify**, page 175.

Crystal

If you dream of a crystal, you might be seeking a rock-solid foundation to support your relationship. Because crystals are natural conductors of energy, you may be feeling your intent, goal, or desire being energized, motivated, transformed, or amplified.

Cup

Dreams of a full cup signify that your relationship cup runneth over; you are experiencing a high level of fulfillment, optimism, and prosperity in your relationship. If your relationship cup is half empty, it may mean that your empty relationship is leaving you wanting.

Curtain

Dreams of curtains signify a desire to either reveal or conceal. This dream could indicate a need for privacy, or that you want to maintain some mystery in your relationship. Perhaps you are not ready for full disclosure or authenticity in your love affair. Consider what the curtain is hiding.

Dessert

Dreams of dessert signify a reward for your hard work, a desire for some sweetness, affirmation, healing, and joy. This dream may be a message to take time to savor your just desserts and the deliciousness of your love or sex life.

Diamond

Dreams of a diamond represent your exponential value, as well as your multifaceted, multidimensional, magnificent soul. This dream might suggest you could use a bit of polish to shine your full splendor in this relationship. It may be reminding you that you are precious, invaluable, and brilliant in your own unique way. Additionally, a diamond is the ultimate symbol of alchemy, as it starts off as a carbon-based sediment that is forged through tremendous heat, mined from the Earth's surface, and is thought of as unbreakable. Perhaps your relationship has been through hell and back, and this dream is affirming its incalculable value as an unbreakable bond you can truly count on and display proudly. See also **Jewelry**, page 116.

Diary

Dreams of a diary signify your true, unedited, unscripted, and raw feelings. If you dream that someone takes your diary, you may be feeling ashamed and exposed. A diary in a dream could also be a message for you to be mindful with whom you share your secrets.

Dildo

See **Sex Toy**, page 127.

Dinner

See page 74.

Diploma

Dreams of a diploma signify completion and the acknowledgment of how far you've come. Perhaps you have a desire for proof that you've graduated beyond the types of relationships that used to test you, and you've earned your degree in higher love. See also **Graduation**, page 80.

Dirt

Dreams of dirt symbolize that you may be feeling dirty, soiled, or dishonored, as if your relationship has run your heart through the mud. Perhaps you or your partner broke a promise, and your self-esteem feels like it's temporarily at rock bottom. Consider what you need to do (forgive, make amends) to clean this up. Also, dirt is related to the element of Earth, which may be a message from your subconscious mind to get grounded, connect with your roots, and plant new seeds that can grow into something that will nurture you and your relationship. See also **Earth**, page 79.

Doll

If you dream of a doll, it could signify perfectionistic tendencies, a desire to please and to fit into an idealistic mold that may keep you from the intimacy, authenticity, and depth that comes from being yourself. Additionally, a doll signifies that your childlike essence is engaged in this relationship and there's a desire to play and use your imagination with your lover (playmate).

Door

Dreams of a closed door may reflect that you're feeling closed down or closed-minded. Perhaps you are feeling the need to set a boundary with your lover to protect your feelings or preserve your sense of self. Perhaps you've been keeping your heart under lock and key, and thus slamming the door and sabotaging your ability to open up to intimacy. If you dream of an open door, you may be opening yourself to a brand new experience of love, sexual experience, and open-mindedness in your relationship. This may be an indication that you and your lover have an open invitation to explore further in your love affair.

Drawer

Dreaming of a drawer suggests that you want to keep an aspect of yourself out of view, tucked away and kept secret from your lover. This may represent a desire to get organized, to sort and compartmentalize aspects of your love life to feel a sense of control in your relationship.

Dress

Dreams of a dress signify your self-image or the persona by which you want others to identify you. Depending upon the type of dress, it can reflect various aspects of femininity. A corporate power suit may represent confidence and an ability to strategize. A frilly dress imparts girlish, youthful, and playful qualities. A mini-skirt represents sexy and sensual aspects, suggesting a femme fatale. And a long, flowing dress represents the romantic and idealistic. See also **Clothing**, page 106.

Drug

Dreams of drugs are the ultimate symbol of the high that comes from the peak of ecstatic connection. This dream could also reflect that you are picking up the pieces after an addictive relationship has crashed and burned. You might be evaluating whether the rush was worth the price you've paid. As you re-establish your conscious connection with your source energy, you'll find yourself graduating from relationship rehab.

Egg

In dreams an egg is a symbol of fertility, possibility, and hope about what is to come. Additionally, an egg symbolizes that a fertile new life is possible between you and your lover, whether that means an actual baby or a new aspect of you to be born. Conversely, this dream may be cautioning you not to be overly optimistic or dependent and put all your eggs into one basket. The egg is also a symbol of your ego's fragile, breakable, protective shell, safeguarding the golden spirit within you. See also **Baby**, page 30.

Elements

Dreams of the elements signify that you are connecting to what is most natural, intrinsic, and crucial within you and your lover. See also **Earth**, page 79, **Fire**, page 112, **Metal**, page 120, **Wind**, page 161, and **Water**, page 93.

Elevator

See page 79.

Escalator

See page 79.

Exam

See **Test**, page 130.

Faucet

Dreams of a faucet signify your ability to turn yourself on or off. A faucet can be a phallic symbol; if it is running at full force, it might signify that you are turned on in your relationship, feeling maximum arousal. If the faucet is leaky, you may be wasting your sexual energy with people who don't turn you on or who drain your energy. If there's no water coming out of the faucet, it might symbolize that you need to tap into a higher source that won't leave you high and dry. See also **Water**, page 93.

Fire is an ancient symbol of transformation, love, sexuality, anger, creation, destruction, and power.

Fire

To dream of fire could denote either that you are burning with passion or that it's time for a radical change in your love life. Fire is an ancient symbol of change, transformation, love, sexuality, anger, creation, destruction, and power. With power comes the need for responsibility, maturity, and balance. This dream might be telling you to find a safe and private place to get your ya-yas out of your system (e.g., take a dance class to express the unabashed zeal of your heart and the scorching embers of your deepest emotions, whether they be passion, anger, or lust). It could also be supporting you to burn away (release and let go) the ties that bind you to past hurts or dysfunctional relationship patterns. If you dream of something burning, it may reflect transformation, initiation, healing, purification, alchemy, passion, and releasing whatever no longer serves you. See also **Breakdown/ Breakthrough**, page 171.

Fireworks

Dreams of fireworks signify a blissful orgasmic explosion, great sex (either currently or on the horizon), liberation, or a joyous expression of deeply felt love and romance. Perhaps this dream reflects the fact that you are exploding in romantic delight, are newly in love, or are falling back in love with a long-time partner. See also **Ejaculate,** page 178, and **Orgasm**, page 188.

Flashlight

Dreams of a flashlight signify that you are doing shadow work, shining a light into dark places within yourself or your relationship's basement. You may be having a dark night of the soul, and this dream illuminates hope and rekindles your spiritual awareness, which will allow you to navigate through the dark times of relationships and find your way to the light at the end of the tunnel.

Flower

Dreams of flowers signify that your romance is in bloom. Regardless of the stage you are in (seed, gestation, blossom, or returning to the soil), the message of this dream is to honor the process and know that you and your romance are flowering.

Food

Dreams of food are reflective of your appetite, sexual or otherwise, and could indicate whether or not your relationship is feeding your soul. Consider the old adage, "You are what you eat." That goes for food as well as your thoughts and belief systems. This could be a message to be mindful of what you are truly hungering for—feed your body/mind/spirit only what empowers, fortifies, and uplifts you. If you are uncomfortable in the dream, you may be attempting to reject the belief systems you've been swallowing. If you are enjoying a healthy dream meal, you have found a recipe for relationship success.

Fruit

Dreams of fruit signify that you are coming into a healthy and delicious time in your love life. Perhaps you are finally seeing the fruits of your labor. In addition to fruit signifying abundance, sweetness, and fertility—as in the horn of plenty—fruit can also represent sexual organs, such as:

Cherry (page 105): the hymen or virginity

Melon: breasts or fertility

Banana: penis

Peach: rear end

G-Spot

Dreams of the G-spot signify that you've found the bull's-eye of mating and relating for which you've been aiming. You are right where you are supposed to be in your life and in your relationship. You've blossomed into the fullest nectar of expression, and have the mastery to send yourself and your lover over the moon in ecstasy. This dream could signify the sacred connection between you and your lover.

Game

See page 182.

Garbage

Dreams of garbage suggest that you are releasing and letting go of that which no longer serves you. The dream could be calling you to expel toxic feelings, drop pessimistic negative beliefs, and purge the nonsupportive habits that keep you from having the love, sex, and relationship you desire.

Garlic

Dreams of garlic reflect a need to keep away intrusive people, lovers, and unsavory types. Perhaps you're feeling the need to protect yourself against impure energies, or your lover is being too needy and vampire-like, and you'd like to be alone. See also **Vampire**, page 67.

Gate

Dreams of a gate can signify either an opening or a barrier to your heart or to your sacred sexual center. If the gate is closed or locked, it signifies that you may not be ready to bring in your partner. If you come upon a closed gate, your lover may be testing you to see how strong your desire or commitment is. If the gate is open, the opportunity has come to enter a new level of intimacy. Additionally, a gate could represent the challenges you and your loved one face as you prepare to cross the threshold into a deeper realm of intimacy.

Gift

Dreams of a gift symbolize an insight, opportunity, or even pregnancy. If you dream that you are giving a gift, this signifies you are appreciative of your beloved. If you dream of receiving a gift, this is a message that you are being recognized, loved, and appreciated by your lover. Allow any issues of unworthiness to be dissolved. Remember, because you've unwrapped your true feelings, you've earned the blessings that are now beginning to arrive, seemingly out of thin air. It is time to be present in your love life.

Gloves

Gloves in a dream can symbolize a desire to protect or separate yourself from being enthralled in an intimate encounter that might leave you cold. Additionally, a glove (or condom) can be symbolic of a desire to prevent pregnancy. A glove could also be a sign that you are attempting to be unmarked, unscathed, and unblemished by the heat of this relationship. See also **Condom**, page 108.

Gold

Dreams of gold denote wealth, abundance, opulence, trust, and your soul. You are realizing that you are in the midst of a golden opportunity, and you've struck it rich with this love affair.

GPS

Dreams of GPS or other navigational systems signify that you are attempting to find your bearings in your relationship. Perhaps you've strayed from home (your comfort zone) and are feeling lost. This dream could be reassurance that your center is always just a breath away. Or maybe you've been so focused on your destination (a relationship or sexual goal) that you've forgotten to enjoy the ride. Keep in mind that the most interesting relationship journeys are the ones with the most detours. See also **Map**, page 119.

Ground

Dreams of the ground signify the need to get grounded in your love affair. Additionally, they might suggest that you come down to Earth from your lofty, visionary perch and get in touch with your animal instincts. See also **Earth**, page 79.

Guitar

Dreams of a guitar signify that you are in touch with what is most instrumental in your love life. You are in harmony with and are attuned to your and your lover's bodies and rhythms. A guitar can be both a metaphor for the curves of a woman's body (a desire to play with the poetic, romantic, feminine aspect) as well as a phallic symbol, a desire to make love and beautiful music together. This can also be wordplay for gutter (as in "get your head out of the gutter"). See **Music**, page 152, and **Musical Instrument**, page 122.

Gun

A gun is a symbol of the need for drastic measures to radically change or end a pattern. Perhaps you feel the need to blow off steam, you're done playing Mr. or Mrs. Nice Guy, or you've been shooting your mouth off. A gun can also be a phallic symbol and may reflect a pent-up, out of control, or even destructive sexual desire. See also **Shotgun**, page 127.

Handcuffs in a dream suggest you feel that your hands are tied in your relationship.

Gutter

Dreams of a gutter signify that you are feeling the need to release and let go of negative thinking about your relationship. Perhaps you've fallen off track, off the wagon, or lost sight of the guidance of your soul. Additionally, gutter can be wordplay for guitar, so this dream might be suggesting that you play a new tune and start fresh.

Hall Pass

Dreams of a hall pass reflect that you may feel the need to roam beyond the boundaries of your relationship, and want approval about your desire to have your cake and eat it too. This dream could be a reality check that inspires you and your sweetheart to renegotiate your relationship agreements. See also **Hallway**, page 82.

Handcuffs

Handcuffs in dreams are a symbol of punishment, shame, and powerlessness and often suggest a guilty conscience. Perhaps you have been withholding love because you don't approve of how you or your lover handled a situation, which you feel deserves more than just a slap on the wrist. You may feel that your hands are tied in your relationship. Alternatively, this dream might reflect an interest in bondage and discipline and the thrill of either being in complete control or submitting to your lover's will. See also **BDSM**, page 168, and **Jail**, page 83.

Hat

Dreams of a hat, depending upon the type of hat, signify a slightly different perspective than you might normally have. In dreams, anything related to your head is about your thoughts, so a hat might denote that you're being closed-minded about a particular issue related to love, or you may be avoiding a certain process. Additionally, a hat might suggest that you feel the need to protect yourself from the influence of your partner or of those around you. See also **Head**, page 49.

Heart

See page 49.

High Heels

Dreams of high heels reflect a desire for higher self-esteem and to stand taller in your relationship, elevate your status, and lift the vibration of your relationship. This dream might indicate your desire to get a rise out of your partner or to stand on higher ground and take control of your relationship situation.

Hill

See **Mountain**, page 83.

Hole

Dreams of a hole represent receptivity, femininity, and a space being held for new life. However, if you dream of feeling empty, hungry, or needy, you may be expressing feelings of lack or loss. Keep in mind that as you grow in your realization of your spiritual wholeness, you will discover that you are whole, and never empty.

Horn

Dreams of a horn could be a message that you're feeling horny, or that you're feeling the call to take charge of your love life. Additionally, horns could symbolize that you've been hurt by someone's bullishness. It may be a hint of the beautiful music you and your lover could make together. See also **Music**, page 152, and **Musical Instrument**, page 122.

Ice

Dreams of ice might signify that you've been playing the ice king or queen in your relationship. Perhaps you've been protecting your tender heart with a frosty and aloof exterior. This dream might suggest that you should allow your defenses to thaw and heal the places of sexual inhibition. As you develop self-love, you'll be able to warm up slowly and take baby steps back toward the heat of romance.

Instrument

See **Musical Instrument**, page 122.

Island

Dreams of an island can be shining a light on the fact that you've been reclusive and distant. Conversely, your dream could be telling you that you and your lover need some private time away—to honeymoon and bond, away from the hubbub of the wild and noisy jungle of life. Because islands are formed from volcanic eruptions, this dream could be showing you the new life that can spring from disaster. See also **Beach**, page 74, **Honeymoon**, page 82, and **Ocean**, page 85.

Jewelry

Dreams of jewelry might signify that you're feeling the need to hold on to what's valuable to you. Because jewels must be excavated, often they're symbolic of the price you pay for your earned wisdom. Perhaps you've just come into a joyous time in your relationship, taking stock of the preciousness of your connection with your loved one. Conversely, this dream might be a message to see past the status symbol or the bling to the real gold beneath the surface of your partner, or a potential lover who might be a diamond in the rough. Additionally, dreams of jewelry can represent extravagance, prosperity, abundance, lavishness, and qualities you cherish. If you dream of draping someone in jewels, this might symbolize your desire to claim them, make your mark on them, or have them beholden to you. If you are the recipient of the jewelry, perhaps you want to be possessed (e.g., an engagement ring marks your partner as belonging to you). Also, because "family jewels" is a reference to male genitalia, see **Penis**, page 57, and **Testicles**, page 65. See also **Diamond**, page 109, **Gold**, page 114, and **Ring**, page 124.

Key

Dreams of a key symbolize that the answers, opportunities, access, secrets, freedom, control, knowledge, responsibilities, and power you seek are in the palm of your hand. You may be trying to lock a part of yourself away, or you are realizing that you hold the key that can set yourself free. A key can also be a phallic symbol, where the lock or keyhole is an entry point to a woman's sacred and secret space. This dream signifies that you are either in control or seeking control. Additionally, this may be a message to open up and share your secrets, resources, and beauty with your loved one or a trusted someone.

Knife

Dreams of a knife signify that you may be feeling the need to cut someone out of your life, or you may be attempting to heal the stabbing pain of rejection. A knife can symbolize the use of force or violence to create a drastic end to a cycle in your relationship, or a desire to cut off an unhealthy pattern. If a knife is being used against you, it might be alerting you to nonsupportive energy in your life. Additionally, knives can symbolize the male genitalia—powerful, strong, and erect. See also **Amputate, Amputation**, page 165, **Castrate, Castration**, page 172, and **Cut**, page 176.

Knot

Dreams of a knot suggest that things have become complicated. A knot implies permanence and the commingling of each other's lives, so perhaps you desire to get married, or tie the knot, with your partner to make your love official. Conversely, you may be confused, or tied up in knots, as you attempt to sort out the decisions you need to make. Perhaps there are opposing forces pulling at you, representing your own conflicting needs and emotional entanglements. The wordplay should remind you to ask if you've been naughty (knotty) or if you're thinking negatively (not) about something. See also **Cord**, page 108, and **Marriage**, page 83.

Ladder

If you dream about a ladder, this could imply that you have what it takes to reach higher ground (e.g., find a partner of a higher caliber or take the status of your relationship up a notch). Additionally, dreaming of climbing up a ladder could imply insatiability, a desire to gain a higher perspective about your love life, or growth beyond your relationship's status quo. If you are climbing down, this could be a message to curb your ambition and handle the ground-level issues of your relationship, or to stop climbing altogether and accept what you've got and where you're at. As with any ambition for improvement, this dream could be a message to make sure the ladder you are climbing is leaning up against the right wall.

Laundry

Dreams of doing the laundry or of being at a laundromat represent an attempt to clean up your act. Perhaps you've had a fight with your loved one, made a mess, and need to forgive or ask for forgiveness. Maybe you've had dirty thoughts that don't align with your relationship morality. This dream may be an attempt to help you iron out a conflict or hang a bad habit out to dry, so that you can emerge clear and new, with a fresh, clean slate. Because clothes symbolize your public persona, this dream could be about wanting to clean up your image. See also **Clothing**, page 106.

Lettuce

See **Vegetable**, page 133.

Lift

See **Elevator**, page 79.

Lingerie

Dreams of lingerie can reflect a desire for romance; you may be in the mood for love or willing to spice up your love life. Because lingerie is an embellishment—something you wear on top of your nakedness as a cover-up—this might signify that there is an aspect of your sexuality you'd prefer to hide. See also **Naked**, page 186, and **Underwear**, page 132.

Lock

Dreams of a lock signify a desire for secrecy and privacy, or the fact that you don't feel safe enough to let it all hang out in your love affair. Perhaps you've had heartbreak or trauma in the realm of romance, and this dream is a reminder that you've locked a part of yourself away—and to not forget about it. Once you've established a sense of emotional safety, you'll realize that you have the key to freedom. Also, because a key in lock can symbolize sexual intercourse, this dream may reflect frigidity or sabotaging yourself from intimacy. See **Drawer**, page 110, **Key**, page 117, and **Safe**, page 126.

Love Letter

Dreams of a love letter symbolize that you may be looking for the words to describe your romantic feelings, or that you desire particular words to be said to open your heart. When you praise your lover or receive praise, it inspires more of what you love to grow and flourish. This dream may be a message that you are coming into alignment with what you truly desire and want to create more of in your love life.

Luggage

If you dream of luggage, it signifies that you may be carrying your past baggage (hurts, heartaches, memories, accomplishments) into your present relationship. Consider the contents of your luggage. Alternatively, this dream could signify that you are seeking to bring the wisdom of past experiences into your current relationship so as not to repeat past mistakes. Keep in mind that the ultimate scenario is to incorporate your wisdom, trust that it's encoded within you so you can drop all heavy burdens, and travel lightly along your relationship hero's journey. See also **Bag**, page 99, and **Purse/Wallet**, page 124.

Mail

Dreams of mail (besides being wordplay for male) are about receiving a message. Consider the contents of the letter or parcel. This may reflect that a gift or blessing is forthcoming. Because you live in this modern age, dreams of mail could denote a desire for an old-fashioned courtship. See **Email**, page 178, and **Love Letter**, page 118.

Makeup

Dreams of makeup could signify your desire to mend a breakup or make up after a fight—to forgive and forget. If you dream of cosmetics, you may be trying to play up your best features, while covering up those that aren't as appealing. This dream might beg the question, "What are you trying to make up (compensate) for to appear more appealing?" Keep in mind that self-love and acceptance are the best beauty boosters. See also **Mask**, page 119.

Map

Dreams of a map suggest that you are getting your bearings and a sense of orientation in your love life. This dream may be helping you navigate in a particular direction that could change the entire trajectory of your romance. See also **Compass**, page 108, and **GPS**, page 114.

Mask

Dreams of a mask signify that there may be something you or your lover is covering up, hiding, or pretending to be. Perhaps the mask in your dream is helping to peel away the erroneous belief that your natural self isn't good enough to be loved. Keep in mind that the authentic you is more lovable than any mask you could wear. Alternatively, this dream could represent a desire to be uninhibited, because the disguise can hide your identity. Consider what kind of mask this is to understand how to express yourself better. See also **Costume**, page 108, and **Makeup**, page 119.

Match

If you dream of matches, you may be playing with fire and taking chances where the risks are great. Perhaps this dream is showing that you and your lover are a perfect match, or that you could get burned with your risky behavior. Alternatively, this dream suggests a desire to meet your match (the love of your life). You might check out an online dating site. See also **Online Dating**, page 186.

Mattress

Dreams of a mattress could signify that you've been lying down on the job or perhaps looking for a little nurturing cushion or a safe place to land in your relationship. They also symbolize a desire for comfort, rest, and a break from a relationship. Give yourself a little TLC. See also **Bed**, page 100.

Meat

If you dream of meat you might be craving more substance in your love life; you want to get to the heart of the issue. Or you might consider whether or not you've been feeling like a piece of meat in your relationship—without a soul, substance, or depth. Perhaps you've been relating to yourself on the physical level and forgetting that there's more to you than the sum total of your physical attributes. Alternatively, meat could symbolize that you are feeling like your relationship is hearty and delicious. See also **Food**, page 113.

Medicine

Dreams of medicine signify that the healing you've been praying for is at hand. Additionally, love brings up everything unlike itself in order to be revealed and healed. There can be no poison more toxic than a relationship that doesn't honor your soul, and there is no medicine better than a relationship that does. See also **Doctor**, page 41.

Melon

See **Fruit**, page 113.

Menu

Dreams of a menu represent the many choices you have in your love and sex life. This dream could be telling you that you have a say in what you fill your time and your plate with to nourish your mind, body, and soul. See also **Food**, page 113.

Metal

Dreams of metal may reflect that your relationship mettle is being tested and that you should hold strong to what you believe in. Conversely, this dream may reveal that your defense mechanisms are in place and that you are being rigid in your beliefs, unbending in your need for certainty and structure, or as tough as nails with your partner. Additionally, this dream may be showing you that your commitment can weather any storm.

Milk

Dreams of milk signify a need for nurturing. Additionally, they indicate that your inner child (or baby) needs more care in this relationship. This dream could also be a message to not cry over spilled milk—don't fret over what's happened in the past. And don't forget to milk the good times for all their worth. See also **Breast**, page 33.

Mirror

Dreams of a mirror signify that your lover is reflecting back attractions and repulsions. A mirror is the ultimate symbol of a relationship. If you like what you see in the looking glass, it suggests you have attained inner harmony, acceptance, and self-love. If you don't like what you see, it reflects shame or blame— you have shadow work to do. Alternatively, this dream might be a symbol of self-awareness, vanity, and a desire to ensure a positive outlook on life.

Mobile Phone

See **Phone**, page 123.

Money

Money dreams symbolize issues of power, survival, security, resourcefulness, and relationship mojo. If you dream of having a lot of money, then you're feeling powerful, capable, successful, and worthy of love. If you are at a loss for money in your dream, you may be grappling with feelings of powerlessness, worthlessness, and low self-esteem. Consider this to be a venting dream where you are letting go of poverty consciousness (feeling like there's never enough). Alternatively, if you dream of being paid to do something that feels like a compromise, consider that you might be grappling with the prostitute archetype. See also **Lottery**, page 185, and **Prostitute**, page 59.

Moon

The moon is an ancient symbol of intuition, mystery, passion, soul, the seasons, cycles of your relationship, as well as your feminine power. Dreams of the moon reflect the goddess aspect of you (whether you are a man or a woman), the season you and your loved one are in, or your ability to shine a light during a dark night of the soul.

A **new moon** is a time to set intentions about a new relationship or a new phase in your relationship. Allow yourself to be in the dark and to find peace in not knowing how it will turn out.

A **waxing moon** is a time for hard work to stay the course. Stick with your relationship, even if it's difficult. Have patience and keep your focus.

The **full moon** is when your wishes come into fruition and fullness. Give thanks for the blessings showing up in your relationship. Let your inner lunatic howl as you celebrate the blessings in your relationship.

The **waning moon** is a time to let go of what you think you know, re-evaluate your relationship structure, and become willing to give up your point of view in favor of something better.

The moon is an ancient symbol of intuition, mystery, passion, relationship cycles, and feminine power.

Motorcycle

Dreams of a motorcycle can be symbolic of a desire for a wild ride, the need for speed, or rebellion against relationship norms. Perhaps you yearn for wild abandon, to throw care to the wind, and to do things your way.

Mud

Mud is a symbol of messy relationship thoughts or resignation (i.e. being stuck in the mud). Conversely, because mud is made up of the elements of water and earth, this dream might mean that signals you are sending are blurred and muddied and it's time to clean up your communication (e.g., make amends or forgive a transgression). Alternatively, because mud can be used to dry out and remove toxins, this dream could be symbolic of the early stages of a healing process. See also **Dirt**, page 110, and **Shadow**, page 156.

Musical Instrument

Dreams of a musical instrument signify the sweet sound of success blowing in your ear. Musical instruments, because of their sensual qualities, can be phallic symbols. Additionally, because music is the universal language of love and a musical instrument is a delivery device, the instrument you dream of may be providing you the experience of feeling the more subtle vibrations between you and your lover. See also **Music**, page 152.

Needle

A needle is symbolic of something painful that has gotten under your skin. You might fear being invaded, hurt, or emotionally punctured. Needles are also phallic symbols, telling you that your lover has been a little prick lately. Or perhaps you've been feeling the stabs of unrequited love or betrayal. Conversely, a needle is an instrument for repair, which suggests that your relationship (or broken heart) may need some mending.

Nightgown

Dreams of a nightgown signify a desire to maintain a slight veil of mystery in your relationship, an opaque covering to hide your authentic nakedness (true feelings). If the nightgown in your dream is sexy, then this might be a message that you are embellishing your sexuality. If the nightgown is frumpy, then it could reflect that you've been hiding your sensuality. If so, let this be a reminder to come out from under the covers and allow your true sexy self be revealed. See also **Lingerie**, page 118.

Obstacle

Dreams of an obstacle suggest that you are being challenged in your relationship. Keep in mind that there would be something wrong if you didn't encounter blocks from time to time. Contemplate your strategy for dealing with this obstacle—do you go under or around it, confront it head-on, or avoid it? Your dreamtime strategy might give you a clue how to best surmount any challenges you stumble upon along the journey of love. Consider that obstacles can be blessings in disguise, as they can be predecessors to depth, closeness, and intimacy. See also **Barricade**, page 99.

Overpass

Dreams of an overpass may be symbolic of your desire to ignore the gridlock of past resentments and override your feelings by taking an emotional bypass. Remember, you can't heal what you can't feel. This dream could also be symbolic of your willingness to take the high road and not get caught up in the traffic jam (the thick of things) you and your lover have been arguing over.

Panties

Dreams of panties, because they cover up your private parts, can be symbolic of an attempt at disguising or covering up a sexual secret or feelings you don't feel safe enough to express. Panties can also reflect a desire to embellish your natural (naked) sexual feelings. Panties represent girlishness, innocence, virginal attributes, or seduction. See also **Lingerie**, page 118.

Pantyhose

Dreams of pantyhose signify your desire for support in standing up for yourself, in a feminine way. Pantyhose reflect a desire to appear softer and smoother than you actually are. If pantyhose are being removed in your dream, this might be symbolic of stripping away your inhibitions as you prepare for a deeper experience of intimacy. See **Lingerie**, page 118, **Panties**, page 122, and **Stockings**, page 129.

Peach

See **Fruit**, page 113.

Pearl

A pearl is made from grains of sand that act as an irritant in an oyster, which produces this treasure. In the same way, dreams of a pearl may reflect something that has been irritating you. Perhaps your heart was broken or your dreams were dashed, but you survived and are now wiser, brighter, smoother, and more luminous than before. A pearl is symbolic of a sacrifice or difficulty that proves to have been worth it in the end.

Phallus/Phallic Symbol

If you dream of a snake, rocket, gun, tall building, sword, key, musical instrument, rooster, carrot, or any other phallic symbol, it relates to potency, power, aggressiveness, sexual desire, fertility, masculine mojo, virility, strength, and a feeling of being competent in the world. You may be having this dream because you are sexually aroused, need a boost of confidence, or could use a reminder that you are desirable and capable of manifesting your relationship dreams into reality. See also **Penis**, page 57, and **Sex**, page 192.

Phone

Dreams of a phone denote a desire to reach out and connect with your lover. If you dream of trying to dial someone but can't reach them, you are grappling with interference on the line of your relationship and are trying to figure out how to get in touch. If you reach the person, you have a harmonious connection with the person you are calling and/or the qualities they represent. Either way, this dream is a message that you are becoming more telepathic and empathic and are polishing your communication skills. See also **Texting, Text Message**, page 197.

Photo Album

Dreams of a photo album signify certain memories from your past that may be attempting to shed light on a relationship pattern. Or this dream may be revealing that you are carrying your past relationship filters (baggage) into your present relationship. A photo album can also signify a desire to know and be known in your relationship—a desire to share your history and explore a deeper level of awareness of your partner's past.

Photograph

Dreams of a photograph signify self-awareness, lucidity, and a desire to capture a moment in time from your past, present, or future. This dream might be a freeze-frame from your life that highlights a special image to frame your current circumstances. Conversely, this dream might be cautioning you about perfectionism, as in expecting your relationship to always look like a picture-perfect holiday card. See also **Photo Album**, page 123, and **Selfie**, page 191.

Plant

Dreams of a plant may be a message to bloom where you're planted, as opposed to feeling the need to uproot yourself every time you encounter a difficult outgrowth in your relationship. A plant could be a message to connect with your organic nature and not be so mesmerized by all the bright and shiny people, places, and opportunities in your outer world. Each type of plant carries its own unique message and symbolism. See also **Flower**, page 112, and **Garden**, page 80.

Pornography

See page 154.

Poop

Dreams of poop signify that your relationship may feel that it has gone to crap. Poop is often symbolic of wealth and financial prosperity because it suggests that you have successfully released blocked energy. Alternatively, ask yourself if you've been dumping on your lover (complaining, nagging, and unloading your negativity). Remember, an intimate relationship is a place to work out your problems and issues—our shit, and we all have it—and it's better out than in. See also **Bathroom**, 74.

Present

See **Gift**, page 114.

Purse/Wallet

Dreams of a purse or wallet symbolize your personal power. Because of what it holds, your purse or wallet is an extension of yourself and your power, as well as your ego-identity. It is a nightmare (in real life and in dreams) when a purse or wallet is lost or stolen, and this may be a message to get a grip on your finances. If you dream of someone stealing your purse or wallet, this may signify that your lover is lying, manipulating, or taking advantage of you (stealing your trust). However, if you dream of finding your purse or wallet,

this may represent a renewed sense of self-appreciation, self-worth, and the ability to value the essential aspects of you and your lover that may have previously been taken for granted.

Quilt

Dreams of a quilt signify feeling blanketed in love, warmed by the story you're spinning about your relationship. A quilt, composed of elements significant to you and your life, is symbolic of self-integration, and that your relationship—or the one you are stitching together—is inclusive enough to embrace all aspects of yourself into its warmth. See also **Blanket**, page 101.

Rag

Dreams of a rag signify that you may be feeling torn between whether to toss out or mend your relationship. Perhaps your relationship has become worn out and threadbare due to overuse or neglect. This dream might be a message to make a choice about how to honor an aspect of your relationship that has become old and tattered. Or if you are a woman, it might soon be menstruation time ("on the rag") and thus a time of heightened sensitivity.

Red Light

Dreams of a red light could signify that you may be doing something to sabotage the progression of your relationship, or it could be a sign to stop your relationship, put on the brakes, and re-evaluate what's been driving you. Alternatively, a red light, as in the Red Light District, could symbolize that you've been selling yourself out in your relationship, and it's time to discover what you're really worth. See also **Prostitute**, page 59, and **Red**, page 155.

Ring

For many people a ring—in dreams and in waking reality—represents that you are loved, lovable, belong to someone, have been claimed, or are worthy of belonging to someone. It's a status symbol and a marker of prestige, wealth, and a place in society. If you dream of giving someone a ring, you may desire to possess. A dream about a ring could be prompting you to look before you leap to make sure my lover is who they say they are and not an imposter ("ringer"). Ask yourself, "Do the promises your lover makes ring true?" Most often, however, a dream of a ring is a wish-fulfillment dream, if your desire has been to be engaged or married; your wildest dreams may be coming true. For ring (verb), see **Call**, page 172. See also **Jewelry**, page 116.

Rod

Dreams of a rod, besides being a phallic symbol, can reflect a need for discipline, masculine power, sexual force, or domination. This dream might reflect that you are feeling a surge of strength in your relationship, or maybe you've been unbending about your boundaries or desires. Consider the saying, "Spare the rod and spoil the child." Perhaps you've been too harsh with yourself or your partner, and it might behoove you to try a little love, kindness, and appreciation of yourself and your loved one to see an improvement in your love life. See also **Penis**, page 57.

Rope

Dreams of a rope can signify a desire to be tied down (in a committed relationship), where you feel the ties that bind. Or perhaps you are feeling fit to be tied (your relationship is driving you crazy), or you may be at the end of your rope (feeling desperate) and are starting to unravel. Alternatively, this dream might imply a bondage fantasy. Either way, this dream is helping you maintain your connection to your lover. If you are walking on a tight rope, then your partnership is in a very precarious situation. See also **Cord**, page 108.

Rose

Dreams of a rose represent love, blooming romance, and an open heart. Everything is "coming up roses" during this flowering time in your love life. A rose bush represents exponentially growing passion. Consider the color of your dreamtime rose to gain a deeper understanding of the particular expression of love being conveyed:

Burgundy represents deep passion.

Orange symbolizes a playful connection.

Pink reflects sweetness or girlishness.

Red connotes devotion, desire, or romance. A single red rose may mean "I love you."

White signifies innocence and purity.

Yellow means joy or optimism.

Rubber

Dreams of rubber symbolize resilience and your ability to bounce back after a difficult situation. Additionally, rubber is slang for condom, which might be a reminder to use protection in your sexual adventures, or that you are being careful to keep intimacy at bay. See also **Condom**, page 108.

Rubbish

See **Garbage**, page 113.

If you dream of giving someone a ring, you may desire to possess this person or leave your mark.

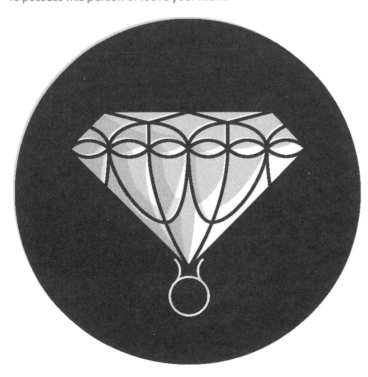

Rug

Dreams of a rug signify that there may be something you or your lover is hiding or sweeping under the rug. This dream may be a message to get a reality check, so that the rug doesn't get pulled out from underneath you. Additionally, a rug is symbolic of a desire to soften the edges or cover up an unpleasant issue you'd prefer not to see about your relationship.

Sacred Text (Bible/ Koran/Torah/ Tipitaka/Vedas)

Dreaming about a sacred text suggests a desire to spiritualize your relationship and perhaps dedicate your sexuality to the sacred within you. Conversely, dreams of spiritual and religious literature might signify a need to reconcile the holy versus the human desires within you. You may be exorcising guilt and shame you've carried from a fundamental belief system regarding sexual desire. If you dream of a specific passage from a holy scripture, it may be advice that you would be wise to heed in waking reality. This dream might lead you to explore your personal code of conduct (however you define it, spiritually or otherwise) with regard to your love or sexual relationship.

Safe

Dreams of a safe, a place to keep valuables, signify that you may be feeling vulnerable and are trying to hide your deeper feelings away under lock and key. This may be a message to find a safe word or a way to communicate your boundaries or the aspects of your body, mind, or spirit that feel fragile or sensitive or that may be healing from a traumatic experience. Additionally, this dream may be a message for you to value yourself, to be mindful, and to treasure yourself as you discern whether or not your partner is worthy of seeing your inner gold. If you dream that you are safe, emotionally relaxed and comforted, this may reflect a wish fulfillment, reveal your personal access to develop your own inner sense of security, or be a message that your relationship is a safe place for you to let down your guard. See also **Vault**, page 92.

Sat Nav

See **GPS**, page 114.

Screw

See **Sex**, page 192, and **Tool**, page 130.

Seed

Dreams of a seed signify a new thought, idea, vision, fertility, or even pregnancy. A seed symbolizes that a new beginning could be sprouting if given a chance. Additionally, it reflects a vulnerable, embryonic season in your relationship. This dream may be a message to take the time to cultivate your relationship's roots within your inner greenhouse before you present yourself to worldly elements. See also **Flower**, page 112, **Gardener**, page 45, and **Semen**, page 126.

Selfie

See page 191.

Semen

Semen (ejaculation) in a sexual dream reflects a desire for an orgasmic release, whether it is physical or emotional. Semen can also symbolize pregnancy or a desire for pregnancy, creative expression, or the fact that you are truly turned on in your love life. The wordplay in semen could be about you wanting to see men; This might symbolize that you have a desire to play the field or behave like a sailor and have a "lover in every port." See also **Ejaculate, Ejaculation**, page 178, **Orgasm**, page 188, **Sailor**, page 60, and **Sex**, page 192.

Sex Toy

Perhaps your attempts at intimacy have been feeling forced or disingenuous, or this dream reflects your willingness and ability to be self-sufficient and take care of your own pleasure. Dreams of a vibrator may be symbolic of a desire to amplify the vibration of your relationship mojo. Perhaps you've become numb or unfeeling toward your partner's or even your own advances. Perhaps this dream is a message to take some alone time. Additionally, it could be a nudge to put yourself in the hot seat and turn up the voltage of your love affair with yourself by recharging the batteries of your wildest fantasies. This dream may be permission to feel the sweet buzz of your own sensuality.

Shield

Dreams of a shield signify that you're feeling the need for protection. Perhaps you're feeling vulnerable (unsafe) in your relationship and you need reassurance. There may or may not be a good reason to be on the defensive. Or this dream may be helping you to become aware of your ego's sabotage mechanism that keeps you safe but keeps love at bay. See also **Safe**, page 126.

Shoes

Dreams of shoes suggest that you are taking a stand in your relationship. If you dream that your shoes are off, then perhaps

If you dream about sexy shoes, perhaps you are preparing to step into your sensuality as you make forward strides toward intimacy.

you are getting grounded as you find your comfort zone in this relationship. If you are putting shoes on, you may be preparing to leave, or take an assertive step toward a relationship. If your shoes are new, then you may be trying to "break in" a new relationship. If you dream of old shoes, this may signify that you've been feeling so comfortable in your love life that you may be taking it for granted, or perhaps you're the one who is feeling unappreciated (like an old shoe)—you may be getting the message to repair your relationship. If you dream about sexy shoes, perhaps you are preparing to step into your sensuality as you make forward strides toward intimacy. If you dream of boots, you may be protecting yourself. Boots can also suggest that you are taking an empowered stance in your love life. Alternatively, boots can signify that you may be trying to cover up your vulnerability so as to avoid getting hurt—perhaps you're feeling a desire to leave an uncomfortable relationship. See also **Foot**, page 45, and **High Heels**, page 116.

Shotgun

Dreams of a shotgun might signify that you or your lover is taking the passenger's seat in your relationship. This dream might be revealing the end of a pattern of recklessness and codependence. Perhaps you're feeling under the gun to make a commitment (a shotgun wedding). If so, before barreling through with it, make sure your actions honor your needs, not just your family's. See also **Gun**, page 114.

Shower

See page 194.

Signature

If you dream of signing your name on the dotted line, you may be dealing with commitment issues, or figuring out whether you truly endorse the relationship you are in. In dreams and in waking reality, the act of writing your name is symbolic of a promise, intent, or an agreement. This dream may be helping you to become lucid, so the agreements you make truly feed your soul. Consider what is being signed or agreed upon in your dream, and if you feel integrity in giving your word or lending your name to this partnership.

Silver (metal)

Dreams of silver are symbolic of strength under fire, beauty, and elegance. Perhaps your loved one is testing your mettle—or you may be coming into an awareness of how precious you and your relationship truly are. See also **Silver (color)**, page 151, and **Jewelry**, page 116.

Skeleton

See page 61.

Smoke

Dreams of smoke suggest a fear of your relationship going up in flames. Where there's smoke, there's fire, so this dream could also indicate that a passionate love affair (that is smokin' hot) is forthcoming. This dream might be helping you reveal and release any unhealthy sexual patterns that make you feel like you've blown it. If you dream of smoke signals, you may be looking for help in navigating your relationship. Or, you may think someone's using excessive flattery ("blowing smoke"). See also **Cigarette**, page 106, and **Fire**, page 112.

Snow

Dreams of snow signify emotional frigidness, rigidity, and aloofness. Perhaps your heart was broken (or bruised), and the shock has turned you into an ice king or queen. This dream may be shining a warm light on the issue so that you can find a gentle way to thaw. See also **Winter**, page 93.

Snowboard

Dreams of a snowboard signify skill, agility, and a willingness to traverse chilly emotional terrain, within either yourself or your partner. A snowboard suggests an athlete or warrior's attitude toward finding adventure in an emotional snowstorm. See also **Snow**, page 128, and **Winter**, page 93.

Soap

Dreams of soap indicate that you are cleaning, purifying, and releasing old thoughts and habits in your love life. Perhaps you are coming clean about a secret that's been cluttering your relationship sanctuary. Dreams of soap might signify a desire for a fresh start, with sparkling clean agreements and renewed commitment to keep the lines of communication open, honest, and respectful. See also **Clean**, page 174.

Sperm

See **Semen**, page 126.

Staircase

See page 88.

Star

Dreams of a star signify that you are being guided on your relationship path by a higher source. Perhaps you've been praying for navigational advice in your love life, and this dream may be illuminating the way, giving you a burst of confidence or a sense of divine direction and intervention. Additionally, you may be coming into your true power and lighting up your life so brightly that the love you desire will have no choice but to find you. If you are currently coupled, then your relationship is providing the right kind of space and support to kindle your luminosity. If you dream of a movie star, see **Celebrity**, page 36.

Stockings

Dreams of stockings, besides being wordplay for stalking, signify that you are seeking support to stand up for yourself in your relationship. You may not be wearing the pants, but you have the strength to stand tall and take charge. Fishnet stockings signify a desire to hook the sexual attention of your lover. See also **Pantyhose**, page 122.

Stoplight

Dreams of a stoplight signify someone or something may be trying to curb your enthusiasm. Or perhaps you're feeling frustrated that you can't immediately manifest the relationship you desire or fulfill your sensual needs in this moment. Keep in mind that infinite patience yields immediate results. Alternatively, ask yourself if you've been feeling rejected or thwarted in making a move. This dream may be a message from your higher self to stop what you're doing before getting in any deeper. See also **Park**, page 188, and **Red Light**, page 124.

Stream

See page 90.

Sugar

Dreams of sugar signify that you are connecting with your sweetness. Perhaps your relationship is bringing out your inner nectar. You may be experiencing the deliciousness of your connection with your honey, or enjoying your just desserts for an arduous relationship journey. Additionally, this dream may reveal that though this love affair is sweet, like a sugar rush, if it isn't backed by protein (real caring and depth) you will burn out. See also **Dessert**, page 109, **Drug**, page 111, and **Reward**, page 190.

Suitcase

See **Bag**, page 99, and **Luggage**, page 118.

Sun

A dream of a sun symbolizes enlightenment, a spiritual awakening, confidence, power, radiance, and lucidity. You, in this relationship constellation, are attuned to source energy. Perhaps your lover lights up your life. Dreams of the sun are an auspicious sign that you are in the right place at the right time with the right person, and that the sunlight of the spirit is shining upon your romance.

Sweets

See **Candy**, page 104.

Tattoo

A dream of a tattoo reflects the messages that have been deeply etched on your heart and soul. Consider what the tattoo is, what part of the body it is on, and the feelings it evokes. This dream may be showing you that you leave a lasting impression on your lover, and to be mindful of what you do or say because it could have a permanent effect. This dream might also indicate a tribal rite of passage or your affiliation with a particular tribe or group consciousness. See also **Body**, page 32, and **Pierce, Piercing**, page 188.

Television

If you dream of television, just as in watching a play or theatrical performance, this could be shedding light on archetypal patterns and processes you and your loved one are playing out. Additionally, if you are on television, this can be symbolic of your desire for self-expression, prominence, success, and recognition. Perhaps you are preparing to become more public with your relationship. See also **Actor/Actress**, page 28, and **Celebrity**, page 36.

Test

To dream of being tested suggests that you may be in the midst of a learning and growing phase in your relationship; perhaps you are discovering answers and resources you didn't know you had. You may be processing or venting fears of failure, or pressure to make the grade. Additionally, this may be a make-it-or-break-it moment in your relationship. Keep in mind that the strongest bonds are forged through fire, pressure, and unthinkable obstacles. See also **School**, page 88.

Thermometer

If you dream of a thermometer, consider that this dream is reflecting emotional temperature in your love affair. If the temperature is fiery hot, this relates to your level of passion. If the temperature is ice cold, then you may be feeling chilly, perhaps due to emotional aloofness or a lack of intimacy. Your dream might be showing you that it's time to heat things up or take a chill pill. See also **Freeze/Frozen**, page 181, and **Heat**, page 149.

Thorn

Just as the saying goes, "Every rose has its thorns," you might be realizing that with great love comes great sacrifice. Dreams of thorns can symbolize a martyr complex in a relationship, as in Christ's crown of thorns. Ask yourself, "Where do I feel unworthy of getting my needs met?" If this resonates, then your work is in dropping your Christ complex as you realize that your human, sexual needs are God-given. See also **Rose**, page 125.

Toilet

Dreams of a toilet could signify that you're in the midst of letting go of resentments that no longer serve you in your relationship. Maybe you've been pissed off and are in need of a good release. This dream might indicate that you could use some alone time to allow yourself to unclench, let go, and claim the throne of your greatest power in your relationship. See also **Bathroom**, page 74.

Tomato

See **Vegetable**, page 133.

Tool

Dreams of tools signify that something needs to be repaired. Perhaps trust has been compromised or an agreement has been broken. This dream might be making you aware of how resourceful you truly are, as well as revealing your strategies and coping mechanisms. If your tools are in good shape, then you can feel confident and competent to handle the challenges you face. If they are broken or not working correctly, then it's time to open yourself up to discovering a new strategy. Keep in mind that every challenge you face in your relationship affords you an opportunity to discover some new inner resource. Alternatively, a tool is slang and can be symbolic of the penis, so contemplate whether or not you feel like a tool that is simply servicing your lover.

A **hammer** may mean a desire to get your point across and a willingness to use force.

A **nail** signifies getting caught in the act (nailed). You now know that you are correct in your assessment of your relationship—you've hit the nail on the head.

A **screw** or **screwdriver** can be a symbol of the sexual act, and it can also signify that you feel cheated, taken advantage of, or screwed over.

A **wrench** signifies taking back something you didn't mean, or sabotaging your love life.

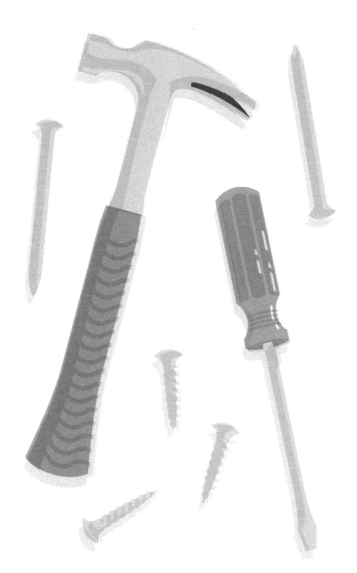

Dreams about tools signify that something—perhaps a broken promise or relationship—needs repair.

Toy

Dreams of a toy signify that it's time to enjoy your relationship, have fun, and play. However, this dream may be cautioning you not to treat this relationship like a plaything. See also **Sex Toy**, page 127.

Trash

Dreams of trash might signify that you feel trashy, perhaps because of behavior you're not proud of. Maybe you've been trashing yourself or your partner, or not treating each other with the respect you each deserve. This is a wake-up call to stop wasting your time on thoughts and people that don't empower you. See also **Garbage**, page 113.

Treasure

Dreams of treasure symbolize that you and your loved one have been digging through the surface of ego pretenses and discovered the inner gold. Perhaps you've been sharing and caring enough to let your true feelings be revealed. You are realizing that to know each other is to love each other. See also **Jewelry**, page 116, and **Lottery**, page 185.

A **saw** represents a desire to get rid of something, cut away the fat, or let go of what doesn't serve you; destruction that can lead to creation.

See also **Construction**, page 174.

Torch

See **Flashlight**, page 112.

Torpedo

Dreams of a torpedo, besides being a phallic symbol, can be synonymous with intense desire, intent, will, and masculine strength. This dream might reflect your need or desire to dominate or to create control by removing any interference between you and the love you desire. See **Phallus/ Phallic Symbol**, page 123.

Tree

Dreams of a tree signify that you're feeling rooted and stabilized in yourself, which allows you to feel grounded in your relationship. They are bringing you back to your roots and your true nature, so that you'll intuitively know when it's time to branch out on your own. Additionally, a tree might be symbolic of your family tree and the ways in which you have been influenced by your familial patterns, wounds, and proclivities. You might want to keep some of these, and others you might want to leave behind in the winds of change. In any case, this dream affirms you and sends a message that your relationships will grow once you are grounded yet exalted in your stature.

Trench Coat

Dreams of a trench coat symbolize mystery, a need for protection, or a desire for easy access to drop everything at a moment's notice and reveal yourself to your lover. A trench coat, in waking reality, can symbolize a flasher or exhibitionist, so this dream might show a desire to be more revealing to your loved one, and that you're waiting for the right opportunity to bare all. See also **Clothing**, page 106, and **Coat**, page 106.

Trophy

If you dream of a trophy, you are recognizing yourself for hard work, accomplishments, and all the ways you've grown in your relationship. Additionally, this dream might reveal where you've been seeking external validation (as in a trophy wife or husband). See also **Reward**, page 190.

Tumor

A tumor in waking reality and in dreams can be seen as a trash can where toxic or superfluous energy gets stored. A dream of a tumor could represent unhealthy thoughts that haven't yet found a constructive outlet. Consider what you've suppressed—emotionally and physically—that is demanding to be expressed. Additionally, a tumor could be seen as a phallic symbol, prompting the question, "Have you found yourself attracted to someone you deem inappropriate? And for whom you have been suppressing your sexual needs or desires?" If this resonates, consider looking for a healthy way to vent or to integrate this energy that is beneficial to your whole being and to your love and sex life. See also **Cancer**, page 141.

Tunnel

See page 91.

UFO

If you dream of seeing a UFO, it signifies that you have an open mind and the eyes to see a new and different type of relationship that is truly out of this world. If you dream of being on an actual UFO, you might feel you are being carried away. Your relationship may have you feeling like an outcast—estranged from family and friends. Perhaps your love affair is taking you into uncharted waters and opening you to aspects of yourself that, up until now, have felt alien to you. Some of those aspects might be readily embraced by you, and some of them may be shadow aspects that you reject. See also **Alien**, page 28.

Underwear

Because genitals represent your sexual identity and vulnerability, dreams of underwear signify an attempt at protecting your "family jewels"—your passion and your sensual or sexual feelings—and keeping them under wraps. Perhaps you feel the need to cover up a secret. See also **Panties**, page 122.

Valentine

Dreams of a valentine are about your burning desire for that special one-of-a-kind romance, or improving your own ability to wear your heart on your sleeve. This dream might be a message to love the one you're with, or to go out of your way to express appreciation for your partner and for yourself. See **Love Letter**, page 118.

Vase

Dreams of a vase signify that you are holding space for your relationship desires that you hope will flourish. Because a vase is usually rounded and curvy and contains water and flowers, it is symbolic of the female body and the beauty it can hold. Whether you are a man or a woman, you may be dreaming of the feminine energy you contain. If properly channeled, it can produce and hold the space for your relationship's blossoming. See also **Flower**, page 112.

Vault

See page 92.

Vegetable

We all know what Sigmund Freud would say if he knew you dream of eating carrots, celery, zucchini, or cucumbers! More than merely phallic symbols, vegetables in dreams represent self-love and strength; you are taking care of your body and your relationship. In general, dreams of veggies represent a healthy sexual appetite and the desire for good, clean, sensual pleasure. Here are a few examples of what the veggies in your dreams may be telling you:

With a **carrot**, you are seeing the truth of your relationship more clearly, perhaps seeing the best in your partner. Have you been goal-oriented, as in chasing the carrot of a promised reward that continues to be out of reach? Dreams of a **potato** signify a hearty, earthy, meat and potatoes connection between you and your lover. It may not be glamorous, but it is substantial.

Because a **tomato** looks and feels like the human heart, it signifies that your relationship has heart and is red-blooded, substantial, and healthy.

Leafy greens mean salad days ahead! Lettuce is a symbol of wealth, signifying that you and your partner are rich in love. Conversely, if you dream of eating vegetables and not liking them, it might indicate that you're on the straight and narrow and may have been depriving yourself of some of the sweet and naughty delights your relationship also has in store for you.

See also **Blow Job**, page 169, and **Food**, page 113.

Veil

A veil symbolizes a desire to remain elusive, secretive, or mysterious. Contemplate what it is that you don't want your lover to discover about you. See also **Wedding Dress**, page 134.

Viagra

This dream can mean you are looking for a quick fix for what might be a deeper issue related to attraction, vitality, and desirability. This dream could also be symbolic of your desire for more mojo, vitality, and virility.

Vibrator

See **Sex Toy**, page 127.

Volcano

Dreams of a volcano signify deep feelings that have been suppressed; they may be warning you to find a healthy outlet. This dream might reflect that you have met somebody who turns you on so much that you feel the Earth move under your feet. Dreams of a volcano may also be a warning to become grounded and stabilize yourself before your deep underground emotions erupt. See also **Orgasm**, page 188.

Wallet

See **Purse/Wallet**, page 124.

Washing Machine

Dreams of a washing machine signify that you've got a mess on your hands and you have a desire to clean it up before it leaves a stain. A washing machine signifies a process by which you can forgive, forget, clean the slate, and move on. Perhaps you are in the spin cycle, as you loop over and over again what bothered you. Or perhaps you are working it out in the tumble-dry phase. Either way, you are in the midst of a healing process, so allow it, don't rush it, and let it run its course. See also **Laundry**, page 118.

Watch

See page 93.

Water

See page 93.

Waterfall

See page 134.

Weapon

Dreams of a weapon are symbolic of a defense mechanism in place, perhaps due to a lack of emotional or physical safety in your love affair. This dream may be prompting you to explore whether or not this relationship is a safe harbor for you, or if you've been pushing the limits too far and now feel the need to contract and create boundaries. You may be furious with your lover or feeling the need to protect yourself.

Web

Dreams of a web signify seduction. Perhaps you are dating a spin doctor, someone who knows how to tell a tale and lure you in with his or her web of words. Or this dream might be showing you the art of enticing your loved one into your web of life or lies. Additionally, whether you are male or female you may be aware of your feminine charm, allure, patience, craftsmanship, creativity, and ability to weave the love life of your dreams. Alternatively, you may have become entangled in your lover's life, and this dream is illuminating a way for you to break free. See also **Spider**, page 62.

Wedding Dress

Dreams of a wedding dress signify the fabric of your hopes, dreams, wishes, and aspirations regarding your divine feminine essence, or meeting and marrying your soul mate. Clothing in a dream often represents a role you play—that you can put on or take off as it suits you—as a completely organic aspect of your soul. You may be processing your desires regarding what marriage symbolizes to you (e.g., status, respectability, acceptability in the eyes of society and family). See also **Bride**, page 33, **Princess**, page 58, and **Wedding**, page 93.

Whip

See page 198.

Wine

Because wine is a spirit, your dream may be showing you that your love life is connecting you with your spiritual essence. Wine also indicates that there is something worth celebrating in your love affair. See also **Alcohol**, page 97, and **Drunk**, page 178.

Yacht

See **Ship**, page 88.

Zipper

If you dream of being zipped up in your dream, perhaps you are feeling tentative about revealing your secrets or exposing your true feelings. You may be feeling the need to zip your lips until the time is right to say what you really feel and unleash the beast of your wildest self. If you are unzipped, you may be ready to let it all hang out. Perhaps the superman or -woman beneath your layers of protective clothing is bursting at the seams. If this is the case, then this dream may be a message to drop the buckles, clamps, snaps, and chains that bind and unleash your true feelings, urges, and fantasies and explore a deepening experience of intimacy.

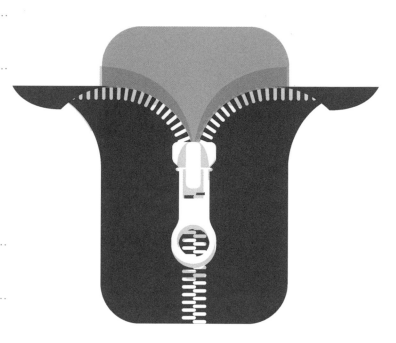

Dreaming of a zipper may suggest you feel tentative about revealing secrets.

Chapter 4

Ideas and Whims

(the Intangible and Hard-to-Pin-Down)

Emily Brontë wrote, "I've dreamt in my life dreams that have stayed with me ever after, and changed my ideas: they've gone through and through me, like wine through water, and altered the color of my mind."

Whether or not we remember them, we've all had dreams like Emily Brontë describes. The best things in life and dreams are not only free but invisible, inaudible, indescribable—and they do change us, if we let them. In fact, our physical body, which may seem to be of the highest importance, is composed of only 1 percent physical matter and 99 percent nonphysical energy, according to quantum physics. With that in mind, we could say that the things we can't touch are the things that matter most, especially when it comes to matters of the heart.

You know you've had a dream that features an intangible idea or whim when you awaken feeling struck by one or more of the following:

- An "aha" moment
- Intense emotion or sensation
- A bizarre sequence of numbers or letters
- A clear knowing, understanding, insight, or thought
- Characteristic, color, quality, or distinction
- Advice from a higher being (or from yourself)
- A new point of view or solution to a problem

When you've had one of these intangible types of dreams—for example, one that features an outstanding color—don't dismiss it simply because it's not as easy to grasp as physical dream symbols. In order for your love life to gain a boost from these dreams, you should ask a few questions upon awakening:

- **How is this dream helping me to see or perceive my relationship from a higher, better, or more creative point of view?**
- **How is this dream helping me to improve my sex life?**
- **What feelings does this idea, concept, or whim stimulate?**
- **What guidance is this dream inspiring me to take?**

Often the problems we experience in our love lives are based on our lack of awareness or creativity. Dreams that feature ideas, whims, and other things we can't touch help us to broaden our minds, solve problems creatively, and become more out-of-the-box thinkers. In fact, I've heard it said that where a thought goes, energy flows, and results show. When you change your mind or gain a new insight, it could make all the difference between shivering in the dark all alone and flipping a switch to shed light on your dream romance.

A (letter)

To dream of receiving an A suggests that you are excelling in your relationship or as a lover. This dream might be an affirmation of your readiness to take your love life to a new level; the work you've been doing on yourself is paying off. Conversely, this dream may be showing you where you are seeking approval outside yourself. Or, as in *The Scarlet Letter*, an A might be a symbol of adultery or sexual shame. See also **Alphabet**, page 140.

Accent

Dreams of a foreign accent signify your desire to spice up your love life. Whether you've dreamed of a foreign tongue whispering sweet nothings in your ear or of adding a splash of color to accessorize an outfit or brighten up a room in your love life, a dream of an accent is about enlivening your romance palette with something or someone new, or reviving a familiar something or someone to be experienced in a new way. See also **Foreign**, page 148.

Account

Dreams of a bank account are a message to give yourself or your loved one credit where credit is due. Dreams of an account or of accounting signify the need to weigh and balance whether or not a relationship is worth the price, risk, or investment. This dream might also be illuminating issues of your own self-worth, and where you need to be more generous with praise and acknowledgment. See also **Bank**, page 73, and **Money**, page 120.

Addiction

Dreams of addiction indicate that you may be feeling strung out on love, or that you are high as a kite and afraid of coming down. They may reveal that you've become addicted to your lover or a habit that can have a destructive effect if not managed properly. Often an addiction in waking life and in dreams reflects a craving for pleasure that you haven't yet managed in a healthy, sustainable way. Ask yourself, what need is this addiction fulfilling? What kind of pleasure does it give me? What life-affirming new habit can I create to override this destructive one? See **Alcohol**, page 97, and **Drugs**, page 111.

Adventure

Dreams of an adventure signify your willingness to live on the edge and have the ride of your life. Conversely, you may be white-knuckling your way through the ups and downs of your relationship. Perhaps you desire a more adventurous love and sex life with a bit more risk. This dream could be a message to stop treating your relationship like it's a problem to be solved instead of the amusement park it is capable of being.

Advice

Dreams where you receive advice signify that your higher self may be attempting to send you a message regarding your love life. The person offering pearls of wisdom, whether it is a life coach, doctor, lawyer, therapist, parent, or best friend, is you. Consider taking this guidance to heart.

Affection

See page 165.

Afraid

See **Fear**, page 147.

Agreement

See **Contract**, page 143.

Dreams of an adventure
signify your willingness to live
on the edge and have the
ride of your life.

Allergy

See **Disease**, page 144, and **Sick**, page 194.

Alone

If you dream of being alone and it feels good, then this dream might suggest you are craving a healthy dose of alone time for self-reflection and self-connection. However, if you dream of being alone and feeling lonely, it suggests a need for self-love and acceptance, and perhaps an opportunity for you to discover your relationship with your higher power. Additionally, your dream might be offering you a strategy for how to enjoy your own company, become more magnetic to attract love into your life, or reveal yourself authentically and soulfully to your partner so that you don't feel so alone.

Alphabet

Dreams of the alphabet signify that you want to spell out what you need in your relationship. Perhaps you've been dropping subtle hints to your loved one—to no avail. Or maybe your love life has become too complicated and your message is to keep communication simple to be understood.

Ancient

See **Old**, page 85.

Anger, Angry

Anger in a dream suggests that what is suppressed must express itself. Perhaps you have suppressed your unpleasant emotions from waking life. Alternatively, if you feel that the anger in your dreams is not your own, it may be helping you to have compassion for an aggressive person you are in relationship with—you may discover a strategy for handling an upsetting situation. Keep in mind that anger, when properly channeled, can be powerful fuel for love. See also **Emotion**, page 145.

Astrology

Dreams of astrology or an astrologer signify a desire to know what's in the stars for your relationship, or to forecast your sexual and emotional compatibility. This dream might be revealing insight about your resonance with each other, as well as the dissonant aspects. Also, dreams of zodiac signs can symbolize relationship success and your desire to allow the heavens to inform your relationship navigation. The following are brief descriptions to consider when these individual astrological signs show up in your dreams:

Aries: courageous, frank, cut and dried, dynamic, naïve, childish, and demanding

Aquarius: idealistic, independent, original, aloof, altruistic, and charitable

Cancer: dreamy, emotional, sensitive, empathetic, crabby, and has strong boundaries

Capricorn: determined, focused, a strong leader, territorial, and ambitious

Gemini: social, communicative, indecisive, quick-witted, and clarity seeking

Leo: royal, regal, confident, charismatic, natural leader, narcissistic, and benevolent

Libra: weighs and balances the pros and cons of a partnership, idealistic, fair, and speaks out on personal convictions

Pisces: emotional, sensitive, adaptive, deep, imaginative, romantic, and spiritual

Sagittarius: inspiring, poetic, deep, romantic, adventurous, charming, and free spirited

Scorpio: powerful, domineering, assertive, possessive, hardworking, and critical

Taurus: grounded, craving emotional (and physical) attention, hardheaded, and safety- and security-oriented

Virgo: analyzing, detail-oriented, serious, practical, and down-to-earth

Big

Dreams of something big (a person, animal, body part, building, or object) suggests importance, power, superiority, influence, domination, or an overbearing aspect of your relationship. If you feel small compared with something or someone big in your relationship, you may be working through issues of inferiority or intimidation. Remember, everyone and everything in your dream is you, so this big thing may be an aspect of you and your shadow not yet embraced.

Birthday

See page 75.

Bisexual

See page 32.

Black

Dreams that feature the color black symbolize darkness, something mysterious, secretive, seductive, and unknown. Black signifies your unintegrated power or the aspect of your shadow you have yet to embrace. This dream could be a message to hold on, because the darkest hour is before the dawn. Additionally, being in the black could point to profit and prosperity. See also **Color**, page 143, and **Shadow**, page 156.

Black and Blue

If your dream features the colors black and blue, it signifies that your heart has been bruised. The pain represented by this dream may be a doorway to ecstasy and surrender (no pain, no gain), as well as a message to give yourself permission for massive doses of self-love, acceptance, and healing. See **BDSM**, page 168.

Blue

Dreams of the color blue symbolize tranquility and peacefulness in your relationship. Alternatively, this dream could indicate that you are feeling blue, or melancholy, due to a rift in your love affair, or that you have a desire to see a blue film (porno). Perhaps you are feeling that the sky of possibility has opened for you and your partner. See also **Color**, page 142, and **Ocean**, page 85.

Body Hair

See page 32.

Brown

The color brown in dreams signifies a grounded, earthy, stabilizing energy. See also **Color**, page 143.

Cancer

Dreams of cancer can reflect that long-held resentment or shame is eating away at you. Perhaps you have negative beliefs or past heartbreaks creating relationship gridlock, needing to be released, healed, or transformed. Consider what negative aspect of your relationship has grown out of control and taken on a life of its own. See also **Astrology (Cancer)**, page 140.

Ceremony

If you dream of a ceremony, you are at a turning point in your love life, moving through a rite of passage and a transformational moment in your relationship, perhaps making sacred your commitment to each other. Consider what you may be releasing and what it is you are making room to embrace. Additionally, this may be a message to acknowledge the new season that you and your partner are growing into. See also **Graduation**, page 80, **Party**, page 86, **Ritual**, page 155, and **Wedding**, page 93.

Chakra

If you dream of a chakra or of the entire chakra system, you may be receiving a message about how to find your energetic alignment, attunement, and balance in your relationship. Additionally, this dream may be showing you where you and your partner are out of alignment, physically, emotionally, mentally, or spiritually. Some say there are between eight to twelve chakras; however, it is most commonly believed that there are seven. Look at the chart below and consider the brief description of what each chakra suggests when featured in a dream.

Circle

Dreams of a circle symbolize wholeness and fullness; your relationship is a space in which you feel a supportive bond of mutuality and fairness. The circle is also symbolic of feminine wisdom, inclusivity, and a safe container for all aspects of you and your partner to be revealed and held. A circle can also represent a repetitious cycle.

Chakra System

Placement in the Body	Qualities/Attributes	Color
1st/Root		
Base of spine	Tribal relations, survival instincts	Red
2nd/Sacrum		
Lower Abdomen	Life force, sexuality, passion	Orange
3rd/Solar Plexus		
Upper Abdomen	Self-confidence, personal power	Yellow
4th/Heart		
Heart/Chest	Passion, love, devotion	Green
5th/Throat		
Throat	Communication, self-expression, words of affirmation	Blue
6th/Ajna		
Head	Mental process, thoughtfulness, collective beliefs	Indigo
7th/Crown		
Above the head	Spirit, transcendent awareness, illumination	White or Violet

Color

Colors in a dream symbolize passion and feeling. If a person or thing in your dream is particularly vibrant, it is worth paying special attention to. Color represents the emotional landscape of the dream. See also specific colors to shed light on what the colors of your dreams may be highlighting.

Conflict

See **Argue/Argument**, page 166.

Constipation

Dreams of constipation could be a message to let go of any resentments you've been holding onto that have been keeping you from being current and in the flow of your relationship. Alternatively, do you feel that someone is lying to you (being inauthentic or full of shit)? See also **Poop**, page 124.

Contest

See **Competition**, page 174.

Contract

If you dream of signing a contract, you are exploring issues around trust, commitment, fairness, and fidelity. It may also be that agreements, both conscious and unconscious, between you and your partner are clamoring to be acknowledged and revised.

Dark

Dreams of something dark often suggest that you are experiencing an aspect of your relationship or your personal power that is mysterious or unknown. You might also feel that you are fighting with dark or negative energies as a result of pain you struggle with in your love life. Keep in mind that something is only dark until the light of your love shines upon it. See also **Shadow**, page 156.

Death

See page 177.

Diet

Dreams of a diet could mean that your subconscious is giving you the message to exert more discipline and self-control regarding your emotional or sexual appetite. Perhaps you've been starving for attention, or you desire to shed unwanted pounds and inches of protective layers that keep you from feeling connected with your loved one, and with a lighter, more elegant version of yourself. This dream could also be a message for you to seek balance (don't take more than you give), or to fast from negative thinking and feast on healthy, affirmative thoughts that fill you up with feelings of attractiveness and confidence from the inside out.

Direction

If you dream of direction it can signify that you are trying to navigate through the cross current of energies in your relationships. You may be seeking guidance and attempting to find your north star to know which way to turn. Consider the following directions:

North: Spend quiet time alone in contemplation and release all false reasons for engaging in your partnership. Let go and trust that what remains (or comes back to you) will be true, solid, and meant to be.

South: Follow your pleasure principle and explore deeper dimensions of your passion and sexuality.

East: Love as if you've never been hurt and with a beginner's mind, take a risk, and try something new.

West: Allow yourself to feel your deeper emotions; honor your tears of sorrow, pleasure, and joy.

See also **Compass**, page 108.

Disease

Dreams of a disease or virus can reflect sexual shame or guilt. Additionally, they might reflect your participation in gossip or be a message that might be harmful to you and your lover. The reality check aspect of this dream would be to see a doctor, get a checkup, and make healthier choices in your love life. See also **Sexually Transmitted Infection/Disease**, page 156, and **Sick**, page 194.

Dreams about seeking directions suggest you're looking for ways to navigate the twists and turns in your relationship.

Down

If you dream of moving down or falling down, it could reflect a loss of control, or that you're feeling overwhelmed, depressed, or sad. This dream could be a message to slow down, connect with your depth, and settle down in your relationship. Alternatively, this might reflect your feelings about going down on your partner (oral sex), or them on you.

Dread

In a dream, dread suggests that you are headed down a path that is not aligned with your highest potential. Consider rerouting or finding an exit strategy. See also **Emotion**, page 145.

Ecstasy

Ecstasy in dreams signifies that you are tapping into your creative brilliance, sexual expression, and eternal and authentic nature. Allow this dream to be a touchstone in your relationship to remind you of your true nature, the feeling tone of your spiritual expression, and a window to insight and enlightenment. See also **Emotion**, page 145.

Eight

Dreams of the number eight signify a full-bodied relationship (mind/body/spirit) experience. Because the number eight symbolizes fulfillment, the dollar sign (material wealth), infinity, and an hourglass figure, perhaps this dream is saying that your hard work is paying off. Isn't it time you feel abundantly loved and cared for? You might also consider the wordplay "ate" or "hate." Are you eating away your feelings? Or are you coming to terms with a hard-to-love aspect of yourself or your lover? See also **Number**, page 153.

Electricity

Dreams of electricity symbolize the level of attraction and chemistry between you and your mate. Electricity in a dream denotes the power and liveliness that occurs when opposites attract. Your dream might be telling you that if you need to be recharged, all you have to do is plug in to the present moment and get current with each other.

Elegant, Elegance

Dreams of elegance signify that your relationship is elevating your status to a higher level, giving your confidence a boost. This dream might also be a message for you to try the less-is-more approach in your romance.

Emotion

Feelings in dreams reveal the true story running beneath the narrative. Emotions run the gamut from hope to pain, and because of your lack of an editing mechanism and inhibitions in the dream state, you will often experience emotional extremes that you may not feel as strongly in your waking state. This is normal, natural, and healthy, as emotions help us to release pressure and awaken in the morning with a clean, clear slate. See also particular emotions.

Empty

Dreams of feeling empty could symbolize that there is a void in your relationship. Perhaps you've been out of balance, feeling lonely or hungry for affection, and this dream is an alert to address it. On the positive side, emptiness can also symbolize openness to growth, change, and transformation.

Engagement

Dreams of an engagement represent grappling with issues of monogamy, fidelity, security, and your feelings about marriage. See also **Commit, Commitment**, page 174, **Marry, Marriage**, page 186, and **Wedding**, page 93.

Ethnicity

If you dream of your own race or ethnicity, you may be connecting to your tribal, cultural roots and family lineage. Perhaps you are drawing on strength or wisdom from your bloodline to support you through a relationship rite of passage. If you dream of an ethnicity different from your own, you may be exploring, incorporating, and integrating aspects of yourself that have been foreign. Your relationship may be inspiring you to expand your knowledge and experience on a fuller spectrum.

Dreams of a fairy tale reveal
that you have met (or desire
to meet) your Prince or
Princess Charming.

Facebook

Dreams of Facebook signify that you may be overly concerned with the way your relationship status looks to others. Perhaps you've been focused on the face value versus the soul of your love life. Conversely, this dream may be a message for you to get off your computer and create some face time with an actual person as opposed to virtual lover. See also **Social Media**, page 157, and **Twitter**, page 197.

Fairy Tale

Dreams of a fairy tale signify that you have met or desire to meet your Prince or Princess Charming. This dream could also suggest that your real life relationship is up against unrealistic, idealistic, or perfectionist standards. Alternatively, you may be in the midst of your epic love story. Consider the feeling tone to help determine the message of this dream.

Fame

Dreams of fame signify an ambition to have your genius recognized and celebrated by your loved one or by the world, or to have your relationship reach a high status in your community. The shadow side of fame is a profound desire to please. This dream could also inspire you to contemplate the question, "How might you behave in your relationship if you knew people were watching, admiring, and seeking to emulate you?" See also **Celebrity**, page 36.

Fat

Dreams of fat or of being fat can signify a need for safety to shield your vulnerability against criticism, rejection, overpowering energy, or emotional pain that you may be afraid or unwilling to feel. This dream might be giving you a warning about excessive or gluttonous behavior so that you can avoid any destructive patterns that sabotage you from having the relationship you most deeply desire. See also **Body**, page 32.

Fear

Fear in a dream signifies an unresolved issue or an unaccepted, unintegrated aspect of your power seeking integration. You may be grappling with a worst-case scenario to make you more resourceful, should this situation actually come to pass. Perhaps you are expressing feelings of inadequacy as you learn to face what you are most afraid of and thus expand your personal power. See also the FEAR formula in the introduction, page 20, and **Emotion**, page 145.

Feelings

See **Emotion**, page 145.

Fetish

Dreams of a fetish reflect that you are in touch with the uniqueness of what turns you on and flips your switch, regarding your quirky sexual and sensual expression. Consider the deeper layers of a dreamtime fetish, where it came from, and what it symbolizes to you. See also **Spank**, page 195.

Five

A dream of the number five might indicate your unbridled passion toward your partner. However, if you feel your passion is blowing the circuits of your relationship, this dream might signify restlessness and a fear of commitment. In essence, dreams of the number five symbolize a desire for freedom and self-expression. See also **Number**, page 153.

Fog

Dreams of fog might suggest that your relationship pattern is feeling hazy because of the mixed signals you're receiving. Or perhaps the smoke and mirrors are coming from you, because you don't want to see what's right in front of your nose. Dreams of fog symbolize a lack of clarity and disorientation; you may be caught in the thick of some heavy moods like depression in your partnership. If this resonates, it may be time for some relationship intervention to clear up any miscommunication.

Foreign

If you dream of a foreign country, language, or person, you're connecting with an aspect of yourself (your power and mojo) that you haven't met—until now. That which is foreign symbolically and literally is often seen as a problem to be solved, as opposed to a new opportunity to explore that might add new spice or at least a subtle accent to enhance your relationship. See also **Accent**, page 138, **Alien**, page 28, **Foreigner**, page 45, and **Shadow**, page 156.

Four

Dreams of the number four can be an attempt to forecast the way your relationship may turn out. The number four suggests that you are craving the strength that comes from commitment, structure, and stability within the four walls of your relationship. See also **Number**, page 153.

Frustration

If you are frustrated in your dream, your intentions have been thwarted. This dream may be revealing a strategy to overcome the obstacles hindering your ability to have the love or sex you desire. See also **Emotion**, page 145.

Gay

See **Homosexuality**, page 149.

Government

See page 46.

Grade

Dreams of a grade represent your perspective on how well you're ranking in this relationship. Perhaps you've been playing tit for tat—keeping tabs on who has the upper hand. Dreams of a grade signal the presence of a judge or teacher—the aspect of you who is discerning, critical, and comparing, who has high standards for what "good enough" looks like in your love affair. Consider whether this process seems to leave you and your partner feeling inferior or superior. Does it encourage or discourage you and your mate from achieving a new level of love? Consider what and who is being evaluated and which grade is given.

Gray

The color gray signifies that you may be feeling hazy, dull, bland, or indecisive about your relationship. You may be feeling uninvolved or like you're going through the motions. Conversely, you may be dealing with fifty shades of gray as you negotiate your relationship contract. See also **Color**, page 143.

Green

Green in dreams signifies that your relationship is feeling sustainable and healthy, helping you to heal from past heartaches. Perhaps your connection with your lover is growing and inspiring you to get in touch with your true, authentic nature, so that the grass is always greener on your side of the fence. See also **Color**, page 143.

Half

Dreams of a half of something could refer to a better half, half empty, or half full, depending on your context. This dream might denote that you're feeling cut off (in half) from certain aspects of your life that you enjoyed prior to your relationship. As it is with anything fulfilling in life, there are times when a sacrifice (to make your relationship sacred) is needed—releasing something lesser in exchange for something better.

Heat

Dreams of heat can signify a sexual charge, as well as feelings of attraction and passion. This dream could be an indication that your lover warms your soul. Heat, like chemistry, happens when opposites attract or have friction. This dream could also indicate that you are being tested to see if you can take the heat of romantic love without feeling the need to run away. However, you might just have too many blankets on you as you are sleeping. See also **Fire**, page 112.

Hollywood

See **Celebrity**, page 36, **Actor/ Actress**, page 28, and **Star**, page 128.

Home Run

Dreams of a home run represent that your relationship is going all the way. A home run can be symbolic of a desire for a full and satisfying sexual experience, as well as reflecting success or victory. You have what it takes to cover all your bases and knock your relationship worries, stresses, and problems out of the park. See also **Sports**, page 195.

Dreams about homosexuality could reflect adoration and high self-esteem.

Homosexuality

If you dream of being homosexual or that someone else is, this could reflect adoration and high self-esteem, or that you are feeling so filled with self-love that you are now free to come out of the closet to express your signature expression of love. Perhaps you have a desire to explore beyond the boundaries of society's parameters. Keep in mind that we all contain masculine and feminine energy, regardless of our sex. This dream could represent an imbalance of either the male or female aspects of your nature, or unresolved issues with your opposite-sex parent. See also the anima/animus discussion in the introduction, page 10.

Horoscope

See **Astrology**, page 140.

Hunger

Dreams of being hungry beg the question, "What are you truly hungering for or craving in your love or sex life? Is your relationship leaving you wanting more, taking you halfway, or simply not meeting your needs?" From a spiritual vantage point you can never get enough of what you don't really need (egoic desires). Contemplate the ways in which you can feed yourself and fulfill as many of your own needs as possible, so you can let your lover be icing on your cake instead of your sole sustenance. Hunger can also suggest that you're feeling a great passion, zest, and vivacity in your love life. See also **Eat**, page 178, and **Food**, page 113.

Impotence

Dreams of impotence could symbolize feelings of powerlessness and emasculation. Perhaps you've been looking for love in all the wrong places and are left feeling limp. Consider the reality check aspect of this dream and take care of your sexual health to get your mojo back. See also **Castrate, Castration**, page 172.

Incest

See page 183.

Indigo

The color indigo in dreams signifies that your relationship may be taking you to higher ground. Perhaps your relationship is helping you to be more intuitive and aware of other realms of consciousness. See also **Color**, page 143.

Internet

If you dream of being online, surfing the Internet, social networking, or blogging, you may be casting your net out to a larger playing field of romantic possibilities. Additionally, this dream suggests that you may be looking for solutions and answers or opening your mind to possibilities beyond those that would have occurred to you under normal circumstances. Additionally, at the root of any pain you experience is the false belief that you are separate from your fellow humans. However, when you remember your oneness with the World Wide Web of life, you awaken to the reality that you exist in a unified field and all of life is ultimately on your side. Allow this awareness to assist you in reeling in an improved way of mating and relating. See **Computer**, page 108, and **Online Dating**, page 186.

Jealousy

Dreams of jealousy reflect that you may be venting insecurities. Jealousy, in real life as well as in dreams, highlights an unfulfilled need or desire. For example, if you dream of another man or woman that has something you covet, this may be a neon sign pointing toward a lack of fulfillment or satisfaction in yourself or your relationship. This dream may be guiding you to ask for reassurance from your partner about his or her feelings, embark on a self-improvement project, or develop self-acceptance and gratitude for what you do have. Jealousy can help you understand what or who you may secretly desire. Consider the person you're jealous of and what they represent to you. Keep in mind that if you see it, you can be it. This dream may be helping you transform from being green with envy to making the grass greener on your side of the street. See also **Emotion**, page 145.

Job

Dreams of a job reflect that you may be goal oriented and ambitious in your relationship pursuit. If this resonates, then this dream may be a mandate to take time away with your loved one and play. Additionally, you may be realizing that a great relationship doesn't just fall from the sky—you have to work for and earn it. If you are sleep-working, this may reflect that your work may be getting in the way of your romance reaching full-time status. Additionally, you may also be processing unresolved feelings about a work-related romance. Keep in mind that in order for your relationship to be in the black, your true job is to incorporate as much of your soul into your love life as possible. See also **Profession**, page 59, **Sex (with the Boss)**, page 192, and **Sex (with a Coworker)**, page 192.

Joy

To feel joy in a dream, as in real life, signifies that you are in alignment with your spirit and you are connected to your vein of gold (the true path of your relationship) that is leading you to the right people, at the right time, in the right way. Consider this dream may be a reward for opening yourself to love and following your heart. See also **Emotion**, page 145.

Judgment

See **Judge**, page 52.

Light

Dreams of light signify a message of illumination. Perhaps you've been feeling in the dark, and this dream may be providing an opportunity to receive an enlightened perspective on the situation you've been grappling with in your relationship. If the light in your dream is flickering or growing dim, it may be a message that you're burnt out and need a getaway (or at least a date night) with your partner. If you dream of a light bulb, you may be having an "aha" moment, an insight or solution that will shed light on your relationship, elevating it to greater potential.

Lonely

See **Alone**, page 140.

Longing

Dreams often reveal the source of our true longing so that we can discover how to fulfill it. Keep in mind that once you discover the origin of your insatiability, you are halfway there. See also **Emotion**, page 145.

Loss/Lost

Dreams of a loss can run the gamut from losing track of time to losing a purse or a person. In every case, this dream is revealing the place in your relationship dynamic where you lose consciousness or lose your sense of self. Additionally, dreams of loss can be a form of soul retrieval, whereby you are taken back to the symbolic scene of the crime to recover the previously lost aspects of your soul. Because you can't heal what you can't feel, this dream may be shining a light so that you can take action in your waking life to regain the pieces of your soul, or at least appreciate and honor what you've got so you can keep better track of it.

Love

See page 185.

Lust

Dreams of lust signify that you may have found someone who truly turns you on, and you may be having difficulty finding the off switch. Lust reflects an urge to merge that may have been suppressed and has now resulted in ravenousness. Remember, energy that is repressed must be expressed. If you're feeling out of control, your dream could be prompting you to find a healthy outlet for your sexuality; do not deprive yourself and honor your pleasure principle before it takes on a mind of its own. See also **Hunger**, page 150, **Nymphomaniac**, page 56, and **Thirst**, page 158.

Masochism

Masochistic tendencies, in waking reality and in dreams, can range from taking slight pleasure in pain or in vulnerability all the way to seeking full-blown torturous humiliation. As is the case with any shadow aspect that comes to call in our dreams, there may be self-hatred begging to be healed or a transcendent intent. At the heart of a masochistic dream is a desire to have all masks of the false self ripped off so that pure surrender to love, liberation, freedom, and expansion can prevail. See also **BDSM**, page 165, **Pain**, page 153, and **Shadow**, page 156.

Movie

Dreams of a movie can symbolize objectivity—the ability to witness the inner workings of your relationship drama. Perhaps you desire to gain a better perspective of the masks you wear, the roles you play, and the script you are writing for yourself (romantic comedy, tragedy, or drama?) so that you can have the kind of romance that movies are made of. See also **Celebrity**, page 36, and **Play**, page 188.

Music

If you dream of music or hear a song in a dream, this signifies that you are in harmony with your soul and higher wisdom as well as your lover's rhythm. Music in a dream predicts prosperity, healing, creativity, joy, and resonant partnership. This dream is a message to sing the song of soul and dance to your unique rhythm. It may be a message to learn to find the melody of your loved one's unique sweet song and combine yours to create a counterpoint in a magical duet.

Naughty

If you or someone else has been naughty in your dream, you may be playing out a parent–child dynamic in your relationship (e.g., the mean mommy and the rebellious teenage boy, or the mean daddy and the sassy daughter). If this is an enjoyable dynamic, then keep it. If, however, the submit-rebel cycle is creating friction, then spank yourselves and awaken to a more mature, adult form of relating. Additionally, dreams of being naughty reflect a need or desire to be punished. Perhaps you or your lover have been coloring outside the lines or staying out after dark, and you know it's only a matter of time before you get in trouble. See also **Spank**, page 195.

Nine

Because dreams of the number nine signify completion, perhaps you're coming to the completion of a cycle with your lover, the climax of your sexual relationship, or a make-it-or-break-it point of no return. See also **Number**, page 153.

"No"

Dreams of saying "No" are about rejecting or resisting a current situation you've been grappling with in your relationship. Perhaps you are feeling that a boundary has been crossed, or that you're headed down a path that doesn't honor your soul in the highest way.

Number

Dreams of numbers represent order, logic, and a desire to figure things out, solve a problem, assign a value, and organize or integrate your heart and mind. This dream might be telling you that you're spending too much time in your head, trying to calculate your next steps with your lover, or counting the days until your next encounter. Or you may be doing the heart math to get grounded after a passionate roller-coaster adventure of spills and thrills, so you can do a cost-benefit analysis. According to numerology, each number is symbolic of its own message. If the number in your dream is more than a single digit, then add them together to get a single digit, for example, 196 would be 7 (1+9+6=16, 1+6=7). See also individual numbers.

Obedient, Obedience

A dream about obedience (displaying the "disease to please") reflects a parent–child dynamic from an early stage of development; you are trying to be a good little boy or girl in your relationship. This dream might also reflect an attraction to bondage and discipline. If so, see also **BDSM**, page 168, **Naughty**, page 152, and **Spank**, page 195.

Obese

See **Fat**, page 147.

Obscene, Obscenity

Dreams of something you deem obscene could be about releasing an attachment to a behavior or thought process that is unhealthy, or that you find unlovable. Or this dream could reveal a shadow aspect of yourself or your lover that you find unacceptable and likely to be rejected. See **Shadow**, page 156.

Obstacle

See page 122.

One

Dreams of the number one could suggest you are feeling at one with your partner. Also, you may be feeling a sense of unity, wholeness, autonomy, and connection to your unique, individual desires. This dream might indicate a competitive spirit, wanting to be the best or number one in your lover's eyes or in your approach to achieving the partnership you seek. If this dynamic works for you, enjoy it. Otherwise, consider that one can be the loneliest number. See also **Number**, page 153.

Online

Dreams of being online represent that you are feeling connected to the World Wide Web of possibilities. Being online signifies being on, plugged in, ready and willing to engage your energy with possibilities of love, romance, and potential partners beyond your current sphere of influence. See also **Internet**, page 150, and **Online Dating**, page 186.

Orange

The color orange signifies that your relationship is juicy. You and your loved one are in an energetically charged, exciting, stimulating, and creative time of your relationship. Orange can also be associated with prison garb; see also **Prison**, page 86. If you dream of eating an orange, see **Fruit**, page 113. See also **Color**, page 143.

Pain

Pain in waking life and in dreams is a red alert that something in your relationship is out of balance. Pain indicates the presence of a neglected need or emotion. It could also signify that you've been storing up feelings of unworthiness, shame, guilt, and self-criticism. Consider the perspective that pain pushes until inspiration pulls. See also **Sadomasochism**, page 155.

Pink

Dreaming of pink evokes your youthful femininity (whether you're a man or a woman) and romantic idealism. Because pink is a blend of red and white, you might consider whether or not you are curbing your enthusiasm (e.g., sexuality or desire for others). See also **Color**, page 143.

Polyamory

Dreams of polyamory could signify that you are feeling ambivalent about monogamy (monogamish). Your dream may be helping you process feeling torn between wanting to be someone's one and only and wanting to play the field. Perhaps you feel that you have more love to give than can be contained. Because everyone in your dream is you, a polyamorous relationship is a metaphor of multiple aspects of yourself seeking fulfillment. Conversely, you might be grappling with issues of monogamy, seeking the most authentic expression of love you can find. You may be realizing that your love multiplies when it's shared. See also **Orgy**, page 188, and **Party**, page 86.

Polygamy

Dreams of polygamy signify that you may be ready to make sacred vows to love the ones you're with, namely, your subpersonalities. Besides the reality check whereby you process your actual feelings about polygamy, this dream is symbolic of responsibility and commitment toward those with whom you feel married or would like to marry (as opposed to polyamory). This dream begs the questions, "Where might you be overcommitting yourself? Is your fear of missing out causing you to spread yourself thin?" See also **Marry, Marriage**, page 186, and **Polyamory**, page 154.

Pornography

Dreams of pornography can represent a desire to explore the boundaries of your wild sexuality. They may be shining a spotlight on your pent-up carnal desires. Conversely, you might feel like you've overexposed yourself or have been exploiting your sexuality. See also **Movie**, page 152, and **Sex**, page 192.

Power

From one perspective, all dreams relate to power—how to get it, keep it, grow it, use it effectively, and empower others with it. They are often revealing your strategy when it comes to power (confidence, self-esteem) in relationships. Dreams of power reflect your desires, attitudes, and personal definition of empowerment, abuse, victimhood, or denial.

Pregnancy

See page 189.

Purple

The color purple in dreams symbolizes spirit, wisdom, and intuition. This dream may indicate that you share a mystical union with your loved one or that you are wearing your purple heart on your sleeve, like a badge of honor. See also **Color**, page 143.

Race (Ethnicity)

See **Ethnicity**, page 145.

Rage

Dreams allow feelings that are suppressed by day to be expressed at night. In dreams, your inner Mr. or Mrs. Nice Guy leaves the building. Perhaps you are furious and don't know how, where, or with whom to express it. Feelings of rage in dreams often rip through the nicest people who would never actually lose their temper in waking reality. Perhaps your boundaries have been crossed by your lover or you haven't felt safe to express yourself. This dream could be a message for you to find a healthy outlet for your pain, or discuss with your partner the best ways to meet your needs. See also **Emotion**, page 145.

Rainbow

Dreams of a rainbow signify hope, good luck, and that even though you may have experienced difficulty, there are bright times ahead. Additionally, the rainbow bridge is associated with a dreamtime place where the dearly departed reunite with those they left behind. The rainbow is also a celebration symbol for those who identify as LGBTQ (Lesbian, Gay, Bisexual, Transgender, and Queer). Perhaps the dream is suggesting it's time to break free from your conventional sexual preference and explore options. Consider the feeling tone and context of this dream. See also **Homosexuality**, page 149.

Red

The color red in dreams signifies that your love is burning. Red denotes passion, sexuality, and excitement. Conversely, like a stop sign, red can be a symbol of the need to put on the brakes. Red might also be associated with a red light district, prostitution, and sex for sale. Or, you may be giving your relationship a red-carpet invitation to your heart. See also **Color**, page 143, and **Red Light**, page 124.

Ritual

Dreams of a ritual often symbolize that change and transformation are on the horizon. This dream might forecast a special occasion in your relationship that's worthy of celebration. In waking life and in dreams, a ritual honors a rite of passage or a special moment in time, as well as an opportunity to gather energy and strength to fuel your relational dreams and wishes. This dream could be prompting you to bring more consciousness to your relationship, to remember to make sacred your unique bond and the special way your intimacy expresses it. See also **Celebration**, page 172.

Sadness

Dreams that feature sadness signify that you may be grieving or moving through a disappointment, heartache, or loss. See also **Emotion**, page 145.

Sadomasochism

Dreams of sadomasochism (finding pleasure in the pain inflicted upon you) may reflect a hidden belief that there is something wrong with you. This dream might also indicate that you have a need to purge or exorcise the demon of self-loathing. If you are into BDSM in your waking life, then this might be a processing dream to help you come to terms with your sexual proclivities. However, if this does not reflect your sexual preferences, then you may be working out guilt or shame so that you can be brutally honest with yourself and find self-acceptance. See also **BDSM**, page 168.

Savage

See page 60.

Search Engine

Dreams of a search engine (like Google) symbolize that you are seeking and finding the answers you crave about your relationship. Any uncertainty is eliminated as you tap into your instincts, intuition, and access to the internal World Wide Web of wisdom, information, hindsight, and even foresight. This dream might mean that you need a reality check, or maybe even a background check, about the status and future of your commitment and depth of your love. Consider what you are looking up in this dream.

Selfie

See page 191.

Seven

Dreams of the number seven signify spiritual connection that appears to be luck and can lead to grace. Alternatively, you might be feeling holier than thou and aloof, which can distance you from the love and connection you desire. See also **Number**, page 153.

Sexually Transmitted Infection/Disease (STI or STD)

Dreaming about an STI or STD can be symbolic of feelings of guilt about being attracted to someone you are not supposed to be attracted to, or for having indulged in sexual activities that your morality deems inappropriate. If you have an STI in waking reality, this dream might be helping you to process your feelings about any wildness that took place in the heat of passion, or your need to punish yourself for expressing your true passion. Keep in mind that your sexuality is a precious gift, and if expressed mindfully and consciously, it can be a tremendous blessing to you and your lover. See also **Disease**, page 144, and **Sick**, page 194.

Shade

Dreams of shade can signify that you are shining a light on your inner shadow, repressed aspects that you previously disowned. Perhaps you are interested in taking a walk on the wild side and exploring your darker nature, so that you may eventually become more whole. Alternatively, you might feel that you've got your love life made in the shade, and it's all going smoothly. See also **Shadow**, page 156.

Shadow

Dreams of a shadow symbolize the aspect of yourself that you've not yet fallen in love with. You are an infinite being—a microcosm of the macrocosm of life. And just as the entire ocean is contained within each drop of the ocean and one ray of sunlight contains all the radiance of the entire sun, within you is the totality of humanity. You, like most humans, identify with aspects of yourself you find most lovable, beautiful, acceptable, and praiseworthy, and have disowned the aspects you find disgusting, repulsive, unlovable, or likely to be rejected. These aspects you resist, reject, or run from are the sum total of your shadow. A dream featuring a shadow might be taking place so you can learn to embrace this orphaned aspect into the whole of your heart. By doing this, you bring a more stable, lovable, integrated (and, yes, more attractive and juicy) energy to your relationship—and you will tend to attract a partner with a similar level of maturity, responsibility, and integrity. True love brings up everything that is unlike love, so that it can be healed in love's embrace once and for all. See the FEAR formula discussion in the introduction, page 20. See also **Chase**, page 172, **Devil**, page 40, and **Shade**, page 156.

A shadow in a dream represents the aspects of yourself that you find ugly or repulsive—the traits you have repressed.

Six

Dreams of the number six may be giving you permission to follow your intuition (sixth sense). Dreams of the number six also represent that you are feeling a maternal, loyal, and protective energy toward your loved one. See also **Number**, page 153, and **Sex**, page 192.

Skinny

Dreams of being skinny represent deprivation of time and attention in your relationship—being starved of love. Alternatively, a thin or skinny person in a dream, in contrast to a fat person, could symbolize your having shed layers of protective armor and feeling safe enough to reveal the bones of your true feelings. Consider the feeling tone. See also **Body**, page 32.

Social Media

If you dream of social media, this could indicate a desire for public approval regarding your relationship, or perhaps that you desire to be noticed, express your true feelings, and seek love. Perhaps you're looking to expand your social circle and spell out what you really want. See also **Online Dating**, page 186.

Sports

See page 195.

Silver (color)

Silver in a dream signifies that you are in a relationship with someone who elevates your status or helps you connect with your own inner wisdom. See also **Silver (metal)**, page 128.

Single

If you dream of being single when in real life you are coupled, this dream might signify the need for freedom, alone time, and your own self-expression. If you dream of being single and in waking reality you are single, you may be exploring strategies to either enjoy your own company more deeply or to attract the partner of your dreams. Dreams of a single thing or object can reflect your feelings of oneness, unity, wholeness, or duality. Or, you might feel that you are being singled out. See also **One**, page 153.

Story

Dreams of a story may indicate that you are awakening to the fact that you and your loved one (as well as all humans) are mythmakers, storytellers, and dreamers. You may be grappling with whether or not you'd like to edit your love story, change the ending, or toss it into the flames and begin anew.

Surgery

See page 196.

Tarot

Dreams of the tarot or oracle cards are symbolic of your desire for higher wisdom, to access your intuitive guidance and see if this love affair is in the cards. This powerful dream reflects your willingness to reach beyond the ego to call on your swords (intellect), cups (emotions), coins (finances), or wands (career), as well as the major arcana (foundations and pillars that hold up the kingdom of your inner being). Perhaps this is a message that you hold the trump cards (power) to manifest the relationship of your dreams. See also **Cards**, page 105.

Ten

If you dream of the number ten (1+0), this could represent perfectionistic tendencies. Perhaps you are trying to have it all in your relationship, placing unrealistic demands on yourself or your lover. However, this dream could mean that you've found a partner that is perfectly imperfect for you. See also **Number**, page 153.

Thirst

Dreams of being thirsty, besides being triggered by having a dry mouth while sleeping, could be symbolic of an unquenched need in your relationship. Contemplate what kind of love or sex relationship you're craving that would truly satisfy you. You may also thirst for knowledge, information, security, and spiritual connection. This dream could be telling you that there is a drought in your relationship that needs to be tended to. Or, perhaps your lover is like a tall glass of water, and you just can't get enough. See also **Water**, page 93.

Three

Dreams of the number three can denote a spiritual, shamanic, or transformational experience in your love life. Additionally, this dream might be shedding light on a love triangle and how to make the most of it, or how to detangle. Three can signify that either you are trying to spread yourself too thin, or you seek a more open (polyamorous) relationship. See also **Number**, page 153, **Polyamory**, page 154, and **Threesome**, page 197.

Traffic

Dreams of traffic symbolize thwarted intentions in your love life, congestion with your communication, or roadblocks and detours in your path. This dream might be prompting you to rethink the route you are taking in this relationship. It might also inspire you to redirect your clogged-up emotions (e.g., stress, anxiety, guilt, and shame) from the past that may be causing gridlock, which could prevent your loved one from finding his or her way to you. See also **Car**, page 104, and **GPS**, page 114.

Trust Fund

Dreams of a trust fund suggest that you've been grappling with trust issues, perhaps wanting reassurance that your lover appreciates you for the right reasons. With this dream you might consider all that you've inherited from your ancestors. What relationship stories have been passed down to you? There may be some of your relationship inheritance that you want to keep and some that you'd prefer to discard. This dream might be preparing you for your true wealth by communicating that the universe has your back. It may be telling you that you are a trust-fund baby; you are taken care of, so you can stop fretting and trust the process. It may be encouraging you to trust the relationship you're in, as it may pay off if you stay for the long haul. See **Money**, page 120.

Turquoise

Because turquoise (or aqua blue) resembles the ocean, it is associated with the feminine, creative expression and intuitive guidance, indicating that you are in the flow of your love life. See also **Color**, page 143.

Two

Number two in dreams is the ultimate partnership symbol. It can reflect relationship harmony; you might be tempted to make your partner your entire world. In any case, allow your intuition to guide you toward fulfillment in your relationship endeavors. See also **Number**, page 153.

Under

Dreams of being under something suggest that you may feel like you are at the bottom in your relationship: overpowered, dependent, in a position of weakness. This dream may reveal that you feel disempowered, not living up to your true relationship potential. Alternatively, this dream could indicate your desire to understand the nature of your relationship and discover the truth that lies beneath the surface.

Violet

The wordplay of violet is violent, so this dream might indicate that your relationship is either infuriating you or elevating you to higher ground. Additionally, a violet flame is indicative of safety, purification, and spirituality. See also **Color**, page 143.

Virus

See **Disease**, page 144.

Voice

If you hear a voice in your dream, consider the words that are being spoken, by whom, and to whom. This may be the voice of wisdom, your higher consciousness, a helpful guide, or a departed loved one from the other side sending you a message or a blessing. See also **Dead People**, page 40.

War

See **Battle**, page 168.

Dreams of wealth are a sign
of good fortune, abundance
of power, blessings, and
positive energy.

Wealth

Dreams of wealth are a sign of good fortune, abundance of power, blessings, and a high state of positive energy. Perhaps your subconscious mind is preparing you to receive more abundance, good health, good luck, love, and happiness in your relationship, and you need to stretch to receive these blessings. Dreams of affluence indicate that you and your partner are dancing in the golden flow of life. See also **Lottery**, page 185, and **Money**, page 120.

Wedding

See page 93.

White

Dreams of white indicate that you may be feeling like a virgin all over again. White symbolizes innocence, spirituality, purity, heroism, and a peaceful intent, as well as new beginnings in a seasoned relationship. See also **Color**, page 143.

Wind

Dreams of wind signify change—as in "the winds of change are blowing"—in your relationship status. Wind is related to the element of air, which signifies thought, so this dream might reflect that your love life is "blowing" your mind, and causing you to think differently about your romance. If you dream of a whirlwind, this might signify that you are overwhelmed by the level of transformation you are facing. Your dream may be giving you the message to find your center, the eye of the storm, a solid place to stand, and a non-resistant attitude that will allow you to be unruffled by the change blowing through your love life.

X-Rated

Dreams of something X-rated may signify your secret feelings and longings that you don't reveal by day. They could also reveal your true sexual desires (e.g., X marks the spot). X-rated could also be wordplay for ex. See **Ex**, page 42, **Pornography**, page 154, and **Sex**, page 192.

Yellow

Dreams of yellow, like the sun, signify personal power, esteem, and an empowered relationship. It would be wise to allow your sunny disposition to guide your relationship. See also **Color**, page 143.

"Yes"

Saying or hearing "Yes" in a dream symbolizes resonance, affinity, a willingness to explore, and a positive feeling as you surrender to opportunities your relationship presents to you. This dream may be helping you become aware of your receptivity and openness to the influence of your lover.

Yin and Yang

Dreams of yin and yang signify an internal sense of wholeness and harmony in your love life and a balance of the masculine and feminine aspects of yourself and your relationship. This dream is like your North Star, pointing toward your desired way of making love and making love stay. See also the anima/animus discussion in the introduction, page 10.

Zero

Dreams of zero might signify a feeling of emptiness, loneliness, or a lack of fulfillment within yourself or in your love and sex life. Conversely, dreams that feature a zero could be preparing you or helping you reject ego in heightened moments of ecstatic joining, fulfillment, and wholeness—which is one aim of a great orgasm or great love affair. See also **Number**, page 153.

Zodiac

See **Astrology**, page 140.

Chapter 5

Actions and Scenarios

(Doing, Being, Mating, and Relating)

Everything we do is an attempt to meet a need. For example, if you dream that you:

- **Run for cover from an angry ex, your dream may reveal your need for safety.**
- **Flirt with the boy or girl next door, your dream may reveal your need for reassurance of your attractiveness.**
- **Tie the knot in holy matrimony, your dream may reveal your need for connecting or belonging.**

In addition to shining a light on the need(s) you are attempting to meet by the action you take or the scenario you find yourself in, your dream will expose your love or sex strategy. This is linked to the role you play in your dreams. You might be:

- **The damsel in distress who is rescued by a knight in shining armor**
- **The knight in shining armor who needs to save others in order to feel valued and loved**
- **A stalker that hunts his prey, needing attention from the one who doesn't want him**
- **A ghost (master of the disappearing act) forever watching the action from a safe, unseen distance**
- **The vengeful victim reliving a painful experience to protect himself from repeating it**

Once you become aware of your strategy, you can unravel it, enhance it, or try something new, in your dreams and in waking reality.

To gain an even deeper understanding of what the action in your dream means, contemplate the following questions:

- **Is the action I'm taking moving me closer or farther away from what I really want or need?**
- **How does this action reveal my strategy for meeting my love/sex/relationship needs?**
- **How might I be feeling competitive or driven to have the upper hand in my romance?**
- **Is this dream revealing that I'm giving my all, or do I have one foot out the door?**

Whether your dream reveals that your relationship is elevating you higher (e.g., flying) or lower (e.g., an elevator plummeting), or your dream takes you forward (e.g., running like a gazelle), backward (e.g., swimming the backstroke), or keeps you stuck in place (e.g., quicksand), your awareness makes these dreams a tool for achieving or improving the loving relationship you desire and deserve.

Abandon, Abandonment

Dreams of being abandoned may help you release your abandonment issues. Your dream may be giving you the message that when you stop leaving (energetically abandoning) yourself, then your fears of others leaving you will cease. Conversely, this dream could be preparing you for the wild abandon you desire—where you are free of inhibitions, and your body, mind, and soul can find its unabashed expression.

Abduct, Abduction

Dreams of abduction reflect that you've been carried away by your feelings, passion, or lust. Perhaps you fear being overpowered and taken for a walk on the wild side or down a dark alley. Often so-called "good" girls and boys are torn between their desire to keep their virginal image and their desire to be ravaged by a torrid affair. If you dream that you are the abductor, you may be processing your desire to be on top or in the driver's seat of your relationship.

Abort, Abortion

Dreams of an abortion symbolize that you are in the early stages of a relationship and are afraid it won't come to term. Or perhaps you feel pregnant with possibilities about a new love and doubt it will have legs to stand. Additionally, this dream may be prompting you to pull the plug on an unhealthy relationship before you're in too deep. Conversely, your subconscious mind may be telling you to check the murky waters of your relationship so the baby (the soul of your relationship, the part that's precious) doesn't slip away.

Abuse

Your dream may alert you that your love life is dangerously out of balance. Don't take this dream lying down. Give yourself the care you desire and demand. If you dream of being the abuser, look into finding a healthy outlet for your rage or your need to control an uncontrollable or unacceptable aspect of your love life. See also **Violent, Violence**, page 198.

Accelerate

See **Accelerator**, page 96, and **Drive**, page 177.

Accident

Dreams of an accident signify a fear of being caught with your pants down or overzealousness in your risky business. When we dream of an emotional fender-bender (or even a physical snafu), we are getting a preview of coming attractions—we can take preventive measures against mistakes so that our love and sex lives might run more smoothly. Keep in mind that accidents in dreams and in reality take many forms—from stubbing one's toe to major oil spills. This dream could be a wake-up call to pay attention and be more present in your romance or your search for a romance.

Accuse, Accusation

Dreams of accusing signify that you may be pointing the finger at or giving the finger to someone in your dream or waking reality, instead of taking full responsibility for your current love-life situation. Keep in mind that most of the time everyone in your dream is you, which means all blame, responsibility, and praise point back to you. If you dream of being accused of something you did (or didn't do), you may be harboring guilt for indulging a forbidden pleasure, or it could be time to make amends if appropriate for past behavior.

Ache

Dreams about an ache in a particular body part are symbolic of imbalance, strain, or stress in the part of the body represented (e.g., a stomachache would be symbolic of not acknowledging your gut feelings). Maybe you've been holding back your urge to merge your body with your lover's (or your animal instincts with your spirit), and this pain is alerting you to channel your energy in a productive and relationship-enhancing way. See also **Body**, page 32, and **Pain**, page 153.

Ace (verb)

If you dream of acing an exam or a situation, your dream reveals your strategy for overcoming and making the most of a challenging situation in your relationship. You are more resourceful than you realize and have what it takes to score the relationship of your dreams. For **Ace (noun)**, see page 96.

Adventure

See page 138.

Aerobics

See **Exercise**, page 179.

Affection

Dreams of kisses, hugs, and compliments symbolize affinity and connection within and between you and a specific aspect of yourself. Keep in mind that the more you love and adore yourself—especially the aspects that have been difficult to love—the more you have to give when it comes to lavishing your lover. See also **Hug**, page 183, **Kiss**, page 185, and **Sex**, page 192.

Aging

Dreams of age reflect maturity or immaturity. This dream could signify that you may be letting numbers on a calendar get the best of you. Or perhaps you've been fretting about whether or not you are too old or too young for your lover. If you dream of a particular age, then you may be processing ego issues symbolic of status, fitting in, or judgment about whether you or your lover is up to each other's standards.

Aggressive, Aggression

A dream that expresses aggression could reflect an unacknowledged or suppressed anger. If this resonates, then your work is to find a way to say what you mean without having to say it mean. If your dream features rough sex, this could reflect a primal urge to break down the walls to intimacy, to be raw and revealed. In Buddhism there is a deity called Vajrayogini, who demonstrates enlightenment via wrath, so if you have recurring aggressive dreams, this could be your path to the high road of love. See also **BDSM**, page 168, and **Violent, Violence**, page 198.

Amputate, Amputation

Dreams of an amputation can signify that you're feeling castrated or cut off in your relationship. This dream could be a message to set boundaries or sever yourself from an unhealthy relationship. Or perhaps you feel that someone has chopped you out of his or her life. In either case, this dream points out that some soul healing is called for to restore a sense of wholeness. See also **Body**, page 32, and **Cut**, page 176.

Applaud, Applause

Dreams of applause could signify an affirmation that you are on the right track with your love life. Perhaps you need a parade, standing ovation, or pat on the back to acknowledge the positive ways you've grown in your relationship. Alternatively, consider whether or not you have the disease to please—you're motivated externally by positive feedback from your lover. If this is the case, this dream may be suggesting you develop a stronger internal reference point.

Argue, Argument

Dreams of an argument symbolize that you are grappling with dissonance in your relationship and are negotiating how to get your needs met in your love affair. This dream might reflect a desire (or need) to release your rage—or your internal struggle as you deal with conflicting needs within yourself. These dreams can be a blessing, helping you work out the issues that block the flow of love in your relationship and helping your communication in waking reality be more peacefully impactful. See also **Aggressive**, **Aggression**, page 165, and **Rage**, page 155.

Arrest

Dreams of being arrested could symbolize that you've been captivated (arrested) by your lover's beauty or sex appeal. This dream could also symbolize a guilty conscience—perhaps a fear of being caught or found out for doing something wrong or punishable. Alternatively, you might be the jailer in this dream, blaming or judging your lover for something he or she has done. Keep in mind that forgiveness is the key that can set you both free. See also **Jail**, page 83, and **Police**, page 58.

Attack

If you dream of attacking or of being attacked, this signifies rage that's been suppressed and is finally expressing itself. Consider who the attacker is and who is being attacked. You would be wise to come to terms with your conflicting (warring) needs about your relationship. See also **Rage**, page 155, and **Victim**, page 67.

Attract, Attraction

If you feel an undeniable attraction in a dream, consider this person (or whatever it is) a mirror of yourself, luring you to explore a lovable, sexual, beautiful aspect of yourself that perhaps you've not yet met. According to the Senoi, an indigenous tribe from the highlands of Malaysia, you

should move toward (as opposed to resisting) the object of your attraction. The aliveness in the body temple that comes from this feeling is the joie de vivre. See also the anima/animus discussion in the introduction, page 10.

Avalanche

Dreams of an avalanche suggest that you've been holding back feelings from your lover and you are at a breaking point. It's natural to want to express what has been suppressed. Keep in mind that an avalanche happens in response to a slight thaw, which indicates frozen emotions are beginning to melt. Your dream may be cautioning you to find a healthy way to express your feelings and avoid an unnecessary meltdown. See also **Breakdown/Breakthrough**, page 171.

Awake

If you realize that you're dreaming while you're dreaming, this is the first step toward lucid dreaming. It is an indication of a high level of awareness, alertness, and even a predecessor to enlightenment. What do you do when you awake in a dream (fly, fall, fight, or another F word)? Keep in mind that as you awaken, your love affair has the potential to rise to a higher level of self-actualization. See the introduction for a discussion of lucid dreams, under "Types of Dreams" on page 19.

Barricade

See page 99.

Baseball

Dreams of baseball may simply be showing you the path to a metaphorical first base (early stages of romance), second base (exploring attraction and comfort), third base (nearing commitment), or a home run (scoring, consummating). The position you play in your dream may be significant:

If you're a **pitcher**, you're the initiator in bed and in most aspects of your relationship

If you're a **catcher**, you are the receiver of advances—do you throw them back, reciprocate them, or drop the ball?

Perhaps you're **up to bat**, readying to swing or hit on someone.

Maybe you're a **spectator** (voyeur), who would rather play it safe and cautious.

This dream may be a message to let go of results and simply go for it! See also **Ball**, page 99, and **Sports**, page 195.

Basketball

Dreams of basketball suggest that the ball is in your court and it's time to get your game on (make your move). This dream might also be telling you that the relationship you are in (or are courting) is a slam-dunk. The action you're taking may be significant:

Dribbling (on offense): looking for or making moves

Guarding (on defense): protecting your heart, deflecting advances

Passing the ball: missing an opportunity, letting others take a shot

Stealing: dating or flirting with a married or otherwise coupled person.

This dream might be telling you to take a shot and express your feelings, offering you a strategy to get past the obstacles that stand in the way of you and the basket. See also **Ball**, page 99, and **Sports**, page 195.

Bathe

A dream in which you are bathing signifies the need for cleansing, releasing, healing, and washing your troubles and worries down the drain. Perhaps you want a clean start. Additionally, dreams of taking a bath in a bathtub can be very sensual, and they may be a message to indulge in more self-care and self-love as you pay more attention to luxuriating in the water element (feminine energy, emotions, and going with the flow) within yourself. See also **Bathroom**, page 74, and **Water**, page 93.

To dream of bathing signifies the need for cleansing, releasing, and healing.

Battle

Dreams of a battle signify that you are in a power struggle, at war with yourself or your relationship. This dream might be help you clarify what's worth fighting for. Also, you may be discovering a way to negotiate a ceasefire between you and your lover, or between your own conflicting needs. You may be at a standoff, willing to fight for what you think is fair as you become ready to defend your boundaries. Like any good general, you should keep the big picture in mind, because you might win the battle, but without a holistic view, you will lose the war.

BDSM

If you dream of BDSM (Bondage, Domination, Sadomasochism), it denotes a desire to explore the kinkier side of your nature. This dream might indicate that you enjoy being wrapped up in (or tied up by) your lover. It may be telling you to define a safe word so that you and your lover understand and respect each other's physical, emotional, and psychological limits. If you dream of being dominated and you like it, this may be a message to give up being in the driver's seat of your relationship and explore the euphoria that comes from relinquishing control. If you dream of being dominated and you don't like it, you may be grappling with a power struggle in your relationship, or you feel tied down or burdened with excess guilt or responsibility. See also **Bondage**, page 170, and **Sadomasochism**, page 155.

Bet

Dreams of a bet signify taking a risk in a relationship. Perhaps you are feeling the need to stack the odds in your favor, or you might simply be willing to throw caution to the wind and trust in Lady Luck. This dream may be a message that you have to be in it to win it: nothing ventured, nothing gained. You may be coming to realize that people are fallible, but if you bet on your higher self, you will always end up a winner. See also **Gamble**, page 181.

Betray, Betrayal

If you dream of being betrayed by your loved one, ask yourself, "Where have I been cheating on me?" Have you settled for less than your worth, or have you dismissed your own inner guidance? This dream might be a message to face your insecurities and embark on the path of self-discovery and healing. Though this dream is typically symbolic, it might represent your fears about your relationship, so consider whether those fears are founded in reality. Remember the wise words of Shakespeare: "To thine own self be true."

Bigamy

A dream of bigamy might suggest that you are grappling with monogamy, commitment, and making room in your heart for two different aspects of yourself with competing needs. This dream might also symbolize insatiability—wanting twice as much love, attention, and romance as you are getting. It may suggest that you suspect your partner of having another lover—even if that lover isn't a person (e.g., a career). See also **Polyamory**, page 154.

Birth

Dreams of birth signify that a new love opportunity has just begun or is about to begin, or that you are feeling the labor pains of a new romance. This dream could also be about a renaissance of the relationship you've been in for a while. It represents renewal, transformation, a fresh start, and the manifestation of a new dimension of yourself being birthed. Keep in mind that though the process is laborious, if you stick with it, the results are worth it. Allow this dream to give you an empowering context to hold while you breathe, spread your arms (and legs), and open your heart, stretching your capacity to love and be loved beyond what you ever dreamed possible. See also **Baby**, page 30.

Bite

To be bitten in a dream is symbolic of an argument, someone trying to get your attention by making a biting (critical) comment or leaving his or her mark on you. Consider what may be bothering (or eating) you. Perhaps this is a shadow energy, like a vampire, trying to devour you, or to get your attention because you have not paid attention to more subtle cues. If you are doing the biting, then contemplate where you're being critical of your lover, or if your communication has a bite to it (reactive and meant to sting or provoke). Ask yourself, "What am I needing or hungering for in my relationship?" Because teeth are related to survival and primitive urges, you may be feeling that either your lover has been encroaching upon your personal space, or you need to do something drastic to assert yourself and put your lover in his or her place. You need to establish your own place in the pack. See also **Eat**, page 178, and **Teeth**, page 64.

Blend, Blender

If you dream of blending or using a blender, it suggests a desire to whip up your sex life—to integrate and mix multiple aspects of yourself into your relationship. Alternatively, this dream could be revealing a strategy for blending your relationship with the rest of your life.

Blind, Blind Date

Dreams about a blind person may signify that you aren't seeing eye to eye with your lover. If you dream that you are blind, then there may be something about your relationship you don't want to see. If you dream that your lover is blind, this may be a message that he or she has selective seeing and is not truly taking all of you in. This dream could indicate a willingness to be seen, or to open your eyes and take a sober look at your relationship before proceeding.

Blow Job

Since the penis is the ultimate symbol of masculine power and desire, and the mouth is the ultimate symbol of communication and self-expression, dreaming of a blow job reflects your desire to communicate what you are passionate about. This dream can also signify issues of giving versus receiving pleasure. Contemplate any issues you might have regarding the power gained from being in control versus the vulnerability of being out of control. Are you on your knees, showing humility in your relationship? Or does having your most intimate sense of self in the hands and mouth of your lover make you feel vulnerable? This dream is a message to use your words mindfully to communicate with your lover, instead of swallowing your feelings.

Bomb

See page 101.

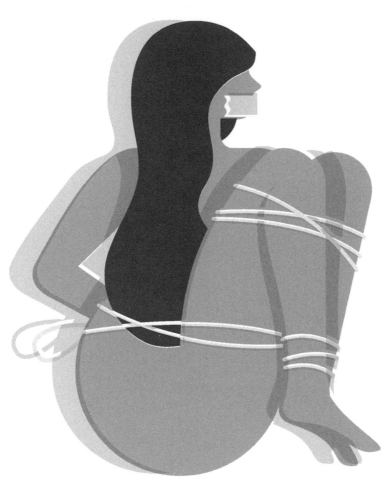

Booty Call

Dreams of a booty call (or a sexual partner calling, texting, or sexting for a late-night hookup) might be about your desire for short-term gratification. This dream may help you come to terms with how to satisfy your immediate sexual longings versus your desire for a long-term relationship. Conversely, this dream might be calling you to kick yourself in the butt and stop being so anal-retentive; cut loose, be spontaneous, and allow yourself to romp and have more fun in your love and sex life.

Break

Dreams of breaking something (or something that is already broken) could signify a broken heart or promise, dashed hopes and aspirations, or that a breakup may be on the horizon. This dream might help you return to the scene of the crime, where innocence was lost and where wisdom can be found in putting the pieces back together. Keep in mind that the places within you that have been broken, when repaired, become places of great strength and wisdom. See also **Accident**, page 164, **Brakes**, page 103, **Breakdown/Breakthrough**, page 171, and **Breakup**, page 171.

Dreams of bondage suggest you may be torn between conflicting needs to stay or go.

Bondage

Dreams of bondage could signify that you feel that your hands are tied. Perhaps you're torn between conflicting needs within yourself about whether to stay or go, to love or leave. This dream may be a message to stop torturing yourself and break the chains that bind you, or to surrender to the fact that you deeply crave the cozy shackles of commitment.

Perhaps you've been overly submissive and you're craving a bit of discipline to dominate your own thoughts that run astray. Alternatively, maybe you've been a control freak in the bedroom and your dreams are showing you the virtues of letting your partner take control. See also **Abuse**, page 164, **BDSM**, page 168, and **Jail**, page 83.

Breakdown/ Breakthrough

Dreams that feature a breakdown or a breakthrough are about the death and rebirth cycle inherent in any love affair. Perhaps you are processing a major transformative change in your life, breaking out of a pattern that no longer fits you. You may be discovering that what you thought was the worst thing that could ever happen is really a blessing in disguise. Keep in mind that a broken heart is an open heart, and wisdom is only earned once you have navigated your way through a difficult time. A breakthrough can be symbolic of the completion of the cycle, illumination, enlightenment, and the reward of wisdom.

Breakup

Dreams of a breakup denote change; a pattern in your relationship, not necessarily the relationship itself, is being reconfigured. However, this could be a rehearsal, helping you process your feelings about how you would handle the end if it did occur. Keep in mind that the best relationships survive many fires on their journey to becoming golden. See also **Breakdown/ Breakthrough**, page 171, and **Death**, page 177.

Breast-Feeding

A dream of breast-feeding or of being breast-fed signifies your need for maternal connection with your loved one. Perhaps you or your lover is going through a rough time, and this dream could reflect permission to baby, pamper, mother, nurture, and care for each other in a way that is gentle, feminine, kind, and that feeds each other's soul. See also **Breast**, page 33.

Breathe, Breath

Dreams of breath and breathing symbolize aliveness, a clean slate, and a new beginning in your love affair. A deep breath could denote relief or exasperation. If you take a deeper look at the word respiration, you'll see that it means to continually breathe in the spirit and stay inspired. This dream could be a message to stop holding your breath as you wait for things to happen. Your life is in session, and this dream can help you face your fears.

Brutality

See **Abuse**, page 164.

Build (verb)

A dream of building something denotes that you are in the creation stage of your relationship, perhaps laying the foundation, working out agreements, and identifying the structure that you want to grow into. This dream might symbolize the blueprint you want to manifest—either a love that will last a lifetime or a short and sweet love affair with no strings attached. See also **Building**, page 75.

Buy

Dreams of buying something may shine a light on the beliefs you've bought into regarding your relationship. If these belief systems bring you peace and joy and feel worth the price you've paid, keep them. If not, this dream may be a message to send it back and get a refund on the money (and time and energy) you've spent. Consider what you are buying. See also **Money**, page 120, and **Shop**, page 194.

Call

To dream of calling someone (by phone or out loud) signifies a desire to connect and communicate with that person or the qualities you associate with him or her. If you call someone in your dream, your telepathic connection has already begun, whether or not they ever officially pick up the line. Consider the scenarios as well as the content of the call to gain a deeper insight into what it communicates. For example, making the call signifies that you may be the initiator in your relationship. Returning a call means you have a mutual attraction and respect, and that you reciprocate the desire to connect. When you let the call ring and go to voicemail, your interest has waned. Continuously calling someone who isn't answering signifies that you are in a one-sided relationship and may be barking up the wrong tree. See also **Phone**, page 123.

Camp

Dreams about camping symbolize your desire for your relationship to get in touch with your wild nature, to go outside the confines of your civilized relationship, or to seek adventure and simplicity. Camping also represents your connection to your survival skills.

Caress

Dreams of a caress can sometimes feel real, because on some level, they are. A touch or caress can signify that you desire to reach out and touch someone. Consider that a caress is a metaphor for intimacy, connection, kindness, and leaving an impact on someone. See also **Hug**, page 183.

Castrate, Castration

If you dream of you or someone else being castrated, it signifies that you are feeling thwarted and emasculated in your intent to move forward in your relationship. Perhaps your lover or your own self-doubt is curbing your enthusiasm, or blocking you from manifesting the love life you desire. This dream can be a blessing, alerting you to become aware of where you are unconsciously giving your power away or are allowing your partner's cutting remarks to injure your self-esteem. If you

are the one castrating someone, then you may be feeling the need to punish, retaliate, or stop your lover in his or her tracks to maintain your sense of empowerment. This dream may be pointing out an imbalance in your relationship with your lover or within yourself, so that you can correct the course before you or someone else resorts to drastic measures. When we feel the most victimized, we can act out and do the most damage. See also **Cut**, page 176.

Celebrate, Celebration

Dreams of a celebration denote that you are worthy of a pat on the back, that you've earned the right to have a party, parade, or glass of champagne to acknowledge how far you've come. A celebration is also indicative of your joy/bliss/pleasure threshold and how much happiness you will allow yourself to have. See also **Ceremony**, page 142, **Graduation**, page 80, and **Party**, page 86.

Chase

Dreams of being chased suggest you may be running from your power or trying to escape unpleasant aspects of your relationship for fear of being overpowered. It is human nature to avoid someone or something

Dreams of being chased suggest you may be running from unpleasant aspects of your relationship.

you consider threatening or out of your league, even if it is an aspect of yourself. When you realize that what is chasing you is an aspect of yourself, you can stop and practice the FEAR formula (page 20). Remember, you are the hunter and the hunted, and you can run but you can't hide from the multifaceted splendor of the whole being that is you. This dream may be telling you to resist the seductive thrill of the hunt. Stand still and allow the disowned aspects of yourself, like puzzle pieces, to magnetically integrate

and click into place. Let them find their home within you so that you can be more powerful in your relationships.

Cheat

If you dream of cheating on your lover, this could indicate dissatisfaction in your relationship and a desire for variety, adventure, and sexual stimulation that you're not finding in your present love affair. This dream could represent your internal struggle with loyalty, guilt, shame, and commitment issues. You

might be thinking that the grass is greener on the other side. This dream may help you process your feelings and get a clearer perspective before you do something that you might regret. If you dream of your lover cheating on you, you are processing feelings of insecurity, inadequacy, and how you might weather the storm should it actually come to pass in waking reality. Remember, seldom are these dreams literal; they should prompt you to ask yourself, "Where am I cheating on me?" Consider whether or not you are dishonoring yourself in this relationship and ignoring your intuitive guidance, needs, and desires.

Choke

A dream about being choked suggests that you are feeling stifled in your relationship, perhaps unable to voice your desires or concerns to your partner. You may be trying to suppress your natural expression, for fear of consequences that could unfold. If you dream of choking someone else, ask yourself what it is that you don't want to hear. You might discover that a comment expressed by your loved one is difficult to accept, or hard to swallow. See also **Body**, page 32, **Neck**, page 55, and **Throat**, page 65.

Circumcise, Circumcision

If you dream of being circumcised, it suggests that you may be curbing your sexual feelings, energy, or potency. In the days of old, a circumcision—a rite of passage—symbolized one's willingness to obey God and be one of the chosen people. Nowadays people associate a circumcision with cleanliness, trimming away all that would be in the way of true connection and intimacy with the divine or with your lover. If you dream of female circumcision, you may be venting sexual shame, religious guilt, or cultural pressure that has undermined your ability to fully revel in the beauty of your sensual/sexual self-expression. See also **Castrate, Castration**, page 172.

Clean

Dreams of cleaning reflect that your relationship may be a bit of a mess. Perhaps there's a communication with your lover that went awry, you've allowed resentments to pile up, you owe your loved one an apology, or you haven't been keeping up your side of the street. This dream may be a message to put on your rubber gloves and do the work it takes to restore your relationship to its natural luster. Alternatively, maybe you've been judging yourself for dirty thoughts or deeds. However, if the space in your dream is clean, this indicates that you or your relationship have honesty and integrity.

Climb

To dream of climbing signifies ambition and that you are achieving your goals in spite of struggles along the way. This dream could also suggest that you desire a higher love that will elevate your status and raise your self-esteem. Climbing in your dream could mean that your relationship may feel like an uphill battle, but you are willing to do the work to rise above your circumstances and reach higher ground. See also **Mountain**, page 83.

Commit, Commitment

If you dream of a commitment, vow, or promise, then you are either craving it or rebelling against it. It's a message to spend some time alone, soul searching to identify your real priorities and which bonds are worth making or breaking. This dream could help you shed light on your willingness to take your relationship to a deeper level. See also **Marry, Marriage**, page 186.

Compete, Competition

Dreams of a competition suggest that you want to achieve a personal best in your relationship. Or perhaps you are trying to win the heart of the man or woman of your dreams away from all other contenders. Additionally, you and your partner may be competing with each other for the upper position in your partnership, deciding who will be on top and who will be on the bottom. This dream may be shining a light on your survival strategy as it asks, "Are you surviving or thriving in your love life?" See also **Sports**, page 195.

Construct, Construction

A dream of construction signifies a time to refrain from presenting yourself in social engagements while you work on your relationship. This dream might be giving you the message to take responsibility for your own internal and external upkeep, while you carry an invisible sign around your neck that reads, "Pardon the mess while relationship renovations are in process." See also **Breakdown/ Breakthrough**, page 171.

Convention

Dreams of a convention reflect your feelings and thoughts about groups, and the conventional paradigm about love, sex, and relationship. You may be comparing (and despairing of) group think and personal desires.

Cook

Dreams about cooking are a message to bring some warmth, deliciousness, and nurturing to your relationship. Perhaps this dream is an incitement to cook up some alone time for you and your lover. Even if you're not rolling in the dough, simple pleasures can feed your relationship's soul. See also **Chef/Cook**, page 36, and **Food**, page 113.

Cover

If you dream of covering something or yourself, it suggests that you are hiding an aspect of yourself from your lover. Consider what you are trying to hide and why. You may find this aspect of yourself unappealing, unattractive, or likely to be rejected. Keep in mind that the partner truly meant for you will be won over by your nakedness (transparency). See also **Blanket**, page 101, and **Costume**, page 108.

Crack

See page 108.

Crash

If you dream of a crash, this could be a warning to slow down in your relationship. It might be a wake-up call, alerting you that you've been falling asleep at the wheel of your relationship. Maybe you've been going too far, too fast beyond your comfort zone and it's time to get back in balance. See also **Accident**, page 164.

Crawl

If you dream of crawling, you may be connecting with the baby aspect of yourself—the part of you that feels small and insecure—as you try to get your footing in a new relationship. This dream could be telling you that at any new stage, you must have patience, take it easy, and remember how important it is to crawl before you can walk.

Cripple

Dreaming of becoming crippled or of someone who is crippled signifies an aspect of you that is unhealed, out of balance, or out of alignment in your relationship. Ask yourself where you've been seriously injured in your love journey, and consider that until this aspect is loved, accepted, or transformed, you are not truly healed. Alternatively, this dream may alert you that you've been relating to yourself as wounded in your relationship(s). If this resonates, do away with your crutches and practice standing tall, presenting yourself in your love life as the empowered, radiant being you truly are.

Crucify, Crucifixion

If you dream of a crucifix or a crucifixion, it suggests that you are struggling in your relationship, feeling betrayed, or being tested beyond what you think you can handle. You may be grappling with your fears about what would happen if you revealed how powerful, beautiful, sexy, or unique you really are. Keep in mind that, archetypally speaking, immediately following the crucifixion is the ascension into heaven, which reflects that your true self can't be harmed. See also **Cross**, page 109, **Crossroads**, page 78, and **Jesus**, page 52.

Cruise

A dream of a cruise signifies a harmonious time in your relationship—it's time to coast for a while. Perhaps you can cruise, relax, and enjoy your love and sex life (what a concept!). Additionally, you may be fantasizing about cruising the streets for an anonymous sex partner. If so, this dream might be a reminder to use protection.

Cry

Dreams of crying symbolize that you are healing, grieving, cleansing, and releasing pent-up energy that no longer supports you, in order to make room for the things and people that do support you. Just as we need rain to survive, we need to cry to cleanse ourselves and our environment and to restore ourselves to balance. This might be a cry for help, revealing where you feel vulnerable and need support to help get you through a challenging time.

Cuddle

Dreams of cuddling symbolize oneness, synergy, and a sense of wholeness and completeness in your relationship. You and your loved one have created a field of safety and warmth, forgiveness, understanding, and acceptance, where you can let down your guard. Dreams of cuddling also signify that you're allowing your most vulnerable aspect into your relationship, which suggests that a profound level of intimacy may be taking place. See also **Hug**, page 183.

Cunnilingus

Dreams of cunnilingus symbolize your connection to the feminine power of receptivity. If you dream of giving cunnilingus, you may desire to please the feminine impulse within you. If you are on the receiving end, then you may be exploring the depth of your vulnerability as well as your ability to give the gift of receiving. See also **Sex**, page 192, **Tongue**, page 66, and **Vagina**, page 66.

Cut

Dreams of being cut might suggest that you are feeling cut off or hurt by something your lover said or did. If you dream of cutting, this could be a message that you desire to end an aspect of your relationship, or at least to take some time away. This might not signify an ending, so much as a desire to simply trim away negative or unneeded parts of your relationship—aspects that don't support your love affair in attaining its highest expression. See also **Amputate**, **Amputation**, page 165, **Castrate**, **Castration**, page 172, and **Knife**, page 117.

Dance

Dreams of dance represent your unabashed, uninhibited, sexual, passionate, primal self-expression; you are finding your rhythm in your relationship. This dream may show you how to be in sync with your inner masculine and feminine, and thus able to have a harmonious psychic and sexual connection with your lover. It might be reflecting that you and your partner are compatible and can express your sensuality with grace, without stepping on each other's toes. See also **Music**, page 176.

Die, Death

If you dream about the death of a loved one, it might indicate an ending of your relationship or of a pattern in your romance. Dreams of death can also be a preparation for coming to terms with the literal death of a person you love. However, usually a dream of death symbolizes the ending of a dynamic in your relationship, and a new phase about to begin. This dream can be a blessing, because it reminds you to be more present and love the one(s) you're with. See also **Breakdown/Breakthrough**, page 171, **Dead People,** page 40, and **Transformation**, 197

Dive

Dreams of diving signify a willingness to commit and jump headfirst into the deep end of your relationship pool or into the ocean of your emotion. Additionally, a dive can be slang for a seedy bar, which could imply you might be seduced into taking a walk into the dark side, to explore the shadow aspect of your relationship. See also **Bar**, page 73.

Divorce

Dreams of divorce indicate a desire to break up or leave behind a way of being in your relationship that no longer empowers you. Perhaps you feel the need to cut yourself off from a particular destructive relationship pattern. These dreams could simply be about processing your feelings about an actual divorce that you have incurred or one that you feel may be imminent. See **Breakdown/Breakthrough**, page 171, **Breakup**, page 171, and **Death**, page 177.

Drink

To drink in a dream suggests you may be thirsting for a deeper, more spiritual connection with your lover. Perhaps you've got an unquenched thirst (an unmet need or unrequited attraction), and this dream is helping you discover what that is. If you are overly indulging in alcohol, see **Alcohol**, page 97, and **Drunk**, page 178. See also **Thirst**, page 158.

Drive

A dream about driving symbolizes that you are engaging your will, motivation, ambition, and intent to get to a destination milestone in your relationship. This dream might also prompt the question of whether your lover is driving you wild or driving you crazy. It may inspire you to get into the driver's seat and get your love life in gear. See also **Car**, page 104.

Dreaming of death suggests the end of a relationship or of a pattern in your romance.

Drown

Dreams of drowning signify that you may feel in over your head in this relationship. Perhaps you are feeling head-over-heels in love, or the intensity of emotions you feel is overwhelming. This dream may be giving you the message to manage your basic needs so you can keep your head above water. See **Death**, page 177, and **Water**, page 93.

Drunk

Dreams of being drunk signify that you've lost control and that you are allowing yourself to drop your inhibitions in love. This might be a message to take a sober look at your relationship and to evaluate whether or not it's healthy for you. If it is, then allowing yourself to be drunk in love can be a courageous step. See also **Alcohol**, page 97.

Earthquake

Dreams of an earthquake symbolize that your love or sexual affair may be rocking your world off the Richter scale. And that's not necessarily a bad thing, since great love brings up everything unlike itself—you can't heal what you can't feel. If you've made your relationship your entire world, this shake-up might ultimately be a message to find balance and stability within yourself first, so that no matter what happens in your love life, your center can't be rocked. See also **Breakdown/Breakthrough**, page 171, and **Earth**, page 79.

Eat

Dreams of eating can reflect what belief systems you are taking in and what relationship or sexual ideas are delicious to you. These dreams help you discover what you are truly hungering for. See also **Food**, page 113.

Eclipse

Dreams of an eclipse can reflect that you may be going through a dark night of the soul. Perhaps it appears that someone or something is blocking your light or getting in the way of your being able to have the love and sex you dream of having. Bear in mind that this is a temporary phase, so do what you need to do to keep your dignity and grace while the cycle passes. See also **Moon**, page 121.

Ejaculate, Ejaculation

Dreams of ejaculation are symbolic of having a full experience, feeling satisfied, and being exalted in your love life. You are releasing your worries, letting go, and allowing yourself to follow your pleasure principle. See the discussion on wet dreams in the introduction, page 24. See also **Orgasm**, page 188, **Semen**, page 126, and **Sex**, page 192.

Email

Dreams of email or text messaging represent communication, telepathy, and a desire to reach out and touch your loved one. This dream might be telling you to be mindful of the messages you send to your lover, because your words create worlds. See also **Love Letter**, page 118, **Mail**, page 119, and **Texting**, page 197.

Erect, Erection

See **Penis**, page 57.

Escape

Dreams of making an escape signify that you may be feeling trapped, smothered, or in fear of being harmed. If this resonates with you, consider that it is difficult to build a loving relationship while you have one foot in and the other foot out. If you dream of your lover leaving, then you may be processing your issues of rejection and abandonment. Alternatively, this dream could be a message that you and your lover need to take a moment away from the world together. Keep in mind that what you resist persists, and you can't hide from yourself. See the FEAR formula discussion in the introduction, page 20. See also **Chase**, page 172, and **Shadow**, page 156.

Exercise

Dreams of exercise could be a message for you to stretch outside your relationship comfort zone and find a positive outlet for pent-up emotional or sexual energy. This dream could also be a message to work out your issues (past wounds and triggers) so you can trim down your defenses and meet your lover heart-to-heart. Keep in mind, relationships are not for the faint of heart; rather, they can be an arduous journey that requires you to be in shape mentally, emotionally, spiritually, and physically.

Explode, Explosion

Dreams of an explosion could signify that your emotions are so intense, you could burst. Perhaps you are past the point of being cool about the way you feel toward your lover. Additionally, an explosion is symbolic of pent-up feelings that will no longer be repressed. This dream could be a message to take preventive action so that your self-expression can be constructive instead of destructive. See also **Emotion**, page 145, **Orgasm**, page 188, and **Rage**, page 155.

Fail, Failure

Dreams of failure could symbolize that your hopes are dashed. Perhaps you've been looking for love in all the wrong places. This dream could be helping you vent out the energy that is caught up in a negative behavior pattern. It could also aid you in coming to terms with a relationship that may be at the end of its cycle. Keep in mind that you are never a failure if you are learning as you fumble forward. See also **Impotence**, page 150.

Fall

Falling can symbolize feeling out of control or over your head, perhaps due to the intensity of your connection with your loved one. This dream might indicate that you could be falling in or out of love. Alternatively, falling is believed by some indigenous tribes (e.g., the Senoi of Malaysia) to indicate that "falling spirits" are calling you to assist you in dropping futher into your depth, becoming more grounded and stabilized so you can handle more of the love you are capable of feeling. This dream might be a reminder that sometimes things need to fall apart before they can come back together in a new and more life-serving way. For fall (season), see **Autumn**, page 73.

Fellatio

See **Blow Job**, page 169.

Fling

Dreams of a fling signify that you may be feeling torn between a momentary pleasure and the long-term consequences and perhaps guilt of your actions. Alternatively, this dream may be a message to love the one you're with. This dream might also be a message to treat whomever you are with (for a night or a lifetime) with respect—and don't just fling them aside when you feel complete.

Float

Floating is symbolic of being connected to the element of air, which symbolizes higher thoughts, divine intervention, and a sense of grace in your relationship. This dream might reflect that you are finding it difficult to keep your feet on the ground in this relationship because you're head over heels in love.

Flood

Dreams of a flood signify that you've been bottling up your feelings, keeping it all buttoned up for too long, and it's time for a release. This may signify that your days of holding back your true feelings (or your orgasms) are coming to an end and it's time to fully express your passion. You also might be in need of a good cathartic cry, a night on the town, or both. If you dream of a storm or tsunami, this might be a message that you will soon be undergoing radical change, so get ready to ride the wave of transformation. See also **Tsunami**, page 197.

Fly, Flight

Dreams of flying signify that your relationship is taking off, reaching higher ground, accessing higher consciousness, and rising to its potential. Flying represents freedom, joy, self-expression, lightness, confidence, creativity, and independence. You are breaking free from physical constraints and fear-based beliefs, and can now feel the breadth of your mighty wingspan and explore the potential of your mind, body, and spirit together in the realm of love.

Flying represents freedom, joy, self-expression, lightness, confidence, creativity, and independence.

Follow

To follow in a dream indicates that you may be abdicating your power, taking a submissive role, and letting your lover take the lead in your relationship. If it's working for you, then keep it up. If it's leaving you feeling like a wallflower, change it up—maybe it's your turn to take the lead. This dream may be a message to follow the clues and messages the universe sends and trust it won't lead you astray. If you dream of following someone on social media, you may be attracted, interested, or exploring a curiosity. If the pursuit is aggressive, see also **Hunt**, page 183.

Football (American)

Dreams of playing football signify your desire to use your brute strength to knock down the obstacles in your way to score a touchdown in your love life. This dream could reflect a relationship fantasy (e.g., the cheerleader and the quarterback) or a sexual fantasy (being the cheerleader tackled by the football team, football player tackled by cheerleaders, or football player tackled by other football players).

If you dream of an **offensive line position** (lineman, guard, or tackle), this dream denotes a willingness to plow through your relational or sexual challenges and tackle them head-on.

If you dream of a **defensive line or cover position** (lineman, tackle, linebacker, cornerback, or safety), this may be a message to stop being a pushover, dig your feet in, and stand your ground.

If you dream of a **receiver**, it might be a message to open your arms and allow yourself to love, or to catch the advances (passes) someone is making toward you.

If you dream of a **quarterback**, you may be carrying the weight of the relationship on your capable shoulders. You've got the ball, and it's up to you to huddle up with your partner and communicate your desires (plays) so that you are on the same page, working together to get your mutual dreams across the goal line. See also **Sports**, page 195.

Football (Soccer)

See **Soccer/Football**, page 195.

Foreplay

Dreams of foreplay might be a literal message to take more time exploring and slowly getting to know your lover, whether his or her body is new or familiar to you. And don't be in such a rush to get to your happy ending. This dream could also be wordplay for making more time for play (sex, fun, alone time) in your relationship. See also **Sex**, page 192.

Freeze, Frozen

Dreams of being frozen signify that hurt has been preserved, you've been slow to forgive, and you've opted to be an ice king or queen, to freeze love out and keep yourself safe yet frigid. This dream might be a message to thaw your heart by warming yourself by the fire of a new love or a dear friend, or by having a good cry.

Gamble

Dreams of gambling suggest that you're willing to take a chance and test your luck, perhaps by trying out a new romance with someone outside your comfort zone. Or maybe you're evaluating whether having an affair might be worth the risk. Make sure to stack the odds in your favor by thinking the situation through before you roll the dice. This dream could also signify risky business in your relationship, that you may be using superstition to guide your decisions, and that you should assess whether the risk is worth the potential loss. In any case, contemplate the motto "Nothing ventured, nothing gained." See also **Cards**, page 165, **Game**, page 182, and **Lottery**, page 185.

Game

Dreams of a game suggest that either you or your lover may be playing mind games with each other, being dishonest, secretive, manipulative, or competitive. If this resonates, consider playing games as a way of distracting you from your own unhealed broken heart. Conversely, this dream could be a message for you and your lover to be more playful and allow the child aspect of you to come out and play.

Help

Dreams of a call for help signify that you may be feeling lost, out of control, or head-over-heels in your romance and need to get grounded. If you are the one providing help, you are accessing your inner hero, compassion, empathy, sensitivity, flexibility, strength, and willingness to step beyond your comfort zone to support another. It could be a test to determine your level of maturity and see if you have the heart for big love. This dream may also be a reminder to call upon a source that is greater than you to see you through the inevitable perils of love's path. See also **Angel**, page 29, and **Victim**, page 67.

Dreams of gambling suggest that you're willing to take a chance—perhaps with a new romance.

Hide, Hidden

Dreams of something hidden could reflect that your lover is keeping a secret from you, or that you don't feel safe enough to lay your cards on the table. Additionally, this dream might be showing you that there are more treasures buried in your relationship than are apparent on the surface.

Hit

If you dream of hitting, punching, or slapping someone, it symbolizes a rejection of what that person represents to you or of his or her energy. This dream may be telling you that you're feeling the need to protect yourself, or you have pent-up hostility that you would be wise to address in waking life. Additionally, this dream may be a double entendre for wanting someone to make a move or hit on you. See also **Violent, Violence**, page 198.

Hitchhike

If you dream of picking up a hitchhiker, remember that you're in the driver's seat. If you don't like how your relationship is going with this hanger-on, you can always pull over and drop him off. This dream might also be a message that you've been taking on your partner's issues and carrying them around as if they were yours. Sexually speaking, this dream might reflect a desire to get out on the open road, take your chances, and have a short-term recreational affair as opposed to one that is long-term and committed.

Hug

Dreams of a hug signify an embrace of the qualities of the person you are hugging. A hug can also signify forgiveness, acceptance, harmony, and integration. This dream may reflect that you are dissolving the barriers that stand in the way of your heart-to-heart connection with your beloved. See also **Cuddle**, page 176.

Hunt

Dreams of hunting signify that you are on the prowl, or that your lover has made you his or her prey. Often in dreams what we hunt or what is stalking us is an aspect of our shadow we've not yet embraced. Hunting also signifies a feeling of desperation that comes from being in survival mode, or a desire and willingness

to go after what you want instead of passively letting your love life pass you by. The shadow side of this symbol could be an attitude of entitlement and a lack of consideration or empathy regarding the consequences of your boldness and its effect on your partner. See also **Chase**, page 172.

Incest

Are you thoroughly disgusted upon awakening from this dream? Don't worry, this dream doesn't mean that you have a forbidden lust for a family member. Remember, your dreams are highly symbolic, and sex is a metaphor for joining and sharing a resonance with the qualities of the person in your sexual dream. Ask the question, "What does this person represent to me?" You may be connecting more intimately with that aspect of yourself and working through unresolved issues with this aspect. Of course, if you have actually experienced this trauma, this dream could be helping you to process and release the pain and come into a place of power. If this resonates, then see also the FEAR formula discussed in the introduction, page 20. The following is a list of examples of the light and shadow side of family members and what they generally symbolize in a dream like this. Consider the feeling tone:

Father: (light) powerful, masculine, security, safety; (shadow) domineering, abuse of power

Mother: (light) feminine, nurturing, caretaking, unconditional love; (shadow) martyr, manipulative, needy

Brother: (light) masculine ally, supportive, protective; (shadow) abusive, aggressive, bully

Sister: (light) young female energy, gentle, kind, caretaking; (shadow) victim, emotional, manipulative

Grandfather: (light) wise, elder, God, masculine, enlightened; (shadow) overpowering, cruel, abusive, sorcerer

Grandmother: (light) wise, elder feminine, goddess, magic; (shadow) witch, evil, bitter, ruthless

See also **Family**, page 44, and **Sex**, page 192.

Inject, Injection

Dreams of an injection signify that you feel that your lover is influencing you, in a positive or negative way. An injection can be symbolic of penetration by your lover's point of view. It can also reflect ejaculation or gaining an infusion of your partner's affection. See also **Medicine**, page 120, and **Sex**, page 192.

Injure, Injury

Dreams of an injury suggest that you may have been overexerting yourself in your love life. A physical injury in a dream could suggest that you're nursing an emotional, psychological, or spiritual wound. It is believed that everything happens first in a dream, so a dream of an injury could be a red flag to pay attention, watch where you're going, and take preventive measures to avoid unnecessary stumbling blocks to love. See also **Accident**, page 164.

Interrupt, Interruption

Dreams of an interruption signify that you feel that someone or something may be getting in the way of your relationship dreams coming true. Ask yourself how you may be sabotaging yourself from having the love, romance, and sexual fulfillment you truly desire and deserve. Additionally, an interruption reflects that you might not be ready for what you say you want.

Intrude, Intrusion

See **Intruder**, page 51.

Invite, Invitation

Dreams of an invitation signify that life is tapping on your shoulder and asking you to dance, to participate. This might also be a message to move when moved, so that you can show up at the right place at the right time with the right people. Consider what the invitation is for and who sends it to you. This dream could be preparing you for an auspicious encounter.

Journey

Dreams of a journey signify your awareness of the path of love you've chosen. You may be coming across hills and valleys, tests, allies, enemies, ordeals, and rewards that are par for the course on a transformational journey. Perhaps you feel like you're on a quest and you wonder if you'll ever reach what you are looking for. This dream might be a message to be patient and access what you seek within you. Additionally, dreams of a journey signify a change in your life direction or relationship, so remain open to the unlimited possibilities that lie ahead. Your lover may be taking you to places you never knew existed within your body, mind, and soul.

Judge

See page 52.

Kama Sutra

A dream of the Kama Sutra might indicate that it's time to change up your position or opinion on sex, intimacy, and connection. The Kama Sutra represents desire for sexual variety, to celebrate your body, and to integrate the sacred and the sexual. This dream might also prompt you to literally try a new way of approaching sex.

Kidnap

See **Abduct**, **Abduction**, page 164.

Kill

Dreams of killing someone signify a desire to get rid of an unacceptable, unpleasant, or unforgiven shadow aspect of yourself, depicted by the person being killed. Death in a dream can also be about a radical transformation—killing off a part of yourself, such as a destructive habit, in order to give birth to another aspect. See **Breakdown/ Breakthrough**, page 171, **Death**, page 177, and **Shadow**, page 156.

Kiss

Because kissing is an activity that involves the mouth, it is symbolic of harmony, intimacy, and communication. A dream kiss could also reflect a desire for a delicious connection, for affection, to see and be seen, and to know and be known.

Laugh, Laughter

Dreams of laughter signify that you are enjoying the light side of your love affair. These dreams reflect happiness, joy, frivolity, taking yourself lightly, and being tickled by your love life.

Lottery

Dreams of winning the lottery signify that you have struck gold in your relationship. Perhaps you've found the man or woman of your dreams, who meets your physical, emotional, and spiritual needs, and you're feeling that you've come into a windfall of blessings. Your lottery dream is not to be taken lying down, as it can create an energetic map from where you are to where you would prefer to be. Just as people who are wealthy attract more wealth and happy people attract happiness, allow this heightened state to make you magnetic to the real life fulfillment of your desires.

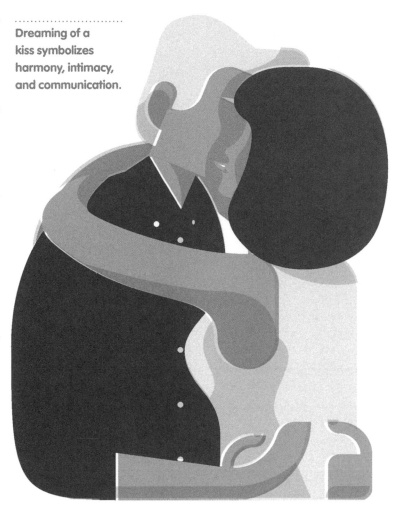

Dreaming of a kiss symbolizes harmony, intimacy, and communication.

Love

Feelings of love in a dream represent connection, integration, understanding, healing, and forgiveness. Love in a dream forecasts that your heart is opening and wonderful things are to come. Conversely, consider if you've been looking for love in all the right or wrong places. Whether you dream about love lost, found, or reunited, these dreams are revealing your strategy to make love stay. If your method is working for you, then keep it. If it's keeping love at bay, then let this dream help you dissolve the blocks to love so that once you find your way back, you can grow and expand beyond where love has gone before. Sigmund Freud said that dreams are the royal road to the unconscious, but they're actually the royal road to the source of life itself. See also **Emotion**, page 145, and **Joy**, page 151.

Lust

See page 152.

Marry, Marriage

Dreams of marriage signify the harmonious blend of opposites, primarily the synergy of your masculine and feminine aspects. This may be a wish-fulfillment dream or a nightmare, depending on your context and who you're marrying. Either way, this dream is leaving clues as to how to heal from the heartaches that might have held you back from marital bliss. See also **Commit**, **Commitment**, page 174, and **Wedding**, page 93.

Massage

Dreams of a massage signify that your relationship agreement is being worked out (massaged) or that you are in need of some TLC—to be touched physically, emotionally, or spiritually. This dream could be a message to release tension and stress in your love life, while you allow your relationship a little recuperation, revitalization, and healing.

Masturbate, Masturbation

Dreams of self-pleasure reflect self-love, self-care, and your awareness that if you love yourself, you become more magnetic and will attract the love you desire. Besides, if you can't be your own best friend, how can you expect someone else to be? This dream might be giving you permission to stop waiting for someone else to take care of your needs and desires, and become responsible for your own joy, pleasure, and fulfillment.

Menstruate/ Menstruation

Dreams of menstruation are symbolic of being in the flow of your femininity, in sync with the ocean tides and cycles of the moon. This dream may represent a time (period) of release (emptying out) in your love life. It could be a message to turn within as you cleanse yourself of limited thoughts, beliefs, and physical or emotional toxins that stand in the way of being your best self in your relationship. Additionally, blood is associated with your personal power as well as your family bloodline, so this dream may help you be aware of your tribal roots and where you bleed out your power and give your energy away in your relationship. Dreaming of menstruation can also signify fertility and be a message to embrace your deeper feelings. See also **Moon**, page 121.

Naked

If you dream that you are naked or naked in public, you might be feeling exposed and vulnerable, emotionally or sexually. If you're comfortable while naked, then you're letting your lover see the true you. If you're embarrassed, ask yourself what you'd prefer not to see about your lover, or what you'd rather he or she not discover about you. This dream can reflect your desire for true intimacy or heart-to-heart communion with your lover.

Nude, Nudity

See **Naked**, page 86.

Online Dating

Dreams of online dating represent your desire to meet someone special and to expand your circle of possibilities beyond your immediate physical experience. This dream may be a message for you to open your mind to the infinite ways that love can happen in your life. Perhaps you are realizing that there is someone out there who would be your perfect match. See also **Date**, page 79, and **Internet**, page 150.

Oral Sex

See **Blow Job**, page 169, **Cunnilingus**, page 176, and **Sex**, page 192.

If you dream that you are naked in public, you may be feeling exposed and vulnerable, emotionally or sexually.

Orgasm

Dreams of an orgasm signify that you are opening yourself to your pleasure principle. Orgasm in a dream or a wet dream signifies fulfillment, wholeness, and your awareness of what brings you to ecstasy. These highly pleasurable dreams are a healthy and natural occurrence, a result of a lack of inhibition during the dream state. See the discussion on wet dreams in the introduction, page 24. See also **Sex**, page 192.

Orgy

Because everyone in your dream is you, an orgy is a metaphor of all aspects of yourself wrapped in an ecstatic, intimate embrace— the ultimate image of self-love. This dream may be satisfying your need for a massive infusion of affirmation, as well as an opportunity for your inner animal to roam wild and make love to all aspects of yourself. Conversely, you might be grappling with issues of monogamy and polyamory (or even polygamy). See also **Party**, page 86, **Polyamory**, page 154, and **Sex**, page 192.

Park (verb)

A dream of parking your car could signify a need to take a time-out from your relationship pursuit. Perhaps you've been driven to find the one you want or to take your relationship further and faster. Your dream is giving you the message to relax from all your striving. Alternatively, if you're someone who has parked his or her love life on the side of the road for too long, this dream might be a message to get back into the driver's seat, get your love life in gear, re-engage in your drive (passion), roll down the windows, and see where the road takes you. See also **Park (noun)**, page 85.

Pee

Besides the fact that it could be prompted by the pangs of a full bladder, a dream of pee signifies that you may be pissed off with your lover. However, this dream could also reflect a need to release and let go of whatever no longer serves you. See also **Anger**, page 140.

Pierce, Piercing

If you dream of a piercing, it suggests that you are bringing power, tribal-level awareness, and warrior-like qualities into your love life. A body piercing can also reflect a rite of passage, a ceremony that transforms you from a younger, weaker being into a stronger, more capable one. Consider what part of the body is pierced. See also **Body**, page 32, and **Tattoo**, page 129.

Play

Dreams of a theatrical play could help you to gain objectivity regarding the drama you and your lover are playing out. You might realize that you are the director (or at least the codirector) of the theater of your life, so if you like it, enjoy the show. If not, consider rewriting and maybe even recasting your relationship drama (or comedy, as the case may be). This dream might also be a message for you and your lover to break away from your busy day-to-day lives, connect with your inner child, and take time to play and enjoy each other. See also **Theater**, page 90.

Polyamory

See page 154.

Polygamy

See page 154.

Pray, Prayer

Dreams of prayer reflect your awareness of your connection with a higher power. Perhaps you are going through a difficult moment in your relationship and are calling on a source of spiritual energy. This dream reveals that you are awakening to the realization that you are surrounded by benevolent beings who are all here to assist you on your journey. See also **Angel**, page 29.

Pregnant, Pregnancy

Dreams of pregnancy signify that you may be feeling pregnant with possibilities, and so ripe with love that you're falling off the vine. They could literally be a wake-up call to take a pregnancy test, to use protection, or to plan for a new arrival. Dreams of pregnancy reflect that this is a fertile time in your life and that your relationship looks like it will go to full term.

Promote, Promotion

If you dream that someone is promoting or marketing something, this may be a message that your potential mate is trying to sell themselves to you or convince you to buy into a belief system of theirs that may or may not be of value to you. Alternatively, if you receive a promotion or a raise, you are gaining an affirmation, recognition, and acknowledgment for how well you are doing in your relationship. See also **Raise**, page 191, and **Sell**, page 191.

Propose, Proposal

Dreams of a marriage proposal reflect your level of desirability and self-love. Perhaps you've been praying on bended knee for clarity about the next stage in your relationship. Perhaps your dream is telling you to be thoughtful, consider your options, and know that the decisions you make at this stage of your relationship will have life-long implications. See also **Contract**, page 143.

Punch

See **Hit**, page 182.

Quickie

Dreams of a quickie might signify that your body is craving a release from sexual tension. Or perhaps you've been in and out of relationships so fast, they make your head spin. The dream may also reflect how your needs are met, physically, emotionally, and spiritually. If this strategy works for you, then keep it. However, if you are unhappy with a quickie in your dream, then it's a reminder to break free from your oversimplified approach and discover a bond with more depth, longevity, and true intimacy. See also **Sex**, page 192.

Race (verb)

Dreams of racing signify that you feel the competitive spirit in your relationship, comparing (and perhaps despairing) your performance. Maybe your biological clock is causing you to feel under the gun to move your relationship faster than its natural pace. If you dream of winning a race, then you may be feeling confident, victorious, and deserving of the success, happiness, and love you have in your life. See also **Competition**, page 174, **Ethnicity**, page 145, and **Sports**, page 195.

Rain

Dreams of rain signify that you may be in the midst of an emotional catharsis. Rain can symbolize tears that need to be shed, whether they are tears of joy or grief. Allow this dream to be a message for you to release and let go of any pent-up feelings from past heartaches so you can stand in the sun of the present moment with your partner or attract the relationship of your dreams with your radiance.

Ram

When you or someone else gets rammed in a dream (sexually or otherwise), it reflects a dominating, mating, or relating strategy. Perhaps you feel that you absolutely must fulfill your longings regardless of their long-term effects. See also **Animal**, page 29, **Astrology (Aries)**, page 140, and **Ram (noun)**, page 59.

Rape

Dreams of rape denote that you feel or fear you have been taken advantage of, had your boundaries violated, or are on the receiving end of an abuse of power. You may be processing an actual rape that happened to you or to someone close to you. In either case, this dream is attempting to help you regain any power you may have lost, so that you can be whole as you traverse your love journey. See also **Abduct**, **Abduction**, page 164, and **Violent**, page 198.

Reject, Rejection

Dreams of rejection could be helping you process a situation in which you were rejected, you could be rejected, or you left someone else feeling that way. Dreams of rejection are a telltale sign that the shadow is present. Ask yourself what aspect of yourself or your lover is being rejected. Once you identify this aspect of yourself, know that self-love is the best antidote. See the FEAR formula discussion in the introduction, page 20. See also **Shadow**, page 156.

Rescue

If you dream of rescuing someone, you may be tapping into your inner hero or heroine, who carries the world on his or her shoulders. Perhaps this dream is alerting you that your partner or an ailing relationship needs attention. If you dream of being rescued, this may be a cry for help from a part of you that has been neglected and is in critical need of support. Additionally, dreams of being rescued can be sexually stimulating and might reveal your relationship strategy involving victim and hero archetypes. See **Hero/Heroine**, page 50.

Reward

Dreams of a reward signify that you are being affirmed, recognized, and appreciated for your heroism. You deserve the well-earned praise you are receiving. Conversely, this dream may be showing you that your eyes are so fixated on the prize that you may miss the preciousness of the moment. You might be trying too hard to orgasm and are missing the journey that takes you there. See also **Award**, page 98, and **Orgasm**, page 188.

Rise, Raise

If you dream of getting a raise, this suggests that you need to gain a higher perspective or recognition for all your hard work. A raise can also suggest an erection or a positive direction in your relationship, and that you are moving upward in your consciousness as a result of your love, sex, and relationship. Keep in mind that as you are lifted in your relationship, everything around you is lifted. See also **Climb**, page 174, and **Elevator**, page 79.

Run

If you dream of running away from someone or something, you are trying to escape an aspect of yourself you deem unlovable, rejectable, or scary. If you are running toward someone or something, you are feeling excitement, longing, and desire for the object or person of interest. This dream might indicate where you are in your pursuit of a lost aspect of your power. See also **Chase**, page 172.

Screw

See **Sex**, page 192, and **Tool**, page 130.

Seduce, Seduction

Dreams of seducing someone or of being seduced can reveal relationship patterns based on power games of fear and control. Even though the energy of seduction can feel delicious, it's not a healthy, sustainable expression of true love. And like a drug, it can string you along and leave you high and dry. This dream may be waking you to destructive relationship patterns, so you can transform them and experience real love. See also **Seducer/Seductress**, page 60.

Selfie

Dreams of taking a selfie might reflect self-consciousness, self-awareness, and maybe even selfishness and narcissism. If pointing the lens of self-love at yourself is a new behavior, keep zooming in to ensure you are taking care of your needs. However, if in waking reality you've been accused of being overly myopic, then this dream might be a message to zoom out, expand your frame of awareness, and consider the possibility that there are other people on the planet to include in the photo gallery of your life. See also **Photograph**, page 123.

Sell

Dreams of selling something could indicate overzealousness in your relationship. Someone selling something to you in a dream could be a message that your lover is trying to get you to buy into a belief system or win over your attention, and there may be an underlying motive or manipulation. If you are the one selling in the dream, consider what you are selling, why, to whom, and the feeling tone of the transaction. Conversely, this dream could indicate passion and a desire to share an insight you feel is worthy. A dream of selling something could also imply the prostitute archetype, which relates to selling yourself out for a price. See also **Money**, page 120, **Prostitute**, page 59, and **Salesperson**, page 60.

Sex

Sex with someone in a dream, whether or not it actually results in intercourse, symbolizes a merging with the qualities that person represents to you. The driver of your sexual dreams is the experience of wholeness (not just orgasm) and your personal power, which must be amplified to create the life of your dreams. See the following for a more detailed explanation of some of the most common sex dream scenarios:

In an adventurous place: Dreams of having a sexual encounter in an adventurous place could be a message to see sex, yourself, and your lover from an out-of-the-box perspective. They may be a prescription from the dream realm to add spice to your relationship, go outside the boundaries of your normal comfort zone, and learn a new trick or two.

Dreams of sex symbolize that you are merging with the qualities of another person.

With an animal: Don't freak out—this book does not advocate bestiality. However, the rules of engagement in dreams are completely different from the rules of civilized society. In dreams, a sensual connection with an animal represents that you are embracing your wild side, as animals represent untamed, undomesticated expression. See also **Animal**, page 29.

With the boss: If you have steamy dreams about your boss or other coworkers, take heart in knowing that these sleep-working dreams are quite common, especially if your job is important to you. It doesn't necessarily mean that you're the type to sleep your way to the top. Dreams of sleeping with your boss could represent that you are craving an intimate connection with your leadership aspect. By incorporating the energy of this dream, you will be one step closer to that raise and to empowering yourself to take charge of your career.

With a celebrity: Sex dreams starring you and a celebrity as your leading man or woman, besides intimately connecting you with the qualities they represent, are helping you celebrate yourself. Sexual celebrity dreams can mean you are connecting deeply with power, influence, and glamour. Consider the qualities you ascribe to this celebrity; they may reveal an aspect of yourself you should embrace in your own life.

With a family member or close platonic friend: Remember that dreams are symbolic and not literal. Did you recently have a fight with this family member or friend? Joining with him or her in your dream could be symbolic of reconciliation, empathy, or merging with and understanding their point of view or the qualities they represent. See also **Incest**, page 183.

With a friend's significant other: In dreams you can explore secret attractions without having to act on them and face the consequences of those actions in the waking world. Remember, when you see this person and blush crimson, you have nothing to be ashamed of.

Sexual problems (inability to perform or sexual deformity): In addition to dreams of sex being symbolic of intimacy, the sex act can often be symbolic of power and potency, or lack thereof. You may have had this dream because there's an area in your life where you feel impotent, powerless, helpless, or ineffective to implement the changes you'd like to see. Or you may be expressing frustration at not being able to rise to the occasion and embrace an opportunity recently presented in your life.

An orgasm that feels real: When you have a wet dream, you are simply giving yourself permission for pleasure (lucky you!). Sometimes when you dream, you are more receptive than you might be in waking reality to explore beyond your typical sensual delights. Thus, a dream sexual experience can be incredibly diverse and satisfying. Take note of the scenario that provided the release, and consider it a window into what turns you on. This may or may not come as a surprise to you, but such self-awareness will no doubt lead you to a deeper understanding of your own pleasure principle.

With someone of the same sex: Dreams of a homosexual nature represent an intimate joining with the feminine or masculine aspect of yourself. Because we all contain masculine and feminine energy, regardless of our sex, this could signify your seeking balance, healing of unresolved issues with your same-sex parent, or the freedom and self-love to explore beyond the boundaries of society's parameters. Such dreams reflect your level of self-love and acceptance about your masculine or feminine energy. They could also reflect high self-esteem or feeling free to come out of the closet to share your signature expression of love.

You might consider this dream symbolic of deeply connecting with the sensual god or goddess within, fulfilling a need for nurturing and gentleness (female) or power and potency (male). See the anima/animus discussion in the introduction, page 10, and **Homosexuality**, page 149.

With an ex: If you dream of sex with an ex, it doesn't necessarily mean that you long to be with that person. Such dreams are often an attempt to retrieve energy, power, or an important aspect of yourself that you may have left behind with your ex, perhaps a part of your heart you feel is missing. Consider that your ex represents an aspect of you (your anima or animus), and it is now time to embrace it. See also the anima/animus discussion in the introduction, page 10.

Shampoo

Dreams of shampoo signify a desire to wash a person or situation out of your hair and cleanse them from your memory. Because hair is associated with thoughts, shampoo in a dream suggests that you are rinsing impure, negative, and toxic thoughts down the drain so you can regain your natural bounce, vitality, and healthy shine. See also **Hair**, page 48, and **Wash**, page 198.

Shave

Dreams of shaving signify a desire to smooth out your rough edges, regain your youthfulness, or release thoughts that age you. Alternatively, because hair can be a symbol of power, a dream of shaving might be about feeling a loss of power. Contemplate whether or not your love life is bringing out your youthful side, diminishing you, or supporting you in letting go of belief systems that used to empower you but have become scraggly. If you're shaving a beard or mustache, this dream is revealing the courage it takes to become exposed, naked, and honest.

Shop

Dreaming of shopping reveals that you have relationship options and a choice in the matter of your love life. This dream could also be a message from your subconscious mind to take your time and shop around before buying into a relationship, job, or other life decision. Perhaps it is illuminating the false belief that something or someone out there will make you sexier, wealthier, prettier, skinnier, smarter, or better than you are. All these superficial, external traits come with an expiration date, whereas your golden, authentic essence accrues interest, becoming more valuable as you cultivate your self-love, talent, and natural genius. See also **Store**, page 90.

Shower

Dreams of taking a shower signify that you are cleansing, releasing, purifying, healing, and creating a fresh start with a clean slate. Perhaps you are at the end of a cycle in your relationship, and you're washing down the drain all that didn't serve you. But you are allowing whatever does serve you to shower down upon you. If you dream of showering with someone, you may be feeling the need to come clean and be honest with that person or rinse the past away and start fresh. See also **Rain**, page 190, and **Shampoo**, page 194.

Sick

If you dream of being sick, there may be something or someone in your life causing dissonance. This dream may be a clue to purge unhealthy habits, negative thinking, or fearful thoughts. You may have judged your sexuality or preferences as sick, and you're venting out suppressed energy. Consider the area of the body affected by the illness, and take preventive measures in your waking life to stay healthy (e.g., wear a condom, wash hands, eat healthy food, get proper rest, etc.). See also **Disease**, page 144.

Sing

Dreams of singing signify joy, passion, freedom, harmony, and a desire to voice your true feelings. Consider the song you are singing and how it applies to your waking life. Are you singing solo, a harmonious duet, or with a choir? This will give you a clue to how this dream applies to your waking relationships. Singing a duet symbolizes that you and your lover are making beautiful music together. You are finding a way to harmonize and synergize each other's best qualities into a partnership that really sings. See also **Music**, page 152.

Slap

See **Hit**, page 182.

Soccer/Football

Dreams of soccer denote a hands-free, aloof, or quick-footed strategy. Perhaps you feel kicked around, or that you've been kicking back and taking it easy, and it's time to use your head. Because in soccer you don't use your hands, you might be feeling frustrated that you can't just reach out and touch your partner in public the way you'd like to.

If you dream you are playing as a **forward**, this could reflect that you've been too overt in your advances.

If you dream of a **defensive position (fullback)**, you are cautious, dependable, and careful.

If you dream of a **sweeper**, you may be the leader (alpha) in your relationship, keeping control and being on the defensive.

If you dream of a **stopper**, you are oppositional to advances your way.

If you dream of a **midfielder**, you're good at handling advances and passing them appropriately.

If you dream of a **striker**, you are goal-oriented and always know when there is an opening despite the obstacles in your way.

If you dream of the **goalie (goalkeeper)**, you are focused on keeping your partner, or anyone for that matter, from scoring or getting the upper hand. Perhaps you've kept your eye off the ball in the past, and you are vigilant that nothing gets past you.

See also **Sports**, page 195.

Spank

If you dream of being spanked, you've probably been a bad boy or girl and you feel the need to be punished or dominated. Perhaps your lover has been treating you like a child. If you are the one doing the spanking, ask yourself if your lover has done something naughty. Or you may be discovering an interest in BDSM fantasies. In any case, consider how the parent–child dynamic may be playing out in your relationship, and that it may be time to tighten or loosen the leash on this pattern. See also **BDSM**, page 168.

Speed

Dreams of speed (going fast) could signify ambition or avoidance. This dream may be alerting you that you have been so focused on arriving at your destination that you're not present for the journey. This dream may be a message to slow down, experience your feelings, and treat each moment like it is precious, because it is. Alternatively, if you've been slow to respond to the cues life is sending you, this dream might be prodding you to get in gear so your love life doesn't pass you by.

Sports

Dreams of sports reflect your attitude about teamwork, competition, winning, losing, and playing the game of love. Consider whether or not your conduct is sportsmanlike, or if you will do whatever it takes to win. Perhaps this dream is a message for you to play your personal best and to be committed yet detached from the outcome so that you can take your losses well, like a good sport. Consider your motivation for being on the playing field—for the glory, the game, or the thrill of victory. Also, if you are more content to sit in the bleachers and be a spectator, this dream might be a message to get down and dirty and play ball. The specific sport you dream about might illuminate further details about your game of love. See also **Baseball**, page 167, **Basketball**, page 167, **Football (American)**, page 181, and **Soccer/Football**, page 195.

Stretch

A dream of stretching might be a message to become more flexible in your thinking, to open your mind, and perhaps to think outside the sexual or relationship box to embrace the ways that your partner is different from you. Conversely, this dream may be showing you that you've been overly flexible and it's time to hold your ground. See **Yoga**, page 198.

Surgery

Dreams of surgery suggest that major healing, transformation, and change are occurring in your relationship, or should be. This dream may reveal where the problem or imbalance is in your relationship so you can address it before more drastic measures become inevitable. Consider the part of the body being operated on and what it symbolizes:

For example, if you dream of **breast surgery**, this may indicate you are healing a challenge related to nurturing, caretaking, feminine support, and mother issues.

If you dream of **cosmetic surgery**, you are concerned with how people perceive you or your relationship.

If you dream of **heart surgery**, it could be a message to open your heart, in spite of having been hurt in love.

Dreams that relate to surgery on **sex organs** can be about empowerment, fidelity, and manifesting your desires.

Dreams about a **vaginal surgery** could suggest the healing of issues of receptivity and openness and being discreet or tight-lipped, rigid, cautious, or discerning.

See also **Body**, page 32, **Cut**, page 176, and **Doctor**, page 41.

Swim

Swimming in a dream symbolizes that you're not afraid to get wet or to dive headfirst into the mysterious waters of intimacy. Swimming also symbolizes that you can hold your own in the water element, which represents intuition, emotions, and the soul of your relationship. You may be navigating feelings about your relationship's soulful depths, reveling in your sexuality, or daring to understand the mysteries of your feminine side. See also **Ocean**, page 85, and **Water**, page 93.

Talk

If you talk in your dreams, consider the content of your speech. Pay particular attention to any strange words or phrases. Speaking in dreams, as in real life, can be ordinary or extraordinary, depending on the context. If you are having a conversation in your dreams, it is symbolic of your desire to communicate, connect, and be understood. If you want to talk in your dream but can't, it may be shining a light on your not expressing your feelings in your relationship. Difficulty with speaking often happens when physical attraction runs high.

Tantric Sex

Dreams of tantric sex symbolize a desire to channel your sexual energy toward a higher experience. This dream reflects that a higher love is available and revealing itself to you and your lover, as you may be seeing the divine in each other. Additionally, because tantric sex requires the discipline of delaying your orgasm, it could be a message to have patience and maturity, and to channel your sexual energy toward higher aspirations.

Tantrum

Dreams of a tantrum could signify that you're tired of holding back your feelings and of being diplomatic. This venting dream may let your inner child release steam about issues in your relationship. Alternatively, it could be revealing where you've overindulged your inner five-year-old, and it's time to give him or her a spanking or time-out, while your inner adult gets strategic about ways to meet your needs. See also **Anger**, page 140.

Texting, Text Message

Dreams of a text message signify telepathy, communication, and a specific message. Perhaps by texting, you are discovering how to spell out exactly what you need/want/desire in this relationship. Pay particular attention to the words you send or those sent to you. See also **Email**, page 178, and **Twitter**, page 197.

Threesome

Dreams of a threesome, or ménage a trois, signify that you may have triangulated your feelings by falling in love with a person other than your significant other. Three is also associated with the holy trinity (father/son/spirit) or another trinity, such as mind/body/spirit or mother/father/child. Your dream of a threesome could suggest that

change is in the midst, especially if there is a third-wheel (a person, project, or even work) getting in the way. This dream might be a message to call on a higher power to create a divine triad for your intimacy. See also **Three**, page 158.

Transform, Transformation

Dreams of something or someone changing radically from one form to another reflect exponential awareness, empathy, and wisdom, perhaps stimulated by issues you are grappling with in your love life. If the transformation is not what you'd consider positive, this dream may warn you to make changes to your relationship. If it is positive, you are exploring an upgrade to a new and improved version of yourself. See also **Breakdown/Breakthrough**, page 171.

Travel

See **Journey**, page 184.

Trip

Dreams of a trip are symbolic of your love life taking you places, or your sex life making you confused or tripping you up. Perhaps you are covering new territory in your love life, which may be an expansion beyond your familiar map. This dream might prompt you to consider whether or not your relationship quest is taking

you to higher ground, or, if you decide to leave the relationship, it could help you avoid tripping as you're trying to get out the door.

Tsunami

Dreams of a tsunami represent radical change in your relationship, and that you are in need of an enormous catharsis. This dream may reflect that, as your world is changing, you'd like someone to save you from an emotionally overwhelming situation. Alternatively, this dream may be revealing that you identify yourself as the hero, whose job is to save the world or at least come to your partner's emotional rescue. See **Breakdown/Breakthrough,** page 171, **Ocean**, page 85, **Rescue**, page 190, and **Water**, page 43.

Tweet, Twitter

Dreams of tweeting or Twitter reflect that you are feeling overly excited (twitterpated), and grappling with the words to spell out what you really feel in your relationship. They might be a message to share your excitement about your love affair with the world in a concise way. See also **Facebook**, page 147, and **Social Media**, page 157.

Undress

Unbuttoning or undressing in a dream is symbolic of dropping a formal facade and revealing your authentic self. This dream may be giving you permission to release your buttoned-up identity, and to trust the process. Consider that you are an ever-unfolding being, with infinite layers of love, beauty, sensuality, and magic to reveal. This dream may signify that you are prepared to be more emotionally and physically naked than ever before with your lover. See also **Naked**, page 186.

Violent, Violence

Dreams of violence, rape, or sexual assault could signify that you are in a healing process as your dreams and subconscious mind attempt to put back pieces that have become lost or scattered. Dreams of violence that take you back to the scene of a crime (a location that resembles a trauma from your waking life) are an attempt to help you re-enter the scene and experience it differently, or to become lucid and change it. A violent dream might also be an expression of pent-up rage or anger you don't feel safe or comfortable sharing in waking reality. This dream might be a message for you to find a nonviolent, emotionally safe way to communicate and vent your frustrations with your loved one.

War

See **Battle**, page 168.

Wash

Dreams of washing signify that you feel the need to clean or clear up a miscommunication between you and your loved one. Perhaps your heart is in a healing or detoxing process, releasing negativity or working out if this relationship can be restored to its natural splendor. See also **Laundry**, page 118, **Shower**, page 194, and **Washing Machine**, page 134.

Wed

See **Marry**, **Marriage**, page 186, or **Wedding**, page 93.

Whip

Dreams of a whip may signify that you've been a naughty boy or girl and feel the need to punish or be punished. They may reveal a kinky BDSM aspect, or show you where your hypercritical self-judgment is attempting to whip you into shape. It's said that every talent we're born with comes with a whip, and we can either use our talent for good or we can torture ourselves with it. This dream may reveal a more gentle approach, which allows you to be more authentically expressed. See also **BDSM**, page 168.

Workout

See **Exercise**, page 179.

X-Ray

Dreams of an x-ray can represent a desire to be seen and known, especially by your lover. If you are uncomfortable being transparent in this dream, perhaps you've revealed too much. Additionally, this dream could be shining a bright light on a chronic issue that gets in your way of a connection beyond the superficial. See also **Naked**, page 186.

Yoga

Dreams of yoga indicate that you are bringing a level of mindfulness and higher consciousness to your partnership. They may be a reminder to breathe and be flexible as you stretch beyond your comfort zone. Yoga is actually Hindu for "yolk," which is means to connect to your own golden center, to align yourself and the body, mind, and soul of your love affair. See also **Stretch**, page 196.

Acknowledgments

Years ago while browsing in airport bookstore I leafed through an eye-catching book and I skimmed the author's acknowledgments section. I read about how she was so grateful to her supportive team for helping bring the dream of her book into reality. I remember feeling a pang of jealousy mixed with a cocktail of inspiration and destiny and declared, "I want to have a team to thank one day!"

It's been a decade since that day, and lo and behold, here I sit, writing the acknowledgments for this book I've been pouring my heart and soul into for the past year (and "field researching" for the last 35 years), and it turns out that I have a team of incredible people to thank. I'm choked up and bleary-eyed as I think about these loving, creative geniuses who support me personally and professionally. Is this real? I must be dreaming (or practicing what I preach about the fact that paying attention to nighttime dreams leads to the life of our dreams). Without further ado, I'd like to acknowledge the following people for helping make the dream of this book a reality.

This book would not be possible if it weren't for my inspiring, talented, passionate—and dare I say, juicy—editor, Jessica Haberman. Words can't express how much I love working with this woman! I'd also like to thank the entire dream team at Quarto and Fair Winds Press: Katie Fawkes, Lydia Finn, Renae Haines, and Jessica Pinault. I'm thrilled to thank my amazing literary agent, Devra Jacobs (and Rebecca Stinson) for such incredible support, psychic guidance, and soul-level sisterhood.

I've already dedicated this book to Dana G. Walden, so I won't write a novel here about how much his love, support, and creative input has fed me throughout this process. To my amazing jewel of a mom who is a best friend and eagle eye first draft editor: Noel Sullivan, thank you for being my personal barista and keeping me caffeinated during my rewrites. To Meesha Walden and all the Sullivans (Dad, Shannon, Jeanene and Granny): Thank you for your support, love and for putting up with me spending so much time with my nose in my computer. To Debbie Spector Weisman for being my partner in shine with Dream-Life Coach Training and a supportive force for dreams coming true in my life; My goddess queen sisters Gypsy Racco, Jo-e Sutton, Wendi Resnick, Suzanne Rock, Jodi Sutton, and Firestar for our deeply soul-nourishing discussions about all things love, sex, relationships, and dreams.

To the young women I have the privilege of mentoring, Mariah (Diamond) Reyes, the young leaders of CHIME IN, and the Fostering a Change young women warriors Victoria, Jaci, Andrea, Jessica, Renashia, Alex, and August: You keep me on my game so I can earn the right to be the wind beneath your wings.

About the Author

Kelly Sullivan Walden is on a mission to awaken the world to the power of dreams. Known as America's premier dream expert, she is the bestselling author of *I Had the Strangest Dream, It's All in Your Dreams, Dream Oracle Cards,* and *Chicken Soup for the Soul: Dreams & Premonitions.* She is also a certified clinical hypnotherapist, inspirational speaker, and founder of Dream-Life Coach Training (**www.dreamlifecoachtraining.com**), a year-long online certification program that empowers people to decode the genius of their dreams and their dreaming minds—and pay it forward to others.

She has reached millions of people with her inspiring message on national talk shows such as *Coast to Coast,* FOX News, Shirley MacLaine's *Independent Expression Radio,* and Michael Beckwith's *Wake Up—The Sound of Transformation.*

She began her dream career at age five, as she and her younger sister shared a room growing up and often shared tandem dreaming experiences. They would discuss their dreams every morning and compare notes about what they thought they meant. Since those early years, Kelly has grown into a trusted advisor, coach, and consultant, enriching the lives of countless individuals, including Fortune 500 executives, UN ambassadors, celebrities, entrepreneurs, inner-city kids, and stay-at-home moms.

She is thrilled to empower you to understand the language of your dreams, so that you can stop taking your dreams lying down, and more powerfully live the life of your dreams. To receive Kelly's dream insights, go to: **www.kellysullivanwalden.com**

Index